Megan Daley is an author, podcaster, teacher librarian and early years educator. She has been awarded the Australian School Library Association Teacher Librarian of the Year, the Queensland School Library Association Teacher Librarian of the Year, and the national Dromkeen Librarian's Award, presented by the State Library of Victoria. A former national vice-president of the Children's Book Council of Australia, Megan is the artistic director of Somerset Storyfest. She is a seasoned speaker and workshop presenter, and the co-host of the *Your Kid's Next Read* podcast. Her other books include *Teacher, Teacher* (Affirm Press, 2023) and *The Beehive* (Walker Books, 2024).

raising readers

How to nurture a child's love of books

MEGAN DALEY

First published 2019 by University of Queensland Press
PO Box 6042, St Lucia, Queensland 4067 Australia
Reprinted 2019, 2022, 2023

This edition published 2025

University of Queensland Press (UQP) acknowledges the Traditional Owners and their custodianship of the lands on which UQP operates. We pay our respects to their Ancestors and their descendants, who continue cultural and spiritual connections to Country. We recognise their valuable contributions to Australian and global society.

uqp.com.au
reception@uqp.com.au

Cover design and illustration by Jo Hunt
Author photograph by Quince and Mulberry Studios
Typeset in 12/16pt Adobe Garamond
Printed in Australia by McPherson's Printing Group

University of Queensland Press is supported by the Queensland Government through Arts Queensland.

University of Queensland Press is assisted by the Australian Government through Creative Australia, its principal arts investment and advisory body.

A catalogue record for this book is available from the National Library of Australia.

ISBN 978 0 7022 6898 4 (pbk)
ISBN 978 0 7022 7048 2 (epdf)
ISBN 978 0 7022 7049 9 (epub)

University of Queensland Press uses papers that are natural, renewable and recyclable products made from wood grown in well-managed forests and other controlled sources. The logging and manufacturing processes conform to the environmental regulations of the country of origin.

For our boys:

Daniel John Daley
Much missed Chief Bedtime Books Reader
10 August 1976 – 29 April 2017
Eternally reading Ranger's Apprentice by John Flanagan

Simon James Dean
5 September 1982 – 28 January 2012
Eternally reading *Looking for Trouble* by John Marsden

Samuel, James and Murray Arkadieff
Reading beside me since 2019

CONTENTS

FOREWORD

Many parents, teachers and librarians will already be familiar with Megan Daley's hugely successful podcast and community group *Your Kid's Next Read*, created with Allison Tait and Allison Rushby. Others may have attended seminars, lectures or professional development sessions with Megan on how to create welcoming library spaces and engage reluctant readers. Moreover, countless authors, illustrators and creators, including myself, have been championed and supported by Megan over the years through her reviews, blogs and book recommendations. It would be very difficult to find someone in the world of kids' books or education who hasn't come across Megan and her work, and *Raising Readers* is the perfect distillation of her years of experience and wisdom, combined with her trademark humour and warmth.

This updated edition of *Raising Readers* is needed now more than ever. Reading rates in Australia have been falling steadily with recent reports outlining the alarming statistics around the number of children finishing school without having the reading skills required for life.

As a children's author, I have spent the past fifteen years writing books to engage our most struggling readers, from the Billie B Brown series to the School of Monsters. As the Australian Children's Laureate for 2024–2025, I have been actively campaigning to ensure that all kids can become readers, so I am delighted to see this edition includes a deep dive into the Science of Reading, as well as exploring recent changes to our education system in the way reading is taught.

For me, this is deeply personal. My youngest son is neurodivergent and has struggled with reading his whole life, unfortunately starting school at a time when it was often assumed that kids would just pick up reading by osmosis. However, despite growing up in a household of books with parents who read to him every night and two older brothers who were voracious readers, for him it just never 'clicked'. By the time he was halfway through high school his self-esteem and self-efficacy were crushed, and it became clear that struggling to read didn't only limit his capacity to enjoy great stories, but also his ability to engage with learning – as every subject requires reading.

With more and more young people identifying as neurodivergent or disabled, it's reassuring to see that the stigma around being 'different' is continuing to lessen – this latest edition of *Raising Readers* supports the social model of disability which, unlike the medical model, encourages us to change the system, not the person. It also includes some excellent reading lists to explore inclusion and diversity with young people. It's been heartening to witness the development of a genuine curiosity and interest by educators as well as children's book publishers about how we can all work harder to create a world where *all* kids can reach their potential.

Alongside a more inclusive and supportive learning environment, there are foundational skills all children need to be explicitly taught – reading being one of the most essential. As Megan outlines in this book, while our brains are wired with the capacity to acquire oral language from birth, reading and writing are not innate skills. What this means is that it is not the responsibility of parents to teach their children to read, just as they are not responsible for their child becoming proficient in physics, piano or French. The teaching of reading and writing is a complex cognitive process best taught by a professional.

However, there are still many things that parents can do at home to prime their child for reading acquisition, as well as support what they will be learning in school. This edition of *Raising Readers* is bursting with creative and informative ways to do this and, perhaps most importantly, to foster and support a reading journey for your child that is also *fun*.

I have no doubt this latest edition will become the go-to guide for parents, carers, teachers and librarians for ideas and inspiration, as well as some brilliant reading lists to suit all types of readers. As challenging as learning to read can be, no child wants to feel that reading is a punishment or a chore, and Megan outlines myriad ways we can create opportunities and inclusive environments to ensure that all kids are raised as readers.

— Sally Rippin, Australian Children's Laureate (2024–2025)
and author of *Wild Things: How We Learn to Read and What Can Happen If We Don't.*

INTRODUCTION

I have loved books my whole life. I was fortunate to be raised in a home that valued words and literature, and my parents read to me throughout my childhood and beyond. I vividly remember my father reading to me in my early teens; though, perhaps, he was reading to my younger brothers and I was just part of the action. Regardless, I was hooked by the sound of words being recited by someone I loved and admired. My mother, also a teacher librarian, filled our house with quality books. She introduced me to some of my all-time favourites, including *Dicey's Song* (Cynthia Voigt), *Came Back to Show You I Could Fly* (Robin Klein) and John Marsden's iconic *So Much to Tell You* – which blew my angsty teenage brain!

When I had my first child it came as something of a shock that others around me were not reading to their babies. And in my role at the time as national vice-president of the Children's Book Council of Australia, I was asked several times over by the media and parents about the 'right age' to start reading to children. The answer seemed obvious to me – from birth, of course! I would tell people that books were an essential newborn accessory. But I also had to be mindful that not everyone had my upbringing or training or knowledge of childhood literacy. On a personal level, fostering a love of reading in my children seemed to be the easiest part of parenting. I find being a parent a very hard job at times and every stage of child-rearing seems to be filled with guilt. I do, however, feel confident that I will be able to look back and say, 'But I read to them and gave them the joy of books' and know that I did my best.

I have been a primary school teacher and teacher librarian for over twenty years now. As a parent and educator, I know how beneficial it is for children to enter the education system bubbling with excitement about words, images and ideas. Flashcards or early online reading programs won't instil this joy in your little one, but gorgeous books will. Immersing your child in language in all forms – stories and songs and nursery rhymes – is one of the best ways you can give them a head start and help them to reach their academic potential. We educators are always so grateful to the families who read to their children and support the education process in this way. It is possible to encourage the joy of recreational reading and still engage with crucial skill development plus meet the demands of the school curriculum and data requirements, but families are instrumental in helping us achieve this.

Raising Readers is a guide for parents and caregivers, and a resource for educators. Like all good non-fiction books (my teacher librarian hat is on now), you can dip into this book as needed or you can read it from start to finish. I will walk you through each stage of a child's literacy development – from birth to adolescence – and offer advice, connect you with the right books at the right times, share pieces of wisdom from my literary friends, as well as some tips and tricks to ensure your family's or classroom's reading journeys are as memorable and as engaging as they can be.

Throughout the book I refer to school libraries and library staff as if they exist in every school. I do this because they darned well should and the research supports this. I don't believe good school libraries and quality teacher librarians and library staff are a thing of the past, but if you are in a school without a library or teacher librarian, I hope that this book offers you guidance. We all have an invaluable part to play in ensuring the young people in our lives fall in love with books. It is a gift they will cherish forever.

CHAPTER ONE

RAISING A READER – THE EARLY YEARS

FROM BABY TO TWO YEARS OLD

Literacy learning begins at birth and the foundations for becoming a reader are firmly established during the early years of life.[1] Shortly after birth, infants respond to sound, often turning towards it, and start focusing their vision. After three to four months of listening and looking at the world, many infants will begin to reach for objects.[2] As they gain control over their movements, babies will explore books in the same way they do a rattle or toy. They will chew them, turn them over and stare at them. They will be intrigued by bright, contrasting colours, and soothed by a calm voice reading a story or singing a song. For babies, hearing the rhythm of words and the expression in voices builds a rich and diverse network of language in their developing brains.

I read a large number of novels when I had newborns as I found myself sitting in chairs rocking or feeding the baby for many hours a day. I became adept at cradling my e-reader in one hand in exactly the right position – at this stage paper books didn't seem safe as I needed to use two hands and no one wants to drop a brick of a novel on their newborn! I mostly read my books aloud and while I'm sure the content was wildly inappropriate, I figured that my babies didn't understand the words. I did know, however, that they were hearing language that was far more complex and diverse than if I was just having a casual chat with them – though, of course, casual chats are also extremely important![3] Some people may feel silly reading to a baby or wonder what the point is, but the key here is exposure. The more you read aloud to a child, the more words they'll be exposed to and the more solid their oral language foundation for future literacy skills will be.

From around six months old, babies who have been read to regularly will begin to identify a book as more than just a colourful object – the book will signal that 'it's time for a story'. This is especially the case when parents or caregivers respond by reading the book whenever the baby hands one to them.[4] Babies may develop a liking for a particular book and frequently pick it up to be read, or become animated and excited when a favourite book is re-read.

Very early on, a baby develops literacy skills using all their senses, including touch. The sense of touch enables babies to attach meaning to objects, from cups and shoes to the pet dog and, of course, books. They explore the mechanics of how books work by turning pages and touching the covers and illustrations. Lift-the-flap and touch-and-feel titles are wonderful for babies and toddlers because they encourage physical engagement with books. Touch and physical contact are finely integrated in language development,[5] from the parent or carer cuddling the child when reading, to the child exploring the physical nature of a book, and then later, as early readers, when they follow words with their finger as they read text or manipulate digital texts on a tablet device. Having plenty of books around the home and within easy access of children provides ample opportunities to hold, explore and play with books.

From around ten months old, babies may comprehend their first word, and by twelve months many will say their first word. Acquiring and comprehending words is a slow process until around eighteen months when many children become rapid word learners.[6]

Toddlers are little sponges, soaking up everything there is to learn. They adore words, nursery rhymes, songs and books. Of course, toddlers can also be destructive! Because they are still learning how a book works and because they use *all* their senses to 'read', chewing and ripping may occur. Do not let this stop you from reading to them. This is the time to get your kids hooked on books.

For younger toddlers I think board books are a great option for unsupervised book time as they are relatively indestructible. However, the text in board books is often minimal, so they should not make up your entire collection for this age group. It's important to also introduce beautiful picture books rich in both language and artwork. Exposing little ones to gorgeous illustrations, exquisite writing and the joy of story is the best way to help them fall in love with books and lay strong oral foundations.

The social nature of reading comes into play around this time, as toddlers become aware of their peers and are able to engage in literacy opportunities in unstructured learning environments.[7] Toddlers in childcare or playgroups may use books in the same way they will use toys – one may show another how it works, there will be tussles over favourites and, *eventually*, there will be sharing and exchanging of books. When toddlers share a book they are supporting each other in their learning,[8] for example, one child might name the animals in the illustrations and the other might make the sounds. In an early education centre, toddlers will often be observed reaching for a book that was previously shared by an educator. They may 're-read' the book for themselves and this independent and unstructured reading time is as meaningful as the group reading session; in fact, it is one of the earliest forms of literate behaviour.

Reading with babies and toddlers

Here are some tips to help make reading with your baby or toddler a fun experience for you both, the operative word being FUN!

- Choose a time when your baby is content and alert.
- Cuddle up with your child. Reading is the perfect time for physical bonding.
- Choose books with fabulous pictures and minimal but engaging text.
- Keep reading sessions short, snappy and regular. Don't feel like you have to finish the book. You might only get through a few pages at a time.
- Babies and toddlers love looking at pictures of themselves and their loved ones, so consider making a photo book – a lovely keepsake as well as a literacy tool.
- Feel free to bounce or tickle or rock your baby as you read – anything that makes reading fun. The same applies to toddlers. Allow them to wriggle and spin as you read. They are (mostly) not going to sit still for the length of a book.
- Modulate your voice and use expression to make the story come alive. Add in animal noises or other sound effects.
- Allow children to chew, touch and smell their books to encourage engaging their senses. This approach may not be ideal in an early-education environment but it's totally okay at home!
- Be prepared to lose a book or two. When there are toddlers in the house, have a selection of books within their reach so they can instigate reading sessions, but keep your precious ones higher up for one-on-one reading time. That said, forget pop-up books for the time being. They'll be shredded in a nanosecond.

- Encourage interaction with the book. Ask questions like: 'Can you point to the horse?'; 'Where is that silly monkey hiding? Can you see him?'
- Show and encourage page turning.
- Be prepared to read books over and over again (endlessly!). It might drive you bonkers but babies and toddlers love repetition – it's how they learn.
- This tip doesn't involve a book per se, but songs and nursery rhymes are incredibly useful oral language and literacy tools, so sing to your child whenever you get the chance. It doesn't matter if you can't carry a tune in a bucket – your kids will love it!

THE IMPORTANCE OF SONG

Like reading, it is never too early to sing to a baby. Parents and caregivers will have experienced how effectively singing a song can calm a baby or entrance a toddler. Song is tightly intertwined with language development and, like books, no child should be without song in their life. Research has found that music is a powerful tool in language acquisition and that the processing of music and language occur in the same areas of the brain and share the same neural pathways.[9] I have been fortunate to work with some talented music educators, including Jennifer Teh. Her Hush Little Baby music classes for babies and toddlers were an important part of our weekly routine for some time, and I have asked her to share her thoughts on the role of song in language development.

Jennifer Teh

Singing is an intrinsic part of raising children. When a baby cries, it feels right to hum a lullaby. We sing action songs and nursery rhymes with our toddlers and young children. Song is a unique way of connecting and communicating, and it carries with it benefits for both the singer and the listener.

Many wonderful things happen when a child is sung to. Songs can be used for storytelling, cultural exchange, to calm, to excite and to incite discussion. For the singer, the act of singing increases cardiovascular function, lowers blood pressure, releases endorphins and lowers stress levels, with a consequent increase in immune function. Singing to babies is particularly powerful. All positive mother–baby interactions lead to the release of beta endorphins for both, promoting feelings of wellbeing and increased relaxation, and this is especially true when a baby is being held and sung to.

There is a direct correlation between singing and the development of language. The folk songs of every culture carry with them the signature inflections of the 'mother tongue' language, and help to wire the child's ear, voice and brain to engage with this language. If you are worried that you don't sing well enough, relax! For your child, your voice is the safest and most familiar sound, and is far better than any recorded music. Just as children learn language in interactive environments by being engaged in live conversation, they will gain the most benefit from being sung to directly by their caregivers.

You can begin singing to your child before they are even born – amniotic fluid is a great conductor of sound. Babies begin to respond to sound in the womb from around eighteen weeks' gestation, and the ability to recognise voices and even songs develops quite significantly by the end of pregnancy. Throughout my pregnancy with my son, Joshua, my husband, Jamie, sang one song to my belly, over and over again. When Josh was born, Jamie held him and sang that song, and immediately Josh stopped crying and stared quietly at him (and our midwife started to cry instead). As an infant Josh would still settle immediately whenever Jamie sang 'You Are My Sunshine'.

Sometimes it is hard to know WHAT to sing to your child, but there are many fabulous books designed to be sung to children of all ages – from illustrated nursery rhymes, to sung stories like *The Wonky Donkey* by Craig Smith (illustrated by Katz Cowley). Other books haven't necessarily been created with the purpose of being sung but seem to naturally lend themselves to it, for example, books written in rhyming verse. But you can sing to your child about everything and anything, so fill your day with music.

All book recommendation lists in *Raising Readers* do not include well-known or classic books. I have instead selected less obvious choices and my personal favourites. Consider each list as a springboard for you to seek out other books that might be a good fit for your young reader.

BOOKS FOR BABIES AND TODDLERS

Baby Business by Jasmine Seymour (Magabala Books, 2019)

Before We Met by Gabrielle Tozer, illustrated by Sophie Beer (HarperCollins, 2024)

Dreamers by Ezekiel Kwaymullina, illustrated by Sally Morgan (Fremantle Press, 2022)

For All Creatures by Glenda Millard, illustrated by Rebecca Cool (Walker Books, 2021)

Good Night, Good Beach by Joy Cowley, illustrated by Hilary Jean Tapper (Gecko Press, 2023)

Good Night, Me by Andrew Daddo, illustrated by Emma Quay (Hachette, 2005)

Kissed by the Moon by Alison Lester (Penguin, 2013)

Little Book Baby by Katrina Germein, illustrated by Cheryl Orsini (HarperCollins, 2024)

Miimi and Buwaarr, Mother and Baby by Melissa Greenwood (HarperCollins, 2024)

Puffling by Margaret Wild, illustrated by Julie Vivas (Scholastic, 2008)

Reading to Baby by Margaret Wild, illustrated by Hannah Sommerville (Affirm Press, 2024)

The Met Colours: A colourful book of art by The Metropolitan Museum of Art, New York (Dorling Kindersley, 2024)

These Little Feet by Hayley Rawsthorne, illustrated by Briony Stewart (Allen & Unwin, 2023)

When I'm Big by Karen Blair (Puffin, 2023)

FROM THREE TO FIVE YEARS OLD

It is tempting as children enter the preschool phase to turn shared reading time into a 'meaningful learning experience' in the belief that a child needs to be 'prepared' to enter the school system. Media representations of parenting are often fear-based, with parents left feeling their child will be disadvantaged if they are not signed up to the latest reading system or online literacy program. Intensive early intervention may produce a child who enters the school system seemingly 'reading' at a higher level, but as their peers learn to read at their own pace and 'catch up', those children with the *experience* of books and oral language exposure and practice are often the ones with higher all-round reading comprehension and engagement with books. By all means, sing songs with your preschooler, discuss books together and encourage them to write their name, but I urge parents and caregivers to keep it playful and be led by your child's interest and enthusiasm. Reading books and developing oral language skills and comprehension is still the single most important activity you can do with your child at this age.

Young children respond with enthusiasm when books are presented in multiple forms or modalities. For example, bring a book to life with props such as puppets, weave in songs, ask children to act out scenes from a story, or get them involved in a hands-on way with felt books. Engaging all of your child's senses in book-based experiences is crucial in maintaining their attention and creating a sense of playfulness.

Technology gives us further opportunities to re-imagine contemporary reading practices. Preschoolers experience story in a different, yet interactive way when they engage with digital texts on touch-based devices. I will never forget when my then three-year-old swiped the paper page of *The Very Cranky Bear* (Nick Bland) in total frustration, trying to make the bear move. I was horrified yet fascinated that she hoped for 'more' from the paper book. The print book will not be replaced, but print and digital stories now share space on the bookshelf.

Children in this age group also often enjoy creating handmade books. Asking your child to tell you the 'story' of their picture and writing this down on the page helps young children make connections between images and words. They will also delight in using their little books to retell their story to a loved adult. This retelling of a story over and over is important in developing the idea of how a narrative works as well as the knowledge that words always stay the same on the page – that the sounds *d-og* will always spell 'dog'. It is an absolute lightbulb moment when a child realises that text, those squiggles on a page, hold meaning, and writing and telling stories together is the perfect way to help your child make this discovery for themselves.

Reading with three- to five-year-olds

Although children in this age group generally have longer attention spans, they are still easily distracted by food, an adored older sibling or any bright shiny object! So keep book time fun to keep young readers interested.

Here are a few tactics I have used with my own young children and in early education centres:

- Turn off the TV and put away the screens. It can be hard to focus on a book when there are colourful, bright images constantly flashing by!
- Kids love humour so put on funny voices or make sound effects

to keep them engaged. Audio books can be a perfect addition for children around this age. They will love the variety in voices and start to understand how tone, pitch and pace can alter the feel of a story.

- Be interactive. Talk about what's happening in the story; ask your child to guess what's going to happen next; point out interesting details in the illustrations.
- Act out or add actions to parts of the story, or ask your child to do so. If you're not confident in this, try using props such as toys or puppets. Some books even come with finger puppets included as part of a pack.
- Talk about the parts of a book and physically point to the cover, pages, text, images and the spine.
- Follow the text with your finger so your child can see the way words flow from left to right.
- Be prepared to re-read favourite books over and over again. I promise they will one day move on to another book – although my now seventeen-year-old still holds onto her favourite dinosaur book from when she was two.
- Tell your kids how much you love reading with them. The emotional bond children form with books, through a loved adult enjoying the process with them and articulating this enjoyment, should not be underestimated.

ESTABLISHING READING ROUTINES

Establishing a reading routine from a young age helps children to develop strong lifelong reading habits. A child's love of books begins with loved adults taking the time out from a busy schedule to read with them. It's a wonderful bonding exercise. Cuddling up and reading with a child allows them to form powerful associations between books and moments of happiness, love and closeness.

But life can be stressful and it can be difficult to keep reading at the top of the priority list when there are work crises to deal with, children to wrangle, bills to pay, and so on. Every family has their own set of challenging circumstances. Making reading part of the daily routine helps to ensure that it happens because it becomes automatic, like brushing your teeth or turning on the dishwasher. But it also means that you're consistently carving out moments for yourself to relax and relish dedicated time with your child.

Bedtime reading is often the easiest routine to put in place as it is already a time of calmness, closeness and winding down from a busy day (more on this soon). However, there may be other opportunities throughout your day where reading routines can be established. There's no right or wrong time. Do whatever will work best for you and your family.

Going to the free 'Rhyme Time' or 'Babies and Books' sessions at your local library is a great way to incorporate fun literacy activities into your schedule. As I've mentioned, songs and nursery rhymes are wonderful tools for a child's oral language development. But sessions like these have the added benefit of filling your little one with the joyful feelings that come from being in a social setting.

Visiting the local library to sign my newborn up for a library card was one of the first outings I had with my children. For many years, my friends and I were in a weekly routine of meeting at the public library for nursery rhyme, music and storytelling sessions with our young babies. Our goal was to expose our children to the sights and sounds of language, but it also became a time for us to discuss, debate and recommend baby books (and some adult ones for ourselves!), leave with armfuls of library loans, and connect with like-minded parents over the trials and tribulations of raising small children.

PICTURE BOOKS FOR EARLY READERS

I don't believe you ever grow out of picture books. Though my children are no longer preschoolers, I will be keeping the books on this list forever. We have created special memories by reading these books together and they have become treasured possessions.

All of the Factors of Why I Love Tractors by Davina Bell, illustrated by Jenny Løvlie (Hardie Grant, 2019)

Do Not Lick This Book by Idan Ben-Barak, illustrated by Julian Frost (Allen & Unwin, 2017)

Good Morning, My Deer! by Mel Amon, illustrated by Sophie Beer (Scribble, 2023)

Gymnastica Fantastica! by Briony Stewart (Hachette, 2023)

Kurrartuwarnti (Brolgas) by June Nixon (Indigenous Literacy Foundation, 2024)

Ladybirds Do Not Go to Day Care (and others in the Preschool Problems series) by Ali Rutstein, illustrated by Niña Nill (Hardie Grant, 2023)

Manyi Nganyjaali (Bush Tomatoes) by Delphine Shandley (Indigenous Literacy Foundation, 2024)

Mayarda (Pelicans) by Patricia Cox, illustrated by Delphine Shandley (Indigenous Literacy Foundation, 2024)

Party Rhyme by Antonia Pesenti (Scribble, 2024)

Rock Pool Secrets by Narelle Oliver (Walker Books, 2017)

Shadow Catchers by Kirsty Murray, illustrated by Karen Blair (Allen & Unwin, 2023)

The Last Peach by Gus Gordon (Viking, 2018)

The Wheelbarrow Express by Sue Whiting, illustrated by Cate James (Walker Books, 2023)

This Is a Ball (and others in the Books That Drive Kids Crazy series) by Beck Stanton and Matt Stanton (HarperCollins, 2016)

Bedtime reading

In our house, my late husband, Dan, was the chief bedtime book reader for many years. At one point the Daddy bedtime books routine was a complicated and strict ritual involving two books, a thumb wrestle, two squashy hugs and something else I don't remember. It was lovely hearing Dan and our girls laugh over funny stories or argue about re-reading a book for the fifth night in a row. I am so pleased my children had these early years with a father who read to them, and this will be a treasured memory they carry into adulthood.

Establishing a bedtime reading routine with my stepsons was instrumental in forming relationships with them, providing an opportunity to be physically close and sharing stories, books and conversation together. Because they were cautious of my presence in the beginning, I read to them in a beanbag on the floor of their bedrooms but away from their bed. Over time, and as we shared books I had especially chosen for them, I graduated to reading next to the bed, then on the bed, and these days my youngest son wraps himself around me or squeezes my elbow as I read to him.

Now, my daughters are often the bedtime readers for their younger brothers and my thirteen-year-old recently swanned into my study brandishing a copy of *Bravepaw and the Heartstone of Alluria* by L. M. Wilkinson (illustrated by Lavanya Naidu). She announced it as their favourite bedtime read of the year and requested I hunt down a similarly adventure filled story.

Bedtime reading is definitely a routine worth aiming for. Sometimes, when I am exhausted by parenting and surrounded by small cranky people, it is so tempting to skip the bedtime books. But when I reflect on the benefits of a bedtime reading routine in my own life, it's clear to me why I make the effort nearly every night to do it:

- Bedtime books make me *stop*. I am on full throttle. All the time.

I sleep very little and I never sit still, but reading bedtime books makes me hit the pause button. Almost instantly I feel my frenetic energy dissipate.

- I have to be present and mindful to read. I can't be on my phone, I can't be washing or working. I have to read the words and engage with the story. I am entirely present with my children and the book we are reading together. For more on mindful reading see chapter 12.
- No matter how chaotic, *loud* and plain horrid the evening has been, bedtime reading is a change of focus and completely resets the mood in the house.
- It (almost) always happens. The routine makes me feel like everything will be okay, like I've *got* this parenting thing. Mostly.
- Books spark conversations. Every afternoon I ask my kids, 'What did you do today?' and *every* day I get nothing. But later that night we might read a book about friends or feelings, and they suddenly start talking about their day at school or an issue with a friend. When my children see their lives reflected in the pages of a book, talk happens.
- Going to sleep with dreams of fairies, dinosaurs or adventures is far better than dreams of being yelled at to floss your teeth properly. It's the last thing you do at night with your children, so make it wonderful.

Despite my lifelong love of books, some nights it is just too much, and I tell my children to read alone or I put on an audio story or streamed reading service like StoryBox Hub – perfectly acceptable alternatives and no guilt needed! However, I can see the benefits, for *myself* as well as my children, so I try really hard, take a deep breath and squash into bed with them. And then we read.

Even if it is only for fifteen minutes, that time spent reading is precious. Being physically close and escaping into an imaginary world through books reduces my stress and anxiety like nothing else I know. Whether you are a single parent, have multiple children or you work long hours, bedtime reading may be the one time in the day when you are completely present with your family. I never regret those fifteen minutes (which often turn into thirty). It's like exercise – you always feel better once you start, or so I'm told.

Challenges to bedtime reading

Time poor. Work on enlisting the help of other loved adults in your child's life, such as neighbours, grandparents or older siblings. For example, if your child has long-distance grandparents, perhaps they could share a book together over the phone or handheld tablet.

Reluctant readers. The thought of an argument just before sleeping time may be enough to prevent a parent from attempting bedtime books with their reluctant reader. The thing to remember is that for a reluctant reader, one-on-one book time with a loved adult can ignite the spark for a love of reading and of story. My advice here is simple – persist, persist, persist. Even when you feel like you are getting nowhere it is worth it, I promise. Choosing books that have a connection with a particular person is a good strategy here. Maybe Nonna always reads *My Nanna is a Ninja* by Damon Young (illustrated by Peter Carnavas) so it becomes 'her' book, or you might have a football-loving family member for whom *Why I Love Footy* by Michael Wagner (illustrated by Tom Jellett) is exclusively reserved.

Choosing the book. Dear glory, the battles we have in our house! We take it in turns, myself included, and we switch it up. Some weeks we will read picture books. Then we might spend a week on puzzle books and then we might have two weeks of reading a longer chapter book. Some people would suggest that the child should choose the bedtime books; but I, with my educator hat on, would argue that bedtime reading is the perfect time to introduce a new genre, explore a book at a higher literacy level, or share one of your own beloved novels from childhood. Taking it in turns means that everyone has choice, but there is also balance, compromise and a variety of reading material.

Incidental reading

Fitness experts talk about the importance of incidental exercise, so surely a teacher librarian can talk about incidental reading?! Incidental reading is all about snatching pockets of time in a busy day to quickly escape into a book with your child. It could be while you're waiting for the bath to fill or while you're killing time before a doctor's appointment. The key to incidental reading is to surround yourself with books so that they can be easily and regularly dipped into.

Place books in baskets or boxes throughout your home, chuck a few board books in the nappy bag, and stash a few in the car. Around the time she was five, my daughter, Ava, decorated an empty shoebox and filled it with board books for her younger sister, Georgia. She asked me to write 'Car Library' on it. We used that box until it fell apart and have had many more 'Mobile Library' boxes since.

I often keep borrowed library books on the back seat of the car, mostly so they don't get lost at home (which happens regularly, despite me being a librarian!). But having books in the car has also been a lifesaver for me. It doesn't always happen, but sometimes I can go on a 30-minute car trip with my children not whingeing, fighting or constantly asking, 'Are we there yet?' It is such a simple thing to do and can work wonders.

It's incredibly easy to model reading as a necessary part of everyday life when you are out and about. Read road signs and menus aloud, or hand your child a catalogue in the supermarket and ask them to read or name the pictures of the items, and then have them add up two or three of them for some numeracy practice.

Six easy 'coffee shop packs' for incidental reading

I'm more than guilty of the 'here, kids, have my phone while I drink my coffee' trick. No one wants to be the parent with the screaming children disturbing the entire café! But I also always carry books in my bag. For 'on-the-go' reading, I like to choose books that can be easily dipped in and out of, like a joke book or poetry anthology or fact book. I also keep coffee shop packs – small bags or zippered folders with a book, pencil, paper and props – in the car. I like to have a number of different packs on rotation so that they retain their novelty value and my kids will stay interested in them. Here are my top six suggestions for easy 'coffee shop packs':

1. **Mini editions of children's books.** These are often sold in school book club catalogues or around Christmas time as gift sets with soft toy characters. When she was young and compliant, my eldest child would neatly line up her five mini Olivia books (Ian Falconer), decide which one to 'read', then settle down to look at the pictures and tell the stories to herself or her mini Olivia finger puppet. Her ability to independently immerse herself in this imaginary world was due, in part, to my mum having read these books endlessly to her. She deeply absorbed the stories, which then informed her play.

2. **Doodle books, colouring books and activity books.** Doodle books are fab. They show a picture idea and the child is encouraged to continue drawing from it. For example, there might be an

outline of a TV screen and the child can draw a scene within it. Just remember to include colouring pencils in the pack. Books of mazes, word games or quizzes are also great for older children.

3. **A few nice picture books that are 'new' to the child.** These might be library books or ones you rotate from home, but the important thing is that they are a bit of a novelty for the child.

4. **'Spot the difference' or other 'finding' books.** These provide hours of entertainment as kids try to find small hidden things. I've set up the idea that my children have to find Wally all by themselves (mainly as I cannot ever find Wally myself!).

5. **Story stones.** These are smooth pebbles with stickers or small paintings of characters, settings and objects, which can be used to tell stories. There are plenty of ideas online for making these yourself or, if craft glue is your kryptonite, you can also buy pre-made ones. At some stage I must have found it quite therapeutic to make these (cut, glue, repeat) as I had about twenty little drawstring bags of different sets of story stones.

6. **Early reader books.** Sally Rippin's School of Monsters (illustrated by Chris Kennett) is a series for young readers which is a midway point between a school reader and a recreational reading text and they have been created with incredible care and attention to detail. A pile of School of Monsters books became our Coffee shop Books of Choice for our youngest son at around five years old; I credit this series with sparking his interest in trying to decode the words on the page. We have many photographs of our eldest daughter reading School of Monsters to James at coffee shops and the photos show his utter engagement in the books, which are in stark contrast to pictures without the books

– imagine food, drinks, legs and arms going in all directions. The Ebb and Flo series by Laura and Philip Bunting also sits in the space between school reader and recreational and not only has the wry humour that Philip Bunting is known for, but the added bonus of stickers – perfect for on-the-go play.

If you are passionate about literacy in the early years and have the desire and capacity to help children and youth living in out-of-home care, consider becoming involved with The Pyjama Foundation. Bronwyn Sheehan OAM founded the organisation with the aim of breaking the cycle of disadvantage experienced by children in care. The Pyjama Foundation trains volunteers, called Pyjama Angels, who are matched with a child in care. Pyjama Angels spend an hour a week with that one child reading books, playing educational games and helping with homework through a lens of connection, empowerment, trust and transformation. Through early intervention, support and mentoring, children in care are able to change their life trajectory; literacy and the immense joy of owning and reading books is a huge part of this. For more information see www.thepyjamafoundation.com.

PLAYFUL READING

My favourite memories of my own childhood are of playing with a huge circle of family friends. Playing was just what we did – it was an organic part of our lives. Our parents never agonised over our choices of games or thought about creating 'meaningful learning experiences'. In those days, everyone seemed to accept that free play was a natural and essential part of childhood.

But of course we *were* learning through our play, as we constructed cubbyhouses and imaginary worlds; experimented with floating and sinking (the caterpillar didn't float – sorry, caterpillar); negotiated with our peers over what games to play next and who was 'it'; practised our numbers while baking and selling mud pies, and empathised with one another as bones were snapped on netless trampolines of the 1980s.

These days, between technology, work, school and extracurricular activities, and the feeling that we must 'entertain and educate' our children at all times, free play seems to have fallen by the wayside. I cannot stress enough how play and literacy development go hand-in-hand. A game of 'shop' may require children to write and read shopping lists or food labels. A game of 'school' will often involve the 'teacher' asking the 'student' to write their own name or listen to a 'modelled book reading'. It is well documented in early literacy development research that parents and educators need to value play as an important and valid part in literacy development as children engage with and respond to stories, create their own stories, and learn about themselves and their world.[10]

Emma Sainty is a kindergarten teacher and advocate for literacy development through play-based learning experiences. Her learning spaces always have books dispersed throughout as well as a book corner or nook which offers children a place to escape the busyness of the classroom, a way to settle into their day, or a space to be immersed in story and imaginary worlds. Emma shares her thoughts below on playful reading in the kindergarten setting.

Emma Sainty

Play is an all-important, and sadly sometimes overlooked, aspect of child development. Play allows children to master social, emotional and academic skills while interacting with peers and the world around them. The mastery of social skills through play develops resilience, problem-solving, empathy and kindness. Through play, children learn to work alongside and with each other, negotiate roles and problem-solve conflicts. They practise their decision-making skills, act out and work through scenarios and interact with a diverse range of peers and adults in a safe environment.

Quality picture books play a pivotal role in play-based learning and oral language development. Children most often role-play situations that they know and understand. Most preschools, kindergartens and prep rooms will have a home corner where you will see children playing various family games. Children take on the roles that they are most familiar with, act them out and make up variations on these games – often informed by the books we have been reading. In doing so, children are developing an understanding of how different roles in the world work, how different families operate, and are challenged by other children when something doesn't go as planned. Role-play in the early years is a way for children to 'try out' the lives of others, such as being a parent and looking after the crying babies (you wouldn't believe how unsettled the 'babies' in my classroom are).

Picture books give young children the visuals for the words on the page. They form an important part of our daily routine and are embedded into our program to support, inform and extend children's play. We read a wide range of books based on the children's interests and every year we find that different groups of children take different things out of the same books.

We have books in outdoor spaces where much play occurs, and while these books will not last as long they are an important component in our play spaces. We often add things to our home corner or change it up completely based on the children's interests and literacy curriculum, which very often stem from a book we have read. I place high value on books and I model this through the way I respect and engage with books. We read every day and children frequently bring in their favourite book from home. These books are carefully placed on the whiteboard each morning, ready to be shared, discussed and enjoyed together. I find that there is often a trend with books that come in from home, demonstrating that children make connections with books we read at kindergarten and similar books they have at home. We may get a run on animal books or books about school or even books by the same author.

Recently we read a Hairy Maclary book in class and the children loved the predictability of the text with the rhyming dog names and were able to playfully join in the reading experience. This one book resulted in an influx of Hairy Maclary books (Lynley Dodd) from home to share with the class. A group of children were enjoying pretending to be dogs and role-playing with their peers. This play was completely organic, and in our classroom we encourage the children to ask their educators for extra props if required. This led to quite a detailed discussion about what they needed for their 'doggie' play. We ended up making a variety of tails, which have been ever so popular, and this imaginative play continued for a couple of weeks. It encouraged children to use verbal and non-verbal language, take turns, share both resources and the different roles they had created within their game, and let us not forget the gross motor skills these children developed when crawling around the classroom!

I almost always use books as the starting point for new topics of interest. A recent unit of work on fairytales involved a huge number of books. Each fairytale was read to the children and they re-enacted the stories incidentally in their play and explicitly through intentional teaching. The language opportunities, storytelling and retelling that flowed from this unit was a delight to witness. We always have a 'small world' area set up in our classroom where children are able to take a set of imaginative play objects and play with them whenever it suits their rhythm. This area is resourced with puppets, objects and props, and during our fairytale unit our small world space became larger than life! Houses were constructed for the Three Little Pigs and puppets were sourced or made to play Little Red Riding Hood and her grandmother.

Some of the children asked if they could act out some of the stories with an audience, so we created a stage and seating; there were even tickets to the show. This simple example of a common unit or area of interest for kindergarten-age children demonstrates the power of books as a starting point for play, acquisition of literacy skills and engagement in the arts.

In a technology-filled and busy world with so many structured activities aimed at engaging young children and their parents, there is something refreshing and comforting about seeing young children playing organically, in their own time, following their own rhythm.

Add books into the mix, and the power of the written word and beauty of the illustrations will take children's play to an even richer and more valuable place.

CHAPTER TWO

READING AND SCHOOL

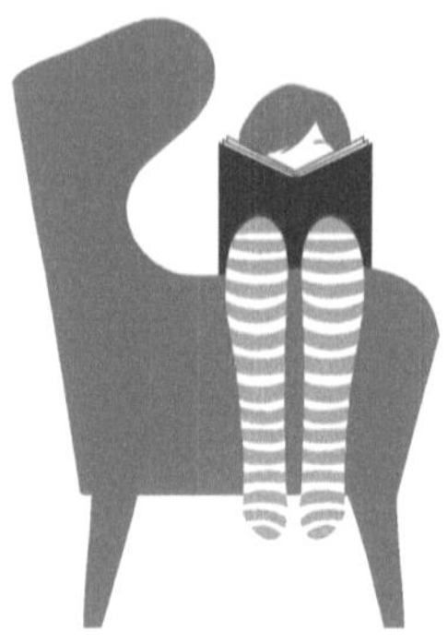

LEARNING TO READ

Learning to read and subsequently being a reader is a skill and a way of life. To me, reading is a way of being; through research we know that reading is central to wellbeing, academic success and job opportunities.[1] Indeed, effective education is classified as a fundamental human right by the United Nations Educational, Scientific and Cultural Organization (UNESCO).[2]

Yet learning to read, for many, is fraught and not an easily acquired skill – high rates of reading failure worldwide is testament to this.[3] Even I, a teacher librarian who has provided my children with the same print- and language-rich home environment as I grew up in (thanks, Mum and Dad), have discovered that for some family members this supportive environment still has not produced readers. I remain convinced that a home environment that fosters both oral and print language is the 'gold standard', and is a significant protective factor in 'raising readers',[4] but we must also consider how our young people are being taught the skills of reading.

Research in education, neuroscience, linguistics and cognitive psychology allow education systems and educators to now understand that, unlike speaking and listening which in most cases are naturally acquired as part of human development, the skills of reading and writing require explicit instruction and knowledge.[5] The educational outcome of this research has produced the Science of Reading. Without explicit instruction, not all children will slip easily into 'being a reader', even when supported with the best of intentions. Some children will learn to read with minimal instruction, but the vast majority need to be taught explicitly.

The shift towards the Science of Reading is slow because teaching is a demanding profession and teachers need time and professional development to take on board the research. My own journey in understanding the Science of Reading and applying it in my teaching practice has been at times challenging, even distressing. I have wrestled with the task of pulling apart and critically examining my own university education, my personal experiences as a reader, writer and parent, and my personal preferences. But when we know better, we can do better.

I find it incomprehensible that our system fails so many young people and allows them to grow into adults still struggling with literacy issues. I have my own literacy challenges (punctuation and spelling – just talk to my mother or my podcast co-host Allison Tait) but the protective factors of my home environment ensured my journey to becoming a reader and writer was a smooth one. Language skills follow a social gradient and a disproportionate number of children from low socioeconomic family backgrounds have fewer protective factors and greater risk factors.[6] Access to quality and early explicit instruction is what we must demand from our education system.

If you are an educator on your own journey of understanding how we teach the code of written English to ensure literacy success, I recommend the podcast *Sold a Story: How Teaching Kids to Read*

Went So Wrong by American educational reporter Emily Hanford. I saw myself in this podcast, I saw my place in the system and how I contributed to challenges for young people struggling to learn the reading code. It also filled me with hope for the future of reading.

As a parent or caregiver, it is important that you understand the skill of reading so you can advocate for your child and support them in the home environment. Further, it enables you to champion skilled classroom teachers, teacher librarians and other allied health professionals.

INGREDIENTS OF READING

The Science of Reading identified the main ingredients required to learn to read and the sequence in which they should occur.[7] I am a keen baker who uses baking to solve most of the problems in my life. As a baker, I understand that making a cake is a science and I can't deviate from the outlined ingredients or the order of the steps, which have been tested multiple times by expert chefs and food scientists. A curry or granola may have a 'little of this and a little of that' to artfully balance flavours, but when baking, one must follow the ingredients and the steps to the letter.

Explicit, evidence-informed reading instruction does not diminish educator autonomy or discard the art of teaching children how to read.[8] Teaching remains an artform and skilled educators consciously and creatively build connection with students, nurturing empathy and persistence, and creating pathways for young minds to bridge key learning areas and maximise learning outcomes.

I may bake a cake based on science but I present it at the table in an artful way so it will be fully appreciated and enjoyed. In the same way, teaching is artful, but parts of it must acknowledge research-based science to ensure successful outcomes.

The ingredients for reading are:

- Oral language
- Phonemic awareness
- Phonics
- Fluency
- Vocabulary
- Comprehension

STEPS FOR TEACHING READING

Learning to read and write independently requires explicit and sequential teaching and guided practice to develop knowledge and skills cumulatively over time.

1. **Soaking in oral language skills.** Nurture strong oral language foundations by absorbing students in conversations, storytelling and listening activities, which fosters a wide vocabulary and introduces sentence structure.

2. **Add phonemic awareness.** Skilfully mix in phonemic awareness – the ability to hear and manipulate the individual sounds in spoken words – by segmenting (breaking down) and blending sounds. This step is crucial as it prepares students to connect sounds to letters, so add gentle heat.

3. **Introduce phonics instruction.** Phonics teaches the relationship between sounds (phonemes) and their written symbols (graphemes). Instruction begins with basic sound-letter correspondences and advances to more complex patterns as all ingredients continue to absorb flavour.

4. **Whisk in reading fluency.** Fluency – reading with speed, accuracy and proper expression – is developed through repeated, guided reading practice. Reading familiar texts multiple times develops automaticity and a smooth consistency.

5. **Add vocabulary.** Liberally sprinkle new words in meaningful contexts to expand the mixture. Include activities that introduce new words in different subjects, and encourage curiosity about language. Rich vocabulary allows students to understand more complex texts and express themselves effectively, and with a depth of flavour and flair.

6. **Fold comprehension through the mix.** Reading comprehension involves understanding and interpreting the meaning of texts. Comprehension is the ultimate goal of reading, connecting all previous steps. Give it a little time and voila! Your independent reader is ready.

An independent reader is a masterpiece – beautiful to behold – and as every lifelong reader knows, the reading recipe will challenge and delight in equal measure and become richer as its flavours develop. In this way, a reader is less like a cake and more like a master stock or a sourdough starter that will, when nurtured, continue to gain value and improve over time.

Just as a baker follows a recipe precisely, educators guide students through these stages with explicit, evidence-informed instruction. By blending science-based methods with artful delivery, educators craft rich and robust learning experiences.

I have worked alongside classroom teacher and curriculum leader Katie Bryant for some years now and she has been instrumental in arming educators, parents and carers with the research and knowledge needed to understand the Science of Reading.

Katie Bryant

As Megan has detailed, there is both an art and a science to teaching young children how to read and write. Teaching is not singing 'Kumbaya' on a ukulele and babysitting until 3 pm, while chanting, 'One, two, three, eyes on me.' It is far more nuanced, and there are many great teachers who have gone before us who have taught children how to read. Well, most of them. But (and here's the thing) we all got very comfortable thinking that everyone learns differently and that some children will struggle and 'that's okay'.

I was asked recently: 'When was the last time you changed your mind about something big?'

For me, it has been hard to accept that some children will always be behind in reading or will struggle with writing. I decided that I didn't agree with this idea. In fact, as Megan has mentioned, learning to read is now recognised as a fundamental human right (UNESCO).

Is my school teaching literacy the 'right way'?

Like Megan, I have become very engaged in the Science of Reading and also the Science of Learning. Okay, well, some people might say I have become obsessed with the topics. My husband always jokes, don't ask Katie a 'light' question about language, literacy or learning and expect 'light banter back'. I love to chat about reading and literacy everywhere I go and hear all the different opinions. Everyone has experience with reading and writing themselves (positive and negative) and as I spend time with other parents, they tell me about the experiences with their own children (positive and negative).

Teachers also have positive and negative experiences when they are teaching reading and writing, and most have honed their craft over time in the classroom. Many have seen different initiatives and programs come and go over the years. Teachers might keep certain parts of a particular program in their repertoire, while others have moved on and started using newer techniques. This invisible 'toolkit' that teachers build can be referred to as their 'pedagogy' or their own style or way of doing things in the classroom. When working with other teachers on literacy, I often ask them about their training and previous experiences to see if they have engaged with the Science of Reading and the Science of Learning. For many teachers, there can be a lag or gap between when new research is presented and when it is practised in the classroom, and I often wonder if this gap is connected to the concept of pedagogy.

Being able to have your own pedagogical style in your classroom is a very accepted practice in the education sector. It's funny, because if we transpose this to other sectors that also have professional standards, we are shocked! Teachers say, 'In my classroom, what I like to do is this' or 'What I've always done is that'. Imagine a doctor explaining that they like to make their patients comfortable with a high-touch approach but try to save time by not washing their hands between patients. Or a pilot who doesn't want to do a pre-flight safety check because it's more important to connect with the crew and catch up on their news. We very quickly point out the professional standards that govern these practices and say, 'Hey, stick to the rules, that's not safe.'

Teaching is also governed by professional standards, and every child deserves a teacher who is trained in the Science of Reading. Children have a finite amount of time before they need to be literate to access the curriculum. We must honour and respect that time and act quickly and purposefully if we notice an issue.

Every teacher agrees that literacy instruction is vital and that reading and writing are difficult skills for students to master. We all want readers who make meaning and writers who convey meaning. This shared understanding is not hard to agree on. However, teachers choose different approaches to teaching literacy; schools often encourage staff to value individualised instruction and differentiation and lean into our own reading experiences to teach students how to read. We often think that because each human is unique, everyone learns to read in their own unique way. In fact, this misconception is part of the problem for parents, carers and teachers.

As French neuroscientist and author Dr Stanislas Dehaene makes clear in his book *Reading in the Brain*: 'It is simply not true that there are hundreds of ways to learn to read … when it comes to reading, we all have roughly the same brain that imposes the same constraints and the same learning sequence.'

When a child starts school, we cannot predict with any kind of accuracy whether they will experience any difficulties in learning to read and write. The shift to becoming a proficient reader and writer is a complex interaction of cognitive activities that continues over a lifespan. By grasping the reciprocal and ongoing relationship of language and literacy, teachers can ensure instruction is impactful so that students not only attain early reading success but continue to develop proficient literacy skills.

It is amazing to look back and realise that reading and writing are relatively new skills and that for thousands of years we did not acquire these skills. While oral language is considered innate and is referred to as a 'biologically primary skill', writing and reading are regarded as 'biologically secondary skills'.[9] Despite this evolutionary difference, the brain can repurpose neural networks utilised for visual recognition rather than creating new ones specifically for learning the secondary skills of reading and writing.[10] This repurposing of the brain takes time and only occurs with explicit instruction. While reading and writing were not prerequisites for survival in earlier societies, these literacy abilities are crucial for survival today.[11] Don't get me started on the horrible and alarming statistics surrounding illiteracy and the pathways here … (my banter becomes less light).

A large proportion of student learning time in schools is therefore dedicated to literacy. What is being taught and how it is being taught are both important parts to an effective literacy program. Teachers who have a strong understanding of each child's skills – their ability to read (decode) and write (encode) – will be best placed to support their development. As significant variation exists in teacher knowledge of the Science of Reading and the Science of Learning, significant changes need to be made to many teachers' pedagogical style and lesson planning habits for literacy.

Here are some key takeaways – you can use these talking points as light banter at your next barbecue (folks love it)!

- **Reading and writing share reciprocal skills.** Reading and writing taught in tandem are mutually reinforcing, as they share many underlying skills.[12] Teaching literacy, through encoding and decoding, will enhance student outcomes.

- **Reading is not simple.** In fact, teaching children to read is one of the most important tasks in primary classrooms as there is an urgent need to reduce the number of people who cannot read. As words are not learnt through a visual process, codification or orthographic mapping is essential[13] and can take up to three years for students to master.[14]
- **Writing is not simple.** In fact, it is probably one of the most cognitively demanding activities students undertake in a day at school. Writing is more than just transcription of spoken language; it is a means of communication that typically involves more complex grammatical structures and a wider vocabulary.
- **Students' cognitive resources are limited.** The mental energy and capacity that pupils employ to think, learn and solve issues is referred to as cognitive resources. Students (and teachers) have finite cognitive resources, which means that the amount of mental ability that can be used at any given time to process information, solve issues and take on new ideas is limited.

Making changes to teaching within schools can be hard. Go too quickly and staff can become confused and vulnerable. Go too slowly and uptake becomes inconsistent. Assessing each teacher's toolkit and figuring out which techniques need to be enhanced and which need to be de-implemented takes time. Schools aren't historically great at de-implementation practices. Letting go of outdated techniques and habits is incredibly challenging and will take time.

Questions for teachers in the staff room

- Do I really understand how a word becomes a sight word?
- Do I know how memory works?
- Do I have a clear understanding of the 'same set of skills' students need to learn to read/write?

Attending various professional development (PD) courses or workshops for staff can be one way to upskill teachers and change teaching practices. Sharing articles and podcasts might be another. Working collaboratively to unpack and assess different programs and how they might fit in your school context is also important. Some students will have complex needs and schools need to be open-minded about engaging with a multi-disciplinary team that includes speech pathologists, occupational therapists, psychologists and paediatricians who can understand student needs. (Look out allied health professionals that come to my school, I use each conversation as my own mini-PD opportunity, peppering them with questionsI).

As a parent of a school-age child, I know trying to decide which school to attend and understand what the school's literacy program is like can be daunting. What is written on a school's website or brochure isn't necessarily the same as what is happening in all classrooms. Remember: a teacher's individual pedagogical style can be strong, so it is important to gain a representative sample of teaching styles before forming a view. Schools are dynamic places that are always changing, so this needs to be understood and responses need to be framed in a flexible way.

Questions to ask your school/child's teacher

- How are literacy lessons structured within the school day?
- What literacy approach does the school follow (e.g. phonics-based, balanced literacy, whole language)?
- How does the school align its literacy instruction with the national curriculum?
- How is phonics taught, and does the school follow a structured literacy approach?
- How are comprehension, vocabulary and fluency explicitly taught?
- What strategies are used to develop students' writing skills?
- How does the school assess students' reading and writing progress?
- Does the school have a staffed school library?

Questions to ask about providing support at home

- What reading materials or recommended book lists are provided for home reading and writing?
- How does the school communicate with parents and carers about their child's literacy progress?
- Are there caregiver workshops or resources available on literacy strategies?
- Is the school library available to the parent and carer community?

My number one piece of advice is to always approach the teaching cohort with curiosity. Every child deserves a teacher trained in the Science of Reading, and while schools are imperfect systems, they are also filled with great humans who want to be there and see students succeed. Good luck – may your barbecue banter be light and your children have a smooth reading journey.

READING COMPREHENSION AND DIALOGIC READING

Katie has outlined what should be happening in classrooms. As young children learn to lift words off the page and decode them, they also learn to construct meaning from a text by making inferences, verifying understandings and repairing their reading. Ultimately, the purpose and goal of reading is to comprehend the text.

Talking about books is one of the earliest ways in which parents, caregivers and educators can engage a child in reading and encourage their comprehension. Reading with young children should not always be a formal learning experience, however it is great to get into the habit of dialogic reading – creating dialogue around books that are read aloud with your child, by asking questions and having informal discussions about the content, context or connections you can make with a book.

When a child starts to decode words in a text, we can get so caught up in the excitement of the word reading, that we momentarily forget that comprehension is an essential element in the process. I see plenty of very young children who can read the words on a page, but if you ask them a few questions about the content of the book, they are at a loss; their deep understanding of a book is not at the same skill level as their ability to decode words. Comprehension is central to reading development.

Reading comprehension is the product of both the ability to *decode words* and the ability to *interpret words* and comprehend language.[15] It is an interaction of skills and cognitive processes that occurs as children achieve mastery of accuracy and fluency with decoding.

When reading and comprehending a text, another protective factor in 'becoming a reader' is the background knowledge a child can bring to the table.[16] Background knowledge is all that a child knows about the world around them through their own experiences, facts they have picked up along the way, and vocabulary they have been exposed to. Obviously, a print-rich home is the ideal environment in which to mentally map background knowledge. Mental maps, constructed by what we know about a topic, are stored in our long-term memory and can be drawn upon when reading and comprehending a text.

For example, I do not have a great mental map for comprehending a book about soccer. I understand very little about the way sporting games work, so my ability to comprehend a book about soccer is impacted. If I wanted to build that area of comprehension, I would need to experience more soccer games (unlikely!) or build my knowledge through books and other resources, such as watching soccer on television.

Parents and caregivers can be of great support in building background knowledge (maps). If you know that your child is learning about a particular topic in school, this is an opportunity to curate a selection of books around that topic. Carefully chosen books can help them to build the requisite knowledge they will need to comprehend work at school and support them in written and other tasks.

Recently, our youngest child, James, was involved in a unit of inquiry looking at celebrations around the world. He has a reading nook under the stairs at home, so I added to this area a selection of books on celebrations from various countries. James and his older brother, Sam, come from Russian and English heritage and James took a keen interest in the customs of these countries. Many of our dinner and car conversations revolved around celebrations he read about in these books. James now has a mental map that he can refer to and apply to other situations.

Around the same time, our youngest daughter, Georgia, was looking at folktales in Year Seven Drama. Again, I added to her reading pile some books with folktales from around the world. She possibly soaked up some of the conversations about Russian celebrations that were occurring at the time, but for whatever reason, she chose a Russian folktale for her assessment piece. The conversations about Russian culture, the shared experiences, the books they had to dip in and out of, all helped to create mental maps for both Georgia and James.

The following list of conversation starters can be used with toddlers right through to independent readers in order to create dialogue around books and increase comprehension. Often, I find that 'reading comprehension' questions related to books elicit a noun response, for example, 'What is the author's name?' Consider how to create a dialogue that will nurture curiosity and comprehension in all ages of readers. The questions below are a mix of 'book knowledge' questions, recall questions, how and why questions, and questions that require a child to predict or explain. Modify as needed and add your own questions into the mix.

Engaging in dialogic reading without making it a chore gives you an insight into your child's level of comprehension and encourages development of critical thinking skills. The idea is not to work through a list of questions after each book is read – that is no fun. But, when your child is in the mood, casually ask one or two questions. In the past, I have written questions on paddle-pop sticks and put them in a bottle and turned it into a lucky dip game. Another suggestion is to make paper chatterboxes where your young reader can pick the question. Get creative and make up board games or cardboard dice with questions written on them. There are no rules and you will know what your own kids prefer.

Dialogic reading question ideas:

- Can you find the author's name on the cover?
- Can you find the illustrator's name?
- What do you think of the illustrations in the book? Are they painted? Drawn? Is it a collage? Photographs? Are they black and white or coloured? How is colour used?
- Which is your favourite illustration? Why is it your favourite?
- What do you think might happen next in the story?
- If you were the author of the story, would you have finished it the same way? How would you change the ending?
- What do you think the author was trying to say to us? What helped you figure out the message?
- What part of the story was the most exciting or interesting?
- When *X* happened in the book, what did you think might happen next?
- Which character was your favourite?

- When character *X* did *X*, what might they have been thinking about?
- Did any of the characters remind you of anyone you know?
- Compare two characters in the book – how do they approach things differently?
- Do you think it would be better for character *X* to do *X*? Why?
- What do you think it would be like to be character *X*?
- Think about the story from the perspective of one of the characters. How might they feel?
- Can you think of any other books that are similar to this one?
- Point to the parts of the book when I call them out: spine, front cover, back cover, blurb, title.
- How did this book make you feel? Was it a happy book? Was it thoughtful? Scary? Adventurous?
- What is the setting of this story? Where else could the book be set? Would that change the story?
- Can you ask me a question about the book we just read?
- Can you retell the story?
- Who is telling the story?
- Can you think of a friend who might like this book? Why do you think they would like it?

READERS AND LIBRARY BOOKS

I often have parents visit my school library early in the year to find books that their child will be able to read by themselves. I take this as an opportunity to talk about the wonder of the school library and the differences between readers (teacher-chosen sequenced readers) and library books (self-selected library books for the purpose of reading for pleasure).

Readers are short texts, specifically designed for the purpose of teaching reading. To the capable adult, readers may appear dull and uninteresting, and the first few years of primary school can seem like a never-ending frantic search for those flimsy school readers that teachers hand out with the reverence of a first-edition classic. Classroom readers are teaching tools that align with a synthetic phonics or code-based approach to reading. Children develop phonological decoding skills and letter-sound knowledge that they will begin to apply independently. They encourage children to sound out words using decoding strategies rather than guessing from pictures or predicting. Readers form part of the 'learn to read toolkit', alongside a suite of other strategies and ongoing reading assessment. The decodable readers that come home from school have already been taught and the 'home reader' is an opportunity for kids to rehearse skills and develop fluency. They can also be a resource for parents and caregivers to use as a spelling guide through practising dictation, as there is a beautiful reciprocity between reading and spelling.

As library lessons begin for the year, library bags full of big picture books are dragged home like treasure sacks and unpacked with excitement. Books borrowed from the school library are self-selected, recreational reads and help young people develop an emotional attachment to reading, lifelong reading habits and reading comprehension skills. Picture books and early chapter books are complex interplays between words and text, and require young people to think deeply, imagine, wonder and interpret (see chapter 4). They contain sophisticated language that requires discussion and increases your child's vocabulary. They are also full of images that add to and extend the text.

Books that your child has chosen from the library are for sharing with a loved adult and are usually a read-aloud experience until your child is reading independently. Even then, reading aloud to your child is something I encourage well into the upper primary years and beyond. Reading comprehension is developed through dialogic reading with an adult and independent exploration by the child.

Young people need both classroom readers and library books/recreational reads – each supports the other but has a distinct purpose. Eventually, reading skills, reading comprehension and, hopefully, a heart-and-soul connection with books will start to intertwine and produce a skilled reader.

BOOKS FOR EMERGING READERS

This list of books is for young readers who are just starting their independent reading journey. A series is great at this stage as there is comfort and familiarity in knowing the setting and characters, and fluency can be practised.

Billie B Brown series by Sally Rippin, illustrated by Aki Fukuoka (Hardie Grant)

Cranky Chicken series by Katherine Battersby (Hachette)

Ebb and Flo series by Laura and Philip Bunting (Hardie Grant)

Ella and the Amazing Frog Orchestra by Cassy Polimeni, illustrated by Hykie Breeze (UWA Publishing, 2024)

Flying High by Sally Morgan and Ezekiel Kwaymullina, illustrated by Craig Smith (Scholastic, 2015)

Fox Kid series by Adrian Beck (Little Learners Love Literacy)

Ginger Green series by Kim Kane, illustrated by Jon Davis (Hardie Grant)

Going Bush with Grandpa by Sally Morgan and Ezekiel Kwaymullina, illustrated by Craig Smith (Scholastic, 2014)

Hey Jack! series by Sally Rippin, illustrated by Stephanie Spartels (Hardie Grant)

Kev and Trev 1: Snot Funny Sea Stories! by Kylie Howarth (Affirm Press, 2024)

Mates: Great Australian Yarns series by various authors (Scholastic)

School of Monsters series by Sally Rippin, illustrated by Chris Kennett (Hardie Grant)

Sporty Kids series by Felice Arena, illustrated by Tom Jellett (Puffin)

Taronga Presents series by Kristin Darell, illustrated by Laura Wood (Penguin)

The Memory Shed by Sally Morgan and Ezekiel Kwaymullina, illustrated by Craig Smith (Scholastic, 2015)

Award-winning children's author Pamela Rushby writes the most beautiful prose, and some of my favourite historical fiction novels for middle-grade readers, but I often find her name on classroom readers. I asked her why and how she writes in these vastly different ways.

Pamela Rushby

I've been writing for both trade and educational publishers for more than twenty years and in that time I've had over 200 educational books published. This sounds impressive until you remember that some of these books are only about eight pages long, and might contain only twenty (or fewer) words. These, believe it or not, are the hardest ones of all to write.

Trade books are the ones you'll find in bookshops, as well as public and school libraries. They're for recreational reading: books you choose and love to read. Educational books are largely found in classrooms.

If you looked at a number of trade books and educational books lined up on a shelf, you might not be able to see much of a difference between them. They're all attractive to children, they're entertaining, they're colourful, they're well edited, they're well illustrated. But there is a difference. Educational books are carefully designed, by educational experts, to give children in classrooms practice in reading, to introduce them to new ideas and concepts, to develop reading skills, to build confidence, and to put children's learning into a broad context.

For a writer, choosing to write for the educational market is a whole different ballgame to choosing to write for trade.

A friend of mine once said that a writer's brain is like a lava lamp. At the bottom there's a whole gooey, pulsating mass of thoughts and ideas. Every once in a while, one idea might go *bloop!* and rise to the top. You'll think about it for a while, it'll change shape, perhaps get bigger, another idea might join onto it. Then it'll sink to the bottom again. But one day, that idea will rise to the top and won't go away, and you'll think, *Aha! There's a story!*

That's the way it works when I write for the trade market. I start out with an idea I've had. It's been blooping around in the lava lamp for quite a while, growing and developing. When it's ready to go, I'll know, because it just won't go away. And soon I'll be writing that story, because I desperately want to write it. (And fingers crossed a publisher will, eventually, want it too.)

When I write for the educational market I'm almost always writing commissioned material. A publisher has decided to produce a new series of books and invited writers to contribute to the series. The publisher will have an absolutely clear idea of what the series is intending to achieve, and the writer will receive a brief that outlines the publisher's needs and expectations. Let me give you an example.

A brief I received for some beginner reading books asked me to write a story about 'weather and its effect on people'. I had 120 to 150 words to do this. I needed to include certain high-frequency words at least eight times in the text. I also needed to include a phonic element and/or a vocabulary element from a given list. Oh, and it would be nice, the brief concluded, if I could manage to be funny too.

Quite a challenge.

After a lot of thought and juggling of ideas and words (and a certain amount of whingeing, whining and despair), it was possible. I did it.

The trick is to approach a brief as if it's a puzzle to be solved. It may take some time, but, like a cryptic crossword, it can be done. It's a totally different way of writing from coming up with your own idea and developing your own story exactly as you want it to be.

One of the misconceptions people have about educational books is that they're boring. Well, in the past some certainly were. You may have memories of some of them. (*See Spot run. Run, Spot, run.*) But writers now see it as a challenge to make the books fun as well as meeting their educational aims. The one I'm working on features Spacegirl, a superhero who saves the universe by lassoing planets. I'm restricted to a very limited vocabulary and word count, (similar to the See Spot Run books), but I'm having fun with it – and I hope the kids will enjoy them too.

Usually, editors from the publishing house will provide suggested topics to write about, although I've found editors to be very open to any suggestions I make too. And boring? Never! In the past few years I've written about the scariest theme park ride in the world; why cows' burps are increasing the levels of greenhouse gases in New Zealand; aquanauts living under the sea for extended periods; and high fashion for dogs – all have been total fun to research and write about.

When your beloved child comes home from school and presents you with the evening's homework reading, you can be assured that they are going to gain from that reading. Because to produce the fifty or so words in that little book, a lot of people – educational experts, designers, editors, illustrators, and writers – have put in a lot of time and effort to deliver a meaningful learning experience.

CHAPTER THREE

THE SCHOOL LIBRARY

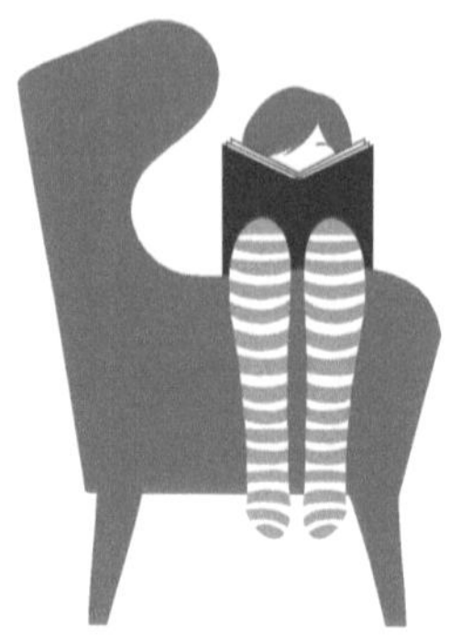

THE SCHOOL LIBRARY AND THE TEACHER LIBRARIAN

Many parents and educators are aware that school libraries are facing challenges of budget and staffing cuts. This trend has been on the rise for some time, but I'm not one to worry too much about trends. I think I rather like to buck them. I am also a firm believer that if you hold onto something for long enough it will come back in style, usually with a few tweaks that make it even better; in short, I reckon libraries are back in vogue. In the 1980s my mother bucked all fashion trends, and I remember being utterly mortified at her turning up to my rowing practice in zebra print jeans and Madonna sunglasses, long before these items were a thing. It is said that we turn into our mothers, and I have most certainly followed in her footsteps, both in becoming a teacher librarian and horrifying my children with my fashion choices.

Well-resourced school libraries and school library staff are worth their weight in gold, and the positive impact they can have on an entire school community is well documented anecdotally and in research. Well-resourced school libraries, with exemplary teacher librarians and library support staff, develop and sustain a vibrant reading culture, promote innovative use of digital technologies and are a participatory hub within schools.

Stepping off my soapbox for a moment, what are the practicalities involved in ensuring the school in your community has a well-resourced library with passionate library staff who work to meet the curriculum and recreational needs of their patrons?

What is the purpose of a school library?

School libraries exist as learning environments providing physical, digital and online spaces to enable access to high quality, diverse collections of resources, activities and services. These appropriately and ethically encourage and support the learning of all who engage with the space. Libraries are community resource centres and operate to contribute to the betterment of their customers, arming patrons with the information they require, and as a social space that can be used for cultural and educational events. School libraries vary in size, funding and staffing but all are focused on supporting student learning and creating lifelong learners and readers. School curriculums are resourced through the teacher librarian, who seeks to extend and support the individual curriculum, goals and ethos of their school. School libraries are wonderful places, the beating heart of many school communities and a refuge for those who need time away from a busy school environment.

What should your school library look like?

A school library does not need an expensive fit-out or architecturally designed space. The very first school library I was put in charge of was a one-room demountable building in the middle of a dusty carpark at the back end of the primary school. Despite the distant location, it was such a hive of activity that we had to hand out numbered cards to monitor the number of students allowed inside at any one time. Those 'today you can visit the library at lunchtime' cards were as valuable as Golden Tickets to Willy Wonka's chocolate factory.

If you are a parent, carer or teacher, the following things are what I believe you should *expect* from your school library. It should:

- Be welcoming, inviting and, above all, accessible. Libraries should provide all community members with equal access to knowledge and physical space.
- Be visible throughout the school. Being visible is not just about building placement, but also about excellent signage and presence both online (school website and social media) and in real life – for example, is your teacher librarian seen at all the major events at school?
- Have library staff who smile and are helpful because libraries are a service to the community. If your library staff are only ever behind a closed office door, you should consider removing that door or moving their work station to the front counter.
- Like a fast-food joint, your school library should be upselling at all times: 'Would you like a magazine with your loans this week?'
- Have a sense of order. I am all for chaos, and my washing pile is a testament to this. Libraries, however, should be easy to navigate with resources that are ordered, searchable and findable.
- Have staff who continually weed and cull their collection with care. The classics will always remain under the careful eye of a good librarian or technician, but it is terribly difficult for young readers to find quality books when they are wedged between mouldy, dusty texts. Damaged or outdated books should be upcycled into artwork or lovingly recycled. Even if your library budget is dire, there is no need to hang on to twenty-five copies of a book that has not been borrowed since 1972.

- Have old and new technologies on display, such as QR codes for students to zap with their devices and stunning picture books treasured as works of art. Print and digital books happily co-exist.
- Be comfortable, and have dedicated spaces for reading and for collaboration. Some students need downtime and solitude in a busy school day and libraries should provide this. They also need collaborative working spaces for the sharing of ideas and creating together.
- Have some noise! Sure, libraries can be calm and quiet at times, but they can also be full of laughter, discussion and debate. If libraries have to be quiet, then I need a new job.
- Be a fine example of a modern learning environment with 24/7 access to parts of the collection available to students through databases, ebooks and a functioning website, and possibly social media streams.

What makes a good teacher librarian?

Let's start at the beginning with what a teacher librarian actually is. I could just reproduce my job description, but real life is far more engaging, so I'm going to use the example of award-winning and well-known Australian teacher librarian Jenny Stubbs.

I first met Jenny when I was starting out as a teacher librarian. Jenny runs the vibrant Ipswich District Teacher Librarian Network which, at her request, now has many local council librarians as members, adding greatly to the information pool. Teacher librarians across Australia are in networks because we are gatherers and sharers of information. One of the jobs of a librarian is to find and access information within a library, but the information gathering goes far beyond the walls of the physical building. Good librarians have curious and enquiring minds and collaborate with their colleagues and the community. Jenny is the master of surrounding herself with like-minded professionals and creatives, who all passionately believe in the power of story to change lives and the importance of literacy.

For over thirty years, the Ipswich District Teacher Librarian Network has published a new book each year based on the Children's Book Council of Australia (CBCA) Book of the Year Awards, an enormous undertaking for the group of educators and librarians who work voluntarily on the project. This book is used in schools throughout Australia and overseas to promote Children's Book Week and to provide resources to teachers and teacher librarians that support joyous and educationally sound exploration of some of the best books in the country.

Jenny Stubbs is the founder of the StoryArts Festival Ipswich, a biennial festival that has become one of the most highly regarded children's literature festivals in Australia. She advocates and builds effective library and literary programs that contribute to the development of young readers. Jenny and her team of dedicated volunteers organise and fund the festival largely through sales of the Ipswich Teacher Librarian Network book, and the festival has enabled tens of thousands of children to experience books and be inspired creatively through a series of free author events.

Jenny embraces any new technology that improves access to information and to story. She is a role model for lifelong learning and a perfect example of how being a teacher librarian involves far more than returning books to shelves.

It must be acknowledged that not all school libraries are managed by teacher librarians, but by teachers, library technicians or other support staff. While a qualified teacher librarian remains the ultimate goal, we should never dismiss the work of others in the library. All dedicated staff can make a valuable contribution.

Students Need School Libraries is an organisation that aims to ensure that every student has access to a dynamic, well-resourced school library run by qualified library staff. The ease of access to technology, online sources and fake news increases the need for qualified library staff who can teach all students the necessary research, online safety and information literacy skills, as well as instil a love of reading. The Students Need School Libraries website offers research, resources and more to advocate in your school.
For more information see www.studentsneedschoollibraries.org.au.

THE SCHOOL LIBRARY AT LUNCHTIME

I can't tell you how many times I've had parents concerned that their child is at the library. Every. Single. Lunchtime. Alone, 'just' reading. I reassure these parents that we see and monitor our 'frequent flyers' to check they are content and not avoiding a social situation or perhaps ruminating on an issue in their life. We sometimes have a conversation with the classroom teacher and school counsellor to check in on the student's wellbeing and, if necessary, we support a student to broaden their lunchtime activities.

I also let concerned parents know that contemporary school libraries are potentially not how they remember them. Our library, I tell them, is like a seething mass of humanity some lunchtimes and somewhat reminiscent of a 1990s rave party – complete with glitter and happy, sweaty people. Many of my students will tell you I am *rather loud*, but I do provide physical nooks of quietude and assess the situation as to whether or not a chat is needed or wanted. I will however, never forget a Year Six child saying to me, 'Mrs Daley, can we talk about books another time? I'm actually trying to read.' It's dreadful being shushed by your own students.

During lunchtime in the library, we witness the most gorgeous imaginary games being played, some of which continue each day for weeks or months; young people laughing and chatting, and sometimes sobbing, being comforted and working through disappointments. We chat with the child who has come to the library to chill out after an altercation during a soccer game, and we quietly support groups of kids who are finding their feet with their friendships and need an adult nearby to keep the game, conversation or art activity on an even keel.

Library staff aim to create inviting and supportive lunchtime environments which meet the needs of a diverse range of students and create a sense of community and belonging.[1] If your school library has a makerspace zone or similar, it is life-affirming to witness the sharing of ideas, discussion, debate and problem-solving that occurs in these spaces – essential social and life skills are being developed.

The library at lunchtime (and, perhaps if you are lucky enough to have a well-staffed school library, before and after school and at morning tea) is a magical place to read, work, play, converse and, yes, sometimes, escape to. There are many reasons students seek them out:

- To have some downtime from the noise and chaos of the playground and classroom. I have a few 'library friends' who I regularly spy under a couch chatting quietly together, a young girl who has a favourite sit spot where she peruses graphic novels for a while before returning to the playground, and a boy who comes in halfway through most lunchtimes to cool down after a frantic game of soccer.
- To escape into a great book. From the comfort of the school library a child can be transported to China, the moon, the future, the past. This is very reassuring for young people who may be having problems in the real world.
- To feel a sense of belonging and community. The library is a great place if a child wants to foster new relationships, nurture an existing one, or if they want to be alone but still around their community.

- To seek out like-minded peers. Countless friendships are formed, reformed and nurtured in school libraries across the world and if you are a 'library person' you will understand this entirely. We're a great tribe.
- To locate and be with friends and family members in different year levels. It's lovely seeing our older students reading to our youngest readers, and my now seventeen-year-old daughter regularly visits my primary library with her friends during lunchtime, giving the youngest students an enormous thrill – 'big kids' are always a highlight of the day. Technically, the seventeen-year-olds are visiting to borrow my sandwich toaster and retrieve their drinks from the library fridge, but I think they also love their celebrity status.

If you have a child or student who you feel is overly attached to the library at lunchtime, talk to their classroom teacher to ascertain why they are seeking out the library, and make yourself known to school library staff. Over the years, I've become really friendly with some of the parents of my 'library friends', mainly because the parents are also readers and lovers of libraries and so are also part of my tribe.

SELECTING QUALITY BOOKS FOR THE LIBRARY

Australia has an incredibly diverse and vibrant children's literary community that produces some of the best children's books in the world. But some people find that when they're presented with an entire wall of books in a store or a library it can be hard to choose and it all becomes a little overwhelming. I choose a children's book in a similar way to how I choose wine; my eye is drawn to the label and its design, then I am won over by how many shiny gold award stickers adorn it, then I consider the price point. It is not an exact science but it often works. For choosing children's books which will be loved, here are my tips:

- **Literary awards do matter.** They point us in the right direction. Awards lists always spark conversation and controversy but these lists are a 'who's who' of children's and young adult books.

- **Phone a friend.** Seriously, go find yourself a book expert at your local school library, public library or bookstore. We bookish types relish opportunities to talk with young readers and recommend books that will keep them reading. Many independent bookstores have children's and YA book specialists on their teams. Public and school library staff are there to help you and if you come across an unhelpful librarian, please feel free to stomp up and down and complain because I strongly believe that we are in customer service and that readers are our customers. Much to the horror of my tween (actually, everything I do horrifies him), if I spot a parent looking confused in a bookstore I usually sidle over to them and help out.

- **Judge a book by its cover.** I do it. All. The. Time. If a book is well designed and the cover grabs you, it generally means that care and thought has gone into not just the cover but also the content. A great cover sums up an entire book in one image.

- **Price point.** This could be controversial but, on the whole, I would prefer to purchase one exceptional hardcover children's book than four or five 'bargain bin' books. Bargain books tend to not remain treasured books. There are, of course, exceptions to this, like the time I found hardcover versions of Blue Willow china–inspired *Little Blue* (Gaye Chapman) reduced to a mere two dollars. After I wept inside that such a stunning book could possibly be reduced to so little, I purchased all thirty-one copies to use as party favours – way better than a lolly bag (said no child ever). If you cannot afford books or would prefer to try before you buy, then give your library card a workout.

- **Take notice of other children.** Not in a way that will cause concern, but stand near children in bookshops and libraries and watch what they borrow. Listen to what books they are talking about. After all, young people are the best guides to the books that will be enjoyed.

SELF-SELECTION AND THE LIBRARY

One of my work goals is that my primary school students will become efficient in self-selection of recreational material by high school. Teacher librarians seek to arm children with strategies for searching out books for themselves and quality library programming ensures that self-selection strategies are explicitly and incidentally taught from a young age.

In the early years, teaching self-selection strategies may take the form of browsing with children through forward-facing picture book boxes and talking about what appeals to them based on the cover. I model this, often through role-playing when choosing a book for myself: 'Oh, here is a book with a cat on the cover, I'll get that one! Oh, hang on ... I really don't like cats at all, I'm a dog person. This one has a lemon tree on the front and the colours remind me of being outside in my garden – this one I *will* borrow because I love gardening.'

I have one-on-one conversations with students whenever I can and regularly insist that each kindy or prep child walks past their teacher or myself on the way out and tells us why they have chosen a particular book. We make a game of this 'march past' and the children hold up their book and loudly tell us why they think it looks like a 'good fit' for them.

There are also patterns when selecting books with young children. If a child has really enjoyed *The Very Cranky Bear* (Nick Bland), this is an opportunity to point out other Nick Bland books and see if children can see the similarities in illustrative style. Likewise, if a child continually borrows books on a particular subject, perhaps dinosaurs, introduce them to non-fiction texts, or expand their horizons and offer them some books on jungle animals – some children feel safe sticking with 'what they know' in books and have difficulty knowing what to move on to.

Throughout the primary school years, teachers, parents and students should have ongoing conversations about why and how we choose books for independent recreational reading. Empowering students to choose their own books sets them up for being lifelong readers and shifts ownership of reading from the adult to the child.

Questions that help with self-selection

- Does the subject matter appeal to you?
- Why do you want to read this book?
- Read the first page – do you understand most of the words?
- Is this book going to challenge you and are you interested enough to accept that challenge?
- Have you read anything else by this author and did you enjoy it?
- Tell me the last book you really enjoyed? Can you find something similar?

Strategies that help with self-selection

- Write down the authors you like and search out their titles.
- Check new book displays in libraries and bookstores.
- Talk with your peers about the books they like to read.

- Scour the shelves at home and find things other family members have enjoyed.
- Ask your friendly school or local librarian for some recommendations.
- Take your time browsing the library shelves and you might notice a gem that you have not seen before.

THE LIBRARY MAKERSPACE

This chapter would not and could not exist without Jackie Child AKA #bestteachingpartnerever. Jackie landed in my world and my teacher librarian life has never been the same, nor would I want it to be. I hired Jackie because I thought we were peas in a pod. Turns out we are polar opposites in just about everything except our passion for primary school education, and for children's literature, and our ability to talk our boss into letting us run with half-crazed ideas.

The half-crazed idea Jackie raised was to introduce some spanners, drills and sewing equipment into the library. She'd seen this 'cool thing' at a conference where libraries in America were inviting the community to work collaboratively on projects that often involved engineering principles and skills; she believed it was a natural fit with school libraries where information is sourced, digitally and physically, and shared among peers. Jackie Child was a rally car driver, engine re-builder and a keen creator of ice-skating outfits *before* she was a teacher librarian, so I did wonder if she was trying to bring her own love of a good tool set into *my* pristine library. Turned out Jackie was onto something and her name has become synonymous with the makerspace movement in Australia.

What is the makerspace movement?

This might sound like a buzzword but the concepts underpinning the makerspace movement are timeless and have been part of the makeup of libraries since their inception.[2] The idea of making, tinkering, engineering and creating is not a new one. Using these elements within a community space forms the conceptual framework for the term 'makerspace'. A makerspace mindset values questioning and inquiry, re-inventing and exploring new ways of doing, and focuses on participating in learning – making and repurposing, rather than consuming.

Under the umbrella term of 'makerspace', there exists several incarnations of the idea, with the Massachusetts Institute of Technology (MIT) considered to be the first to formalise the concept in America. It is generally believed that the makerspace concept evolved from the hackerspaces in Germany as early as the 1950s.[3] A hackerspace is focused on computers and technology, and co-working spaces are shared working environments with shared tools and resources.[4] One of the incarnations is Fab Labs, which are places of fabrication where physical items are produced.

Makerspaces are the perfect partnership for libraries – where information is stored, accessed, shared, explored, pondered and debated. Library patrons can follow their interests and passions, applying knowledge from all areas of their life; personal and educational knowledge, experiences and skills. Informal makerspace activities are probably already occurring in your school or local library; formalising the process is merely a response to what students and customers now expect from modern library spaces and extending our outreach to new library patrons.

Libraries provide equal access to information, resources and technologies and this is particularly obvious in public libraries, where patrons access the internet and computers, assisted in this process by library staff. Increasingly, libraries are providing equal access to hardware such as robots, 3D printers and scanners. It follows that librarians embrace the ideas underpinning the makerspace movement and facilitate community interest in new and emerging technologies and spaces of making and creating.

In our school library, books have been the starting point for nearly all of our makerspace projects. This includes books with characters that think outside the square – Violet Mackerel series by Anna Branford (illustrated by Sarah Davis), *Different Like Coco* by Elizabeth Matthews, the Engibear series by Andrew King (illustrated by Benjamin Johnston), and *Rosie Revere, Engineer* by Andrea Beaty (illustrated by David Roberts) – and books that present opportunities to create new characters or ideas, with technology or physical equipment. For example, when reading *A Very Unusual Pursuit* by Catherine Jinks, we invented our own Bogles, and when reading *Something Wonderful* by Raewyn Caisley (illustrated by Karen Blair) we created our own wonderful machines to solve a problem at home.

Student borrowing of books and their engagement in reading have also increased since the introduction of makerspace ideas in libraries I have worked in. As students tinker and create, there is incidental language learning and the building of literacy across multiple domains. The library becomes a space for all, not just for students who identify as readers. When students enter a library space, they are surrounded by books to tempt all persuasions and more often than not they walk out with one or two books under their arm. Recently, students playing the *America the Wild* game on our Xbox Kinect ended up walking out with the book *The Call of the Wild* (Jack London); librarians are experts at finding the right book at the right time!

For many students who have struggled with literacy and for whom the library is not a space of contentment, a makerspace can be an opportunity to invite them in through a different 'doorway' and for them to shine. There are many different ways to come to a love of reading.

BOOKS THAT SUPPORT THE MINDSET OF THE MAKERSPACE MOVEMENT

Aussie STEM Stars series by various authors (Wild Dingo Press)

Brobot by James Foley (Fremantle Press, 2016)

Can I Build Another Me? by Shinsuke Yoshitake (Thames & Hudson, 2016)

Doll-E 1.0 by Shanda McCloskey (Hachette, 2018)

Engibear's Bridge by Andrew King, illustrated by Benjamin Johnston (Little Steps Publishing, 2014)

Millie Mak series by Alice Pung, illustrated by Sher Rill Ng (HarperCollins)

Our Little Inventor by Sher Rill Ng (Allen & Unwin, 2019)

Rosie Revere, Engineer by Andrea Beaty, illustrated by David Roberts (Abrams Books, 2013)

Something Wonderful by Raewyn Caisley, illustrated by Karen Blair (Puffin, 2018)

The First Scientists: Deadly Inventions and Innovations from Australia's First Peoples by Corey Tutt, illustrated by Blak Douglas (Hardie Grant, 2021)

The Imagineer by Christopher Cheng, illustrated by Lucia Masciullo (National Library of Australia, 2021)

Whodunnit, Eddie Woo? series by Eddie Woo and various authors, illustrated by Mitch Vane (Pan Macmillan)

LITERARY AWARDS

There are many literary awards in Australia shining the light on the best books for children and young adults. The Children's Book Council of Australia (CBCA) Book of the Year Awards is possibly the most long-standing and well-regarded for recognising the talent of authors and illustrators in this country. The awards were established in 1946 with the first winners receiving a camellia flower before generous donations guaranteed a financial prize for each category.

The CBCA award stickers carry weight in terms of literary honour. The Shortlist and Notables lists of the CBCA Awards are used by many parents, teachers and children as a buying guide.

Many other awards fill the literary calendar. Some awards are state-based, while others are more niche and can be hugely beneficial when looking for books of a certain genre or topic. Two examples of niche children's book awards are the Wilderness Society's Environment Award for Children's Literature, and the DANZ (Diversity in Australia and Aotearoa New Zealand) Children's Book Award, which was created to celebrate diverse youth literature.

Each category of an award usually contains a large range of books, suitable for different age groups within that category, and parents/teachers should always assess the themes and content of an individual book before choosing it for their child or classroom. Do not assume that the picture book category will contain books suitable for infants, as many illustrated texts are more suitable for older readers. It is also important to keep in mind that literary awards are based on the literary merit of each book and are not children's choice/popular awards.

However, young readers are able to take part in recognising the books they love best with a number of children's choice awards co-existing within Australia. These awards are an opportunity for readers to make their voices heard. When we ask young people to evaluate their favourite books for an award, we involve them in their reading in a way that asks them to think critically about reading and writing in general, and we provide them with a sense of ownership in choosing the winners themselves.

CHILDREN'S BOOK WEEK

Children's Book Week is the longest-running children's festival in Australia and is managed by the Children's Book Council of Australia (CBCA). The announcement of the winners of the CBCA Book of the Year Awards kicks off Children's Book Week and it is a week of celebrating Australian children's and young adult literature. To be honest, most of us stretch the celebrations out for an entire term with author visits, book fairs, competitions, maker fairs and events in our school communities as well as attending many children's literature functions.

The theme for Book Week is set by the CBCA and each year an award-winning illustrator is engaged to bring the theme to life. Illustrators interpret the theme in their own style, ensuring that each year the posters, banners, balloons and stickers are as individual and unique as each picture book on a shelf. This sends librarians and educators off on happy shopping trips to turn their libraries or classrooms into reading islands, galaxies or deserts, depending on the theme. Libraries and bookstores in your local area will almost certainly be celebrating Children's Book Week. Following the social media accounts of your local library and independent bookstore will guarantee that you don't miss a single literary event.

My mother had the pleasure of being the national merchandise manager for the CBCA for several years and it was an honour to peek behind the scenes. One year she worked with the late Gregory Rogers on the merchandise and his take on the theme 'One World, Many Stories' aligned closely to his book that had won the picture book category in the previous year. His series of illustrations for that theme remains among my favourites. Children's Book Week posters have become collectors' items and everyone has opinions on which posters were the greatest. I use past posters over and over again in my library and also as artwork in my children's bedrooms.

Children's Book Week competitions and dress-up parades are always a key part of Term Three in Australian schools – and the costumes can be as simple or as elaborate as time and craftiness will allow. Discuss which book characters your child would like to dress up as and take it from there. It's fantastic if your child can have ownership over the costume choice and be involved in the creation – just make sure they take inspiration from a book, not their favourite movie or digital game!

My 'How to create a Children's Book Week costume' guide (page 233) is a good starting point if you need a creative nudge.

CHAPTER FOUR

PICTURE BOOKS – READING THE VISUALS

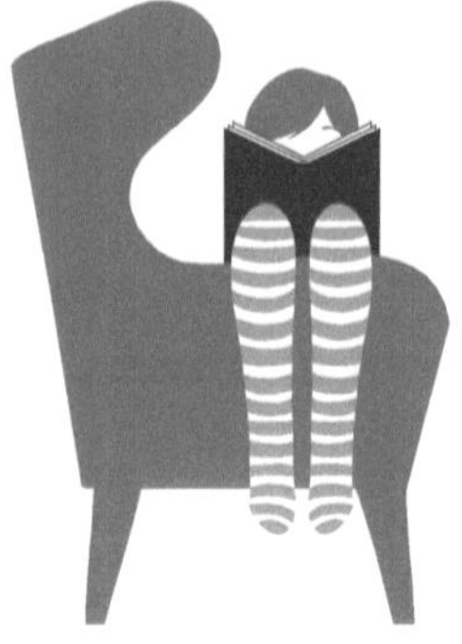

Why anyone would want to leave picture books behind is beyond me. They are works of art and the best way I know to enhance and teach visual literacy. The language in picture books is often complex and the storylines sophisticated and thought-provoking. So why is it that so many parents and educators 'celebrate' a child's move into chapter book territory and then actively discourage the borrowing of picture books? I wish I could say I've seen it only once, but over the years I've seen several versions of certificates handed out to young children with words similar to 'I've graduated from picture books!' This chapter celebrates picture books, but it is important to take a moment to examine why the perception is that picture books are only for the very young.

When I talk at conferences about the importance of picture books I often hold up my favourite one from my childhood, *Little Cloud* by Robert Tallon. I use it as an example of how picture books have changed, although in fairness to Tallon it's actually a rather good book and I can still recite the whole thing by heart so it clearly had an impact on me. Like *Little Cloud*, many picture books of my childhood had beautiful but fairly simple illustrations, mostly a front-facing perspective or view of the character and the setting. Illustrations often existed to merely capture and reinforce what was said in the text. The language was at a level that would have been considered appropriate for a three- or four-year-old, and the storylines often offered a moral lesson or described a simple family occasion. In both overt and subtle ways, picture books were used as a reflection of the expectations and aspirations of society at the time as well as to educate and entertain. I'm certain that many of us have held fast to our pre-conceived notions of picture books formed in our childhoods, and, for the most part, have not had exposure to the richness of contemporary picture books and illustrated texts.

Of course, it is a generalisation that all older picture books are simplistic in nature, with books by Ida Rentoul Outhwaite, Norman Lindsay, May Gibbs, Jenny Wagner and Ron Brooks immediately springing to mind as examples to the contrary. The State Library of Victoria houses over 100,000 Australian and international children's books in the Children's Literature Collection which showcases the wonder of Australian children's illustrated works from the early nineteenth century to the twenty-first century. The illustrations in this collection reflect society at different points throughout history and are fine examples of art at its very best.

HOW TO READ PICTURE BOOKS

When I am reading and working with picture books at home with my own children and at school in library lessons, I always talk about the book as a whole, and follow a similar routine in each picture book session with students from kindergarten to Year Six. It may seem ridiculous to some that I have taken the time to outline 'how to read a picture book', but I firmly believe that so much visual literacy and other learning is embedded in picture books and it seems such a shame to miss any of it. Of course, not every picture book reading should be a formal lesson, and at all times enjoyment of the story should be paramount.

Doing picture books well

Always read a book before you share it with an individual or group of students. Every time I am tempted to grab the closest book and read it to a group of rowdy three-year-olds to calm them down, I remember The Grandparents' Day Incident of 1999.

I was teaching Year Two and I grabbed a picture book about grandparents from the shelf to read to my class and the thirty or so grandparents present. The teacher librarian had helpfully put together a selection at my request. Halfway through reading the book, I realised that grandad was going to die. I kept going until I knew things were about to decline for grandad and then I shut the book and cheerily said, 'And if you want to read the rest of the book, you can visit the school library!' I announced more loudly than was necessary (lest any child ask a question about grandad in the book) that scones with jam and cream were about to be served.

A grandfather sidled up to me at morning tea with a smirk on his face, and said, 'Grandad died, right?' Always pre-read a book for content!

I start most picture book readings with a good look at and discussion of the physical features of a book, explicitly pointing them out and naming them. We then make predictions about what the text might be about and I discuss how the design features help us to form an idea about the book. I conduct a 'picture walk' through the book and have the children predict the story using the images. This helps to introduce the story, settings and characters.

Physical parts of a picture book: how and what to discuss

Title. The typography shape, colour and size.

Front and back covers. What information is contained on each? On the front cover, look at the title and locate the author's and illustrator's name. If the book is from a library, can you see the library barcode? On the back cover, read the blurb, find the ISBN and any other text which identifies the publisher. Is there a photograph of the author and a bio or is this inside the book?

Spine. Just like the spine in your body, the spine on a book holds the book straight and together. Also like your own spine, the book spine needs to be treated with care and respect or we end up with a wibbly wobbly book. If the book is from a library, is there a call number sticker on the spine and what information is on this? Is the title of the book written on the spine? Why is it written in a certain direction?

Endpapers. The pages at the start and finish of a hardcover book are called endpapers. The front and back inside covers essentially help to strengthen the book but of course they really are so much more than this! There are social media accounts dedicated to endpaper design, and astute readers know that the story in a Bob Graham book almost always begins and ends on the endpapers. I myself loudly proclaim every year to the little people at school that when I am a grown-up, I am going to own an endpaper art gallery.

Other physical features. The dust jacket, double-page spread, gutter, recto/verso pages may also contain unusual design features, such as cut pages, pockets, flaps, deckle edges or fore-edge painting.

Reading a picture book

When reading a picture book for the first time I don't stop and start to discuss a point. We explore the entire text in one fluid and expressive reading first. With young students I often begin by saying, 'I'm going to read you the words in this book now and your job is to listen and also to read the pictures.' In this way I make it clear that reading the visuals is as much part of reading a picture book as reading the text is.

On a second and sometimes third (or more) re-reading we will stop along the way and unpack ideas about the intent of the author and illustrator and how they may have used point of view, lines and colours, angles and typography to influence how we read the text. We might consider if the text and images are telling a different or parallel story and we always mull over how the book makes us feel. See chapter 2 for more ideas about dialogic reads of picture books.

VISUAL LITERACY

We access visuals continuously throughout our day, whether browsing the internet or on your computer, seeing advertisements via screens and billboards, the box of your granola, the artwork on the wall in your local coffee shop, and so the list goes on. Spend five or so minutes pondering the visuals you have consumed today and the messages that each artist is trying to convey and you'll soon be acutely aware that we live in an age saturated by visuals. Visual literacy is the term used to describe the skills needed to comprehend, create and communicate with visuals.[1] While text-based literacy instruction is considered essential, visual literacy does not receive the same level of attention in educational settings.

Visual language features: how and what to discuss

There are countless visual language features to discuss when viewing a picture book and a few are outlined in detail below. Also consider other features, such as the use of media, the design and layout of a page or an entire book, and the angles an illustrator has chosen.[2]

Lines and vectors (action and direction of lines or lines formed by shapes). Discuss what sort of lines you see in the images of a picture book. Are the lines formed by the shapes of objects? Are they straight or curved? Could the lines be changed in style and still retain meaning? Do the lines take your eye to a particular part of the illustration? Are there intersecting lines and do they cross at a particular point in the image? Do the outlines of the characters lend a particular mood or feeling – contrast here the open and free lines of the work of Ann James in *I'm a Hungry Dinosaur* (written by Janeen Brian) with the sharp black lines used by Jules Faber in the illustrations in the WeirDo series (written by Anh Do). Find some examples of vectors in picture books – *Sorry Day* by Coral Vass (illustrated by by Dub Leffler), for example – and have children identify the movement and direction which the vectors force in the viewer.

Colour. Colour can be symbolic or used to represent a feeling or mood. It can be used sparingly to great effect or splashed boldly to create a different sense. Different colours evoke different feelings and are often dependent on cultural and historical contexts – for example, Western cultures often use black to represent death whereas many Asian countries use white. The use of red in *And the Ocean Was Our Sky* (Patrick Ness, illustrated by Rovina Cai) and in *Swan Lake* (Anne Spudvilas) are fine examples of colour as strong elements of visual literacy. What does the red represent in each of these books? Consider what red might represent in another context – love or passion, for example; or good luck in a Chinese text. Look at a colour wheel and the spectrum of colours on it – what feelings do these colours evoke in you? Can you find books with similar colours and feelings? Can you find an example of a warm-toned book and a cool-toned book?

Symbols. Symbols and signs are like a text abbreviation and they may represent something from somewhere else (say, a symbol from a well-known fairytale). They may also include icons, such as the Opera House to represent a story being set in Sydney without direct mention of the city.

Can you see any symbols? Do they represent a place? A concept? A feeling (a heart, for example)? Impending danger for a character? Look carefully at the symbols in *Plume: World Explorer* by Tania McCartney and make a list of them. What do they represent?[3]

Point of view. Authors and illustrators position a reader to see subjects and add feelings to the story based on placement; for example, placing a subject down low and looking up can create a feeling of being small and insignificant. Sometimes we are positioned as readers looking in at the action front on and other times we are placed as a character and experience the book from a different point of view.

How are you positioned to view the image? How does the choice of distance affect how you feel? Do you feel part of the action or isolated? Alone or part of a group? Why has the illustrator made this choice? Why might a bird's-eye view be used? Can you find an example of this? Why might a direct gaze be used? How does it make you feel to be up close to a direct gaze? Look at how Tony Flowers uses perspective in *Small Town* (written by Phillip Gwynne) to show different aspects and features of the town.

For more information on picture books I highly recommend *The Grown-Up's Guide to Picture Books* by Dr Lara Cain Gray (illustrated by Lorena Carrington and Timothy Ide). It is a picture book for adults that upskills parents, carers, teachers (or anyone!) to enjoy deeper reading of picture books with children – or just for themselves.

WORDLESS PICTURE BOOKS

Starting my working life in early years education, I discovered that wordless picture books afforded students the freedom to interpret and narrate visual stories and sparked creativity and engagement. I will admit, however, that without a bit of background on wordless picture books, it can be quite disconcerting to open a book without words!

With the complete absence of words, we might wonder what the book wants to tell us, we may worry that we will misinterpret the intent of the story and, as a reader, we need to work harder to decipher the story and pay closer attention to 'reading the images'.

The benefits of wordless picture books

- **Active participation.** The need to lean in, decipher images and discuss wordless picture books requires active participation rather than the more passive act of hearing a story being read aloud.
- **Inclusivity.** The lack of text allows readers to engage with the story regardless of reading ability or cultural language differences.
- **Imagination.** The creative possibilities are endless. A wordless picture book is a springboard for imaginative play and storytelling.
- **Storytelling.** With illustrations not bound by text, we foster imaginative thinking and narrative creation, empowering children to construct their own stories.
- **Oral language development.** Picture books promote language skills through discussion and description of illustrations, enhancing oral communication.
- **Vocabulary expansion.** Readers must work harder to find new words to articulate observations and tell the story, expanding vocabulary.
- **Visual literacy.** Critical visual analysis skills are nurtured, teaching

children to interpret facial expressions, body language and visual cues.

Tips for sharing wordless picture books

- **Encourage imagination.** There are no right or wrong ways to read a wordless book; foster the idea that there are endless ways to interpret and imagine the story.
- **Discuss the relationship between the creator and reader.** The narrative or meaning in a wordless picture book is co-constructed by the creator's artwork and the reader's imagination. The story is only 'complete' (is a story ever complete?) when a reader adds their interpretation, imagination and storytelling skills. The book is almost like a conversation between the creator and the reader.
- **Engage at eye level.** If sharing with a group of children, sit at their eye level, creating a more intimate reading experience that encourages participation.
- **Predict and explore.** Spend time examining the cover and title, making predictions, and taking a 'picture walk' through the pages.
- **Analyse illustrations.** Develop visual literacy skills by discussing the use of colour, light and shadow to convey mood and meaning. Look at the composition and page layout and consider what the juxtaposition of multiple images might mean.
- **Consider themes.** Hunt for clues as to the creator's intent with the book – what might be the major themes of the story? Co-constructing meaning around a book is a great way to develop analytical skills. For example, take a close look at Gihun Lee's *09:47* and students of all ages will quickly pick up on themes of environmental destruction, sustainability and care for the earth.
- **Discuss and connect.** Enjoy the illustrations together, discussing details and making personal connections to the story.

- **Share.** Encourage children to narrate the story in their own words and share their story with their peers.

WORDLESS PICTURE BOOKS

09:47 by Gihun Lee (Gloyeon, 2021)

Anno's Italy by Mitsumasa Anno (Penguin, 1979)

Bee & Me by Alison Jay (Old Barn Books, 2017)

Bunny & Tree by Balint Zsako (Abrams Books, 2023)

Door by JiHyeon Lee (Chronicle Books, 2018)

Flashlight by Lizi Boyd (Chronicle Books, 2014)

Float by Daniel Miyares (Simon & Schuster, 2015)

Flora and the Flamingo by Molly Idle (Chronicle Books, 2013)

Flotsam by David Wiesner (Clarion Books, 2006)

Footpath Flowers by JonArno Lawson, illustrated by Sydney Smith (Walker Books, 2016)

Fox's Garden by Princesse Camcam (Enchanted Lion Books, 2014)

Journey by Aaron Becker (Walker Books, 2013)

Lines by Suzy Lee (Chronicle Books, 2017)

Midsummer Knight by Gregory Rogers (Allen & Unwin, 2008)

Mirror by Jeannie Baker (Walker Books, 2010)

Noah's Ark by Peter Spier (Doubleday, 1977)

Pool by JiHyeon Lee (Chronicle Books, 2015)

Professional Crocodile by Giovanna Zoboli and Mariachiara Di Giorgio (Chronicle Books, 2017)

Quest by Aaron Becker (Walker Books, 2014)

Red Book by Barbara Lehman (Clarion Books, 2004)

Sunshine (40th Anniversary Edition) by Jan Ormerod (HarperCollins, 2022)

The Arrival by Shaun Tan (Hachette, 2006)

The Boy, the Bear, the Baron, the Bard by Gregory Rogers (Allen & Unwin, 2004)

The Chicken Thief by Béatrice Rodriguez (Gecko Press, 2009)

The Girl and the Bicycle by Mark Pett (Simon & Schuster, 2014)
The Hero of Little Street by Gregory Rogers (Allen & Unwin, 2009)
Wave by Suzy Lee (Chronicle Books, 2008)

Tony Flowers is a well-known Australian illustrator with a passion for children's publishing. Tony presents at academic conferences on visual literacy and is an academic at the University of Tasmania, lecturing in design. He also happens to be a dear friend and I will forever be floored by the kindness he extended to Ava and Georgia when my first husband, Dan, passed away. Tony had an established relationship with our girls and started sending them 'Ninja Mail', highly illustrated letters, notes and original pieces of art. It became an absolute highlight in what was a terrible time and the girls still have every single piece of the 'Ninja Mail', including the illustrated envelopes. There is no one else more qualified to add their voice to this chapter on visual language and space.

Tony Flowers

When I was young, teachers scared the bejesus out of me. I was not a good student in the classic sense. I was terrible at spelling, hopeless at complex math, and left school virtually unable to read. My only saving grace was that I could draw. Much to my surprise, I ended up being a lecturer at a university and working in the publishing industry writing and illustrating books. What saved me was my ability to draw and my love of stories. I didn't just love stories; I wanted to know what made them tick. Why did visual stories captivate me so much? How did people draw narratives that are strongly driven by the visual, and could I ever learn to draw in this way? When I first started on my journey into illustration, it was as much about finding the answers to these questions as it was about my love of drawing. I have always approached teaching and learning visual narratives as I would approach learning another language. If you are like me, when you travel, you try to learn a few expressions. For me, that includes how to order a coffee and croissant wherever I go: 'Un caffè e un cornetto, per favore' (when in Rome). But knowing an expression or two doesn't mean you speak the language.

I find teachers and others from outside of the world of art and design visit it much like I would visit a Parisian café. They can see the basics and enjoy the ambience enough to read the scene. But to truly understand what is going on, you need to work on your visual vocabulary and grammar. This allows you to not only see some of the underlying structures, but also start to construct your own visual narratives.

In my classes, over a few weeks, I introduce my students to the elements and principles of design. Think of these as the basic building blocks for all art and design.

The core components of design and art (subject matter, form and content) simply wouldn't exist without these elements and principles of design.[4]

The elements of design include point, line, plane, shape, form, colour, value, tone, texture and space. The principles of design include unity, variety, emphasis, focal point, balance, rhythm, scale and proportion.

Using these elements and principles, along with understanding how we read (decode) information and build stories, helps us both understand and create visual stories. This is visual literacy at its core: the ability to read visual information and visually communicate in a way that others can understand.

Rather than diving into what could be an entire book on visual language for picture book illustrators, I want to focus on one concept that will help you look at illustrations in a completely different way. The concept of 'space' is a great starting point for delving deeper into illustrated works.

Space

For me, as an illustrator, 'space' has three possible meanings: represented space, positive space or negative space.

Represented space. Represented space refers to the scene or environment depicted in illustrations. It's created using elements like line, plane, shape, form, colour, perspective and the visual representation of objects, reference points or known locations. This aspect of illustrating a narrative is all about world-building. It provides the viewer with context, helping them understand where and when the story is set, and whether it's grounded in reality or fantasy.

A great example of this is Terry Denton's world-building in the Treehouse series. Each book, while seemingly sampling in its illustration style, expertly expands on the environment established in the previous ones, creating a rich, immersive world for readers.

In my graphic novel *Divi and Frey*, I strive to build a strong sense of space by basing my stories on real-world locations. I invest a lot of time in researching these locations, and whenever possible, I travel to them in person. This approach helps build trust between me, as the author/illustrator, and the reader, making them feel like they are in the actual setting, not just looking at a postcard version of it.

Positive space. This concept is all about the visual information on the page. Simply put, it's where everything is placed – text, colours, line work, characters. Anything added to the blank page creates meaning and contributes to the story. It's crucial that every element on the page has a purpose and is thoughtfully placed. The placement of these elements is enhanced by design principles like unity, variety, emphasis, focal point, balance, rhythm, scale and proportion.

These principles work together to create a harmonious and engaging illustration. For instance, unity ensures that all elements on the page work together cohesively, while variety adds visual interest by introducing different elements. Emphasis and focal points guide the viewer's eye to the most important parts of the illustration, and balance ensures that the composition feels stable and pleasing. Rhythm creates a sense of movement, and scale and proportion ensure that everything is sized appropriately in relation to other elements.

You can see these principles in action in *You, Me and Community* (by Zanni Louise). In this book, the background narrative shows the construction of a bridge connecting two parts of a geographically divided town. This visual element exists entirely separately from the text narrative, relying on visual clues and the progressive stages of the bridge's development to build the story. By carefully placing each element and considering design principles, the illustrations add depth and enhance the reader's understanding of the narrative.

Negative space. Negative space is my favourite! It refers to all the empty areas on the page. It can be as small as the 'aperture' in the letter 'c' (the gap that prevents 'c' from being an 'o'). It includes the space between letters, lines of text, or any other printed element on the page. Negative space is crucial in good layout design, creating emphasis, focal points or balance. It makes text easier to read and highlights important elements within an illustration. Sometimes, negative space allows the reader to perceive the image and text as a whole, not just as individual elements on a page.

I explored this concept in *Grandma's First Tattoo* (written by Phillip Gwynne), where the absence of information was so pronounced that I created images by leaving blank spaces within the character illustration. Just as positive space must have meaning, everything left off the page should also be intentional. In *Grandma's First Tattoo*, I aimed to visually link the children's concepts and imaginations in the story for the reader, allowing them to project their own imagination into the reading experience.

The true unsung heroes of picture books and masters of managing the balance between negative and positive space are the graphic designers. I have been lucky enough to have the same designer work on my last four book projects, Nicolette Treanor. She takes over the project once the illustrations are done, placing text and images together on the page. Her expertise in handling negative space ensures that every element on the page serves a purpose, creating a visually harmonious and engaging reading experience.

Negative space isn't just empty space – it's an essential part of the design that gives our eyes a place to rest and helps emphasise the important parts of an illustration. It allows the composition to breathe and adds a sense of balance and harmony. By thoughtfully considering negative space, illustrators and designers create images and books that are not only visually appealing but also deeply engaging and meaningful for readers.

So, next time you look through your favourite picture book, take a moment to appreciate the negative space. It's like the silent partner, making sure the positive elements shine and the overall design works beautifully. Now, compare this to a book that you find difficult to read or don't like, but you can't quite work out why. It may well be the use of space through the book that is the problem.

CHAPTER FIVE

SPACES FOR READING

Whether in the home, classroom, kindergarten or library, creating a space all about reading emphasises books and their beauty to children. This can be as important as the learning and language tools an educator uses. Take a look at your child's kindy or school classroom next time you are there. See all the labels? The signage? The posters with words and pictures? That is what we call a 'print-rich environment'. A print-rich home helps young children become familiar with letters, numbers, pictures and words. It tells young children that print is important and has a purpose. My mantra for creating a print-rich environment is: *Display print. Use print. Value print.*

I love nothing better than walking into a kindergarten or childcare centre and being drawn into a fabulous reading space. Libraries with dedicated spaces designed for children are my happy places – and I've been known to say that I could move into my local library book nook. In the homes of my friends I'll be found checking out the books on the shelves in their kids' rooms and gushing over big, comfy reading chairs. I may not notice the designer entry table, but I will always notice the reading spaces and bookshelves.

I don't think there is any better home décor than beautiful books and prints from favourite picture books. I'm also a big fan of forward-facing storage for children's books because not only are the covers works of art that deserve to be on display, but the books are easily identifiable, helping young readers to self-select.

How you organise your books within your space is entirely up to you. I'd love nothing better than my home being organised like my school library but that won't happen. Nor will I ever organise my books by colour because my librarian brain cannot cope with the idea that *A Clockwork Orange* (Anthony Burgess) could sit on a shelf next to *Winnie-the-Pooh* (A. A. Milne). Having said this, I know a Dewey decimal system-loving library technician who has colour coded her books in her new home. I am shocked that a devotee of library rules would do such a thing!

BOOK-THEMED BEDROOMS

Surrounding your child in print and visual-rich spaces is a great way to model your love of books and reading. My children have had book-themed bedrooms several times in their lives. Book-themed rooms are a no-brainer to me as the colour themes, motifs and décor items you choose are decided by the artwork of the illustrator of your favourite picture book or from the world created by your favourite author.

Georgia started life with a nursery based on one of my all-time favourite picture books, *Little Blue* (Gaye Chapman), which also inspired her middle name. Heavily pregnant at a Children's Book Council of Australia conference, I saw the Little Hare publisher stand filled with heavenly posters and postcards from the book and fell hard for it. The book retells the story of the Willow pattern plates. In creating a *Little Blue*-themed room, I used blue-and-white Chinese paintings, as well as a gorgeous soft gum-tree green. This is still my favourite bedroom theme as it was soft and calming. I also had a calico reading tent with Willow pattern cushions and a thick lambswool rug, bunting made from the pages of the book (yes, I cut up a copy) and cot linen in Willow pattern fabric. I colour-matched the blue of the book at a hardware store so the walls were painted the palest and prettiest of blues.

But don't feel as though you have to go to such great lengths. A reading space can be as simple as a chair or window seat near a bookshelf or even a great big beansbag with a basket of books beside it. No matter your budget, a reading nook can always be created.

Kelly McDonough is an expert in spaces for children, tweens and families. Kelly has shared some thoughts on home design and how to maximise space for reading. These ideas can be easily adapted for the classroom or school library.

Kelly McDonough

If I think back to my childhood I remember standing in front of our huge timber bookshelf. It wasn't fancy. I actually didn't even notice the shelves because, let's be honest, kids don't care if it's a designer piece or if you picked it up at a garage sale. They only see the things they love on the shelves.

With such an abundance of home décor inspiration in stores, renovation TV shows and online, it can be way too easy to become lost in the big-ticket items, such as the on-trend 'must have' pieces. These might fill the void (or the room) but there is one thing to remember: they aren't long-term items and they probably won't be part of your child's memories. Books, on the other hand, are stayers. Stories defy age and continue to create an environment that inspires imagination, touches our soul and educates little minds.

Shelving

If you're short on floor space, think up. Shelving is not only versatile, but it's gorgeous and timeless. I love using picture ledges down low so that little hands can find favourite books. Think about retail store displays: the stuff they want seen is kept at eye level. Books shelved spine-out just end up being pulled off bookshelves and left on the floor; books shelved face-out are easily identifiable by their covers so they not only invite the reader to pick them up but also create an instant display.

If you're lacking in toy storage space, some funky baskets or boxes on the shelves is a great way to keep books tidy and stored when they're not being used. And a little tip – rotate the boxes around so that there is always something different on the eye-level shelf your kids go to first.

Colour

Using colour in spaces for kids is like breathing: it happens without thinking. Kids are naturally drawn to colour, but that doesn't necessarily mean a colour assault on the eyes. My advice with choosing colours is to pick three main ones. These could be anything from your child's favourite colour, to a favourite book cover with a dominant colour or a chair or quilt cover in the space.

Once you have these three colours choose three more variations to tie everything together. For example, adding a soft grey to a bright blue will help balance it out. Experiment with sample paint wheels to see what works and challenge yourself to think outside your usual go-to combinations. You'll be surprised at the colours that work together! At the end of your search you'll have six colours to work with. Having different shades of your chosen colours actually helps avoid the room becoming too matchy-matchy, making it kid-friendly and versatile when it comes time to mix things up.

Zones

A reading nook doesn't have to be sized to epic proportions. A cosy cushion and a basket with books placed on a rug or under a canopy draws little eyes instantly. Kids are funny little creatures as they will seek out spaces we don't think of. So don't be afraid to get your child onboard with mapping out a zone. While it's probably not a great move to get them to design the whole layout, seeing a room or area from their perspective might help you to plan and visualise what works best for your child. Well, for that day anyway!

And if you're lacking floor space, areas can always have a double purpose. A little trolley on wheels containing arts and crafts can be brought out to create an instant makerspace and then easily packed away again!

Kids' spaces are about functionality. Your budget, tastes and the purpose of the room are all factors to consider when decorating. Planning out your storage options, zones and colours aren't the be-all, but they are a great place to start when designing an area that you and the kids will all love.

I wish I had a solution for a room that automatically cleans itself – I promise you'll be the first to know if I work that one out!

As Kelly mentions, kids may seek out spaces that seem like odd choices to us as adults. I witness it daily in my school library as children read under desks or in the middle of rows of shelving. Each year I ask my Year Three to Year Six students to close their eyes and imagine their perfect reading space, thinking about its colours, furniture, comfort, sounds and 'feel'. Students write a description and then we either paint or draw this space. If we have time, we create a model using materials from our makerspace. I always imagined that beds would be the favoured reading place of choice, but I am constantly amazed by the variety of spaces children describe. They commonly desire a small and cosy space, often on the floor or under something (tent, blanket, bed, etc) and for it to feel tranquil and calm. Every year a number of children will describe an outside space, such as in a tree or on a deck, and a few children will express a preference for reading on a bus or other crowded space like a shopping centre – usually explaining that they read to 'block out' the overwhelming sensory experience of such environments. The message here is that what we adults see as ideal or appropriate reading spaces may in fact not work for every reader.

Having a discussion with your child or going through a creative exercise as described above can uncover some valuable insights into the readers in your care.

As a blended family we recently built our Very Brady Bunch House. There was a void under the stairs which we considered using for storage but it quickly became clear that in an open plan living area, this was the one nook where the youngest, James, could escape to with a good book. James likes to be among the family rather than in his bedroom (where the teens now seem to be!) but he also likes a space of his own. Using a modular play couch that had previously been used as a lounge, castle, sleepover bed and cubbyhouse, I set up a reading nook. I added strip lighting under the stairs, cushions, a basketful of little rugs and books – many, many books. This has become his favourite place to read and quite a few of the siblings and kids from the street now crash his reading nook. I regularly change the books in the front-facing baskets and have noticed that he does the same. Often, we forget he is reading under the stairs until a little voice calls out in reply to some conversation that is happening around him. It's his private reading nook in a very busy household.

THE READING CLASSROOM

Classrooms need an area or zone dedicated to recreational reading. I vividly recall my first year of teaching and the reading zone I created in my Year Two classroom, because it remains my favourite to this day: acres of deep purple and bright turquoise tulle, ten oversized turquoise cushions covered in purple stars (thank you, Nan, for making those), framed pages torn out of old books and a selection of beautiful books that I changed each week at the school library and displayed in baskets and on the windowsill. When I eventually moved from the classroom to the library, the tulle came with me and my first library was a riot of colour and texture (but, I promise, not an assault to the eyes because I did stick to just a few colours).

While there are some fabulous reading spaces in classrooms all over social media, I think it's important that you work with the interests of the students and allow them to create the space with you. It can even become a curriculum-related task. The main things for students to think about should be how the books will be arranged, how key books will be displayed and 'advertised', how to make the space comfortable (chairs, cushions or beanbags), how often books will be changed and by whom, and what colours or innovative features should be used to invite and welcome readers to the space. When the students are a part of the process, it gives them a sense of ownership and they are more likely to feel comfortable using the space. This is also a perfect way to involve reluctant readers in a reading-related task that will have a positive outcome for everyone.

How you stock your classroom library is also an important consideration and books should be changed up regularly to keep interest high. For most of the classroom libraries at school, we library staff send new classroom reading books each term, ensuring a mix of fiction, non-fiction, chapter books and illustrated texts. There are also a number of classrooms where students are assigned the weekly task of 'librarians'. These students manage the books in the classroom reading zone and swap some out each week, tidy them and refresh displays.

INVITING LIBRARY SPACES

School library spaces are public spaces and should consider the needs of the learners as well as the needs of the educators and the entire school community. Our students need a balance of spaces from expansive, active and social to small, intimate and quiet with technology infused rather than glaringly obvious.[1] Teachers need spaces to withdraw individual students for testing and areas for whole class research. Social learning spaces might be needed for small groups to discuss and debate or for students to read aloud in a group context. Conversely, students also appreciate and seek refuge from a busy day in small reading nooks and quiet, reflective spaces.

In *33 Educational Design Principles for Schools and Community Learning Centers*, Lackney talks of creating 'alcoves for learning' centrally located and close to resources.[2] I love this term and it brings to mind cosy and inviting learning spaces. Many of you will fondly remember those individual, 'walled' library desks from your own school days; your own little private space where you were meant to work in silence. These went out of vogue as education embraced group work, but more recently we have reconsidered the needs of individuals, and for many students there are moments in a school day when being alone (as alone as one can be in a busy school) can be beneficial to think, create and wonder.[3] In one school library I worked in, we created 'booths' reminiscent of milk bar booths where students could work alone or in small groups. They were close to the fiction area of the library and often students chose a book and made themselves comfortable in a booth for study or for recreational reading. These 'alcoves for learning' were probably the best feature of this library despite the initial worry that they would look a little like school libraries of old!

I could talk endlessly about the importance of displays of books in the library, but instead I'm going to distil this information down to one sentence that I hope will stick in your mind: Library displays should be dotted around the library, be ever-changing, professional (embrace Canva), eye-catching with books forwards-facing and able to be borrowed from the display.

A final point on library spaces: if at all possible, extend your space into the outdoors (see chapter 11 for more on this). I worked in a school library at the top level of a building, which is not ideal, but we utilised the lovely outdoor areas downstairs for quiet reading, group reading and workshopping. When we were doing a unit of work on mindful reading, many of the students chose to read near our native stingless beehives or in the grove of palm trees.

Library spaces should be dynamic and constantly evolving as they are meeting the many requirements of a modern learning environment. A library should offer flexibility and access to the varied resources to support a technologically robust community and one which promotes language and literacy learning at all times.

CHAPTER SIX

THE RIGOUR OF READING

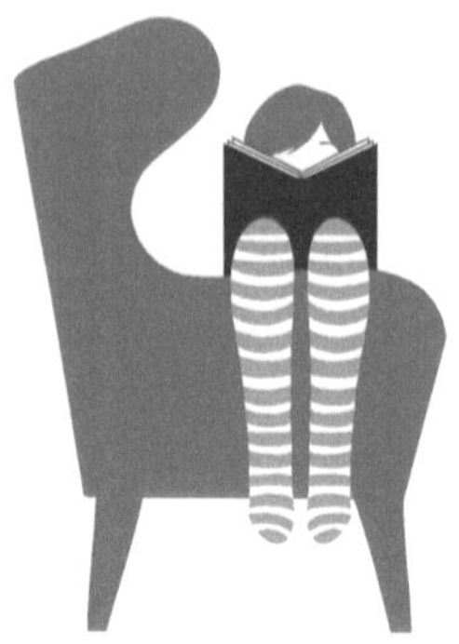

Many of us know from anecdotal evidence that sustained and regular reading, as well as reading for pleasure, contributes to positive academic outcomes, and this is backed by research examining how reading correlates to academic success.[1] We want young people to be highly literate and critical consumers of words; from the novels they read to environmental signage on the streets to marketing images and the analysis required for understanding complex ethical issues. Deep and meaningful reading contributes to language acquisition and the ability to use language in a way that is empowering. But how do we maintain rigour in reading while ensuring that we don't turn reading into a chore? What motivates students to read and continue reading?

As children move into the upper primary years of schooling their reading, by necessity, becomes more purposeful and strategic. The demands of the school curriculum require students to read a large volume of materials, and this only increases as students move into high school. Those who have read with enthusiasm from a young age and have built up a powerful armoury of reading comprehension strategies are in an ideal position to cope with the demands of reading for academic gain. These students build on prior knowledge, and are prepared for rich and thought-provoking analysis and skilled extrapolation of information using techniques such as skimming and scanning, highlighting passages, taking notes, summarising and locating credible supporting sources. Readers understand sentence structure and know where in a paragraph the important nugget of information will be, and they read widely in order to extend their general knowledge, build an extensive vocabulary and achieve mastery in what they read and in the tasks they complete.[2] Those years of reading for pleasure and racing through novels at an astonishing pace pay dividends when high school arrives and the reading volume increases.

Reading for pleasure need not disappear in high school. Fantasy is a great way for teens to escape mathematics study, for example. Or some young people may be comforted by reading contemporary stories of students who, like them, feel overwhelmed by a heavy workload but manage to stumble their way through school and social situations. A ready supply of reading material in the house will ensure that in moments of downtime your child will have a book to provide them with a portal to another world outside of study and school. Reading newspapers, magazines and graphic novels can also be used as escapism. The ability to dip in and out of these short-grab texts can suit busy students, satisfying their need for a quick and interesting read.

A word of caution here to not push your avid reader too much. I can put my hand up for being guilty of this and it really serves no purpose; in fact, it can turn reading from a pleasure to a chore. At all times and in all situations, make reading a joy and remember that even the most avid of readers may go through a rut.

EXTENDING YOUR CHILD'S READING

Once your child hits a certain reading level in those early years of primary school, they will start to crave books with more complex storylines and in their area of passion, be it sharks, fairies, magical tales or true stories of heroes. This is a time when things can come unstuck for parents and educators alike and we stress over questions like: 'What on earth can I give them next?'; 'How do I know what's appropriate?'; 'I know they are only five, but can they read Rangers Apprentice?'; 'Shouldn't they read the classics I read as a child?'

I am of the opinion that reading material should always be age appropriate; however, there are various schools of thought on this, with many parents happy to allow their children full access to their home or public library collection. You know your child best so you are the one best placed to make the decision on their level of reading maturity. In my role as a teacher librarian, I often spend time talking to parents who are keen to extend their child's reading with books aimed at a much older audience. I always point out that while their five- or six-year-old might technically be able to read every word in, say, Harry Potter with great fluency, they may not grasp the content and full complexity of the story – and it always seems such a shame to me to not completely fall in love with a series like Harry Potter. The same can be said for something like *The Wind in the Willows* (Kenneth Grahame) or *Black Beauty* (Anna Sewell). If read at too young an age, while the child may understand the words, they may not fully appreciate the beauty of the language and, at worst, they may end up intensely disliking a fantastic book. The classics are wonderful for older readers but are a slog for young readers still working on the mechanics of reading. In my experience, books are usually only great when they are read by the intended age group, though there are always exceptions to this.

With young people who have an insatiable reading appetite, I always ask parents to continue to encourage their capable reader with their classroom readers as these are designed to teach specific skills. I also urge parents to never let their children leave picture books behind once they've 'moved on' to chapter books. If I had a dollar for every child who said to me, 'Mummy says I have to borrow chapter books because I can read now and don't need picture books', I would be well and truly retired and living in Bali. Picture books have come a long way since our own childhood memories of them. The language in today's picture books is often complex and at a much higher level than that found in an early chapter book, and the storylines sophisticated and thought-provoking. And we haven't even considered the illustrations yet! We live in an age of visuals; picture books teach visual literacy like no other teaching tool (see chapter 4). Avid young readers are often the ones most capable of dealing with the complexity of a picture book ... I could go on and on. Suffice to say, I believe that every child should always have picture books on the go.

There are so many young readers whose reading ability and comprehension is way beyond their years and they can wield a pen as effortlessly as many published authors. While this sounds glorious to many parents, it can be quite the struggle to keep the gifted child engaged and connected with their learning. Tracey Hand has years of experience as a teacher and a particular passion for the learning needs of gifted and talented students. She has the following advice for parents looking to extend their child's reading.

Tracey Hand

It is commonly accepted that the experience of childhood has significantly changed for the twenty-first century child. Many people of my generation recall the sense of fun and freedom that came with being allowed to play outside with the neighbours' kids all day, usually unsupervised, until 'Mum called you to come in for tea'. Books could be described as the 'last frontier' for today's child. Stepping into a book may be the only opportunity many children have now to experience the thrill of adventure and the sense that 'anything could happen'. In my mind, books play a vital role in enriching the life of a child – today more than ever.

As a specialist 'gifted and talented' teacher, I am often asked by parents to recommend 'suitable' books for their gifted reader. My advice to parents is to assist their child to seek out books that cater for their interests and ability level while keeping in mind that many age-appropriate books often lack the depth and complexity young gifted children crave. By monitoring their child's book choices and providing them with the opportunity to indulge their passion for reading, parents are enabling their child's imagination, creativity and critical thinking skills to flourish.

To help extend avid readers you can:

- Support your child's passion for reading by exposing them to a wide variety of text types and topics that will engage them, challenge them, teach them and arouse their curiosities while encouraging them to think deeply and ponder. Providing your avid reader with a wide variety of books is similar to providing them with a drink to quench their thirst.

- Ensure that your avid reader is engaging with books that contain age-appropriate themes and concepts. Many avid readers have the ability to read books written for students much older than they are, which can cause them to become distressed or feel confused by what they have read. I recall a past student who at five years old had the reading age of a fifteen-year-old, and after finding and reading a short article titled 'Fearsome Facts: the Inca' in her school library, she was too traumatised to sleep in her own room for a few months. 'Why did the Incas kill children, Mummy?' was the question this young girl wanted answered.

- Make the time to discuss with your child the books they are reading. Checking in will help you to keep abreast of the themes your child is being exposed to.

- Unless your child objects, continue to read aloud to them regularly. There is an assumption that young gifted children do not need this, but reading aloud not only models reading, it expands their book experience, especially if they are beginning to develop a preference for a specific genre at a young age.

- Ensure you provide opportunities for your child to visit the local library regularly. Get to know your local librarian; they often love to help gifted readers indulge their particular interest and will recommend recently purchased books.

Reading aloud to capable readers is not something we often think to do but, as Tracey says, it should be continued for as long as possible – it helps to build connection and community as readers discuss a shared experience of a book. It is also a great way to level the playing field, with readers of varied ability making meaning together and developing a shared culture of reading.

FROM READER TO WRITER

Research confirms a strong link between reading and writing competency and we know that readers are often the most capable writers. Reading and writing rely on many of the same cognitive processes and the skills reinforce and support each other.[3] One of the ways I often extend my capable readers is through writing, often in response to books they have been reading either recreationally or for school.

Crafting a narrative or penning some poetry fully immerses children in the writing and reading cycle. At school I have, for many years now, worked with small groups of students on extending their writing skills, based on their reading interest or on a book we have chosen together to study. We have innovated on particular texts, co-authored books online with other extension students from local schools, and have contacted favourite authors to interview them about their creative writing process. Creative writing skills and academic writing skills are interconnected and interchangeable, and an extensive vocabulary built through wide reading empowers young people in all forms of writing.

Allison Tait, author of *The First Summer of Callie McGee*, The Mapmaker Chronicles and The Ateban Cipher series, is a talented children's author. Her work at the Australian Writers' Centre (AWC) in helping others to realise their dream of becoming an author is outstanding, and together we co-host the *Your Kid's Next Read* podcast. Allison was the first person who came to mind when I wanted someone to comment on the connection between reading and writing.

Allison Tait

'If you can't see it, you can't be it.' This phrase is generally used in regard to role-modelling careers, but I think it works just as well when it comes to reading and writing. When authors are asked for their top tips for writers, their number one response – and I can vouch for this because I host a podcast in which I've asked hundreds of authors for their top tips – is 'READ'. If someone asks who inspired me to become an author, I talk about the hundreds of books I read as a child.

If someone asks me how I understand story structure, pacing, dialogue and narrative arcs, I explain that most of what I do is innate, instinctive. Why? Because of the thousands of books I've read in my lifetime, both as an adult and as a child. I've read detective stories and romance stories and adventure stories and stories that were beautifully written but didn't even seem to HAVE a story.

Through reading those thousands of books I have absorbed things that I love – and things that I didn't. I have studied, without ever knowing I was doing it, the craft of writing at the hands of masters such as J. R. R. Tolkien, Margaret Atwood, Stephen King, Jane Austen, Judy Blume, S. E. Hinton, Charles Dickens, Mark Twain and [insert the name of your favourite author here because chances are I've read his or her work].

From non-fiction books I have learnt that one tiny fact can be the most interesting thing in a sea of words. From comics I have learnt the importance of a single idea per panel to keep a story moving. From memoir I have learnt that any story can be riveting when the voice is honest and true. All of these things came together when I started writing The Mapmaker Chronicles.

Kids who read know that a story needs a beginning, a middle and an end. They know that a story is not just a description – that something has to happen. Their vocabulary grows all the time, giving them new tools to use in their own writing.

Kids who read know what it is like to be dragged into another world and emerge blinking at the end of a book. When I explain in my school talks that one of the things I love most about writing is that it gives me the ability to control the whole world, they get it.

Reading fuels imagination, ideas and imagery. Being read to has the same effect.

There is more to writing than simply reading. Every craft has its own set of tools, and writing is no different. But if you're a reader, you're not starting from scratch. You are simply building on the big picture that every single story you've read combines to create.

And who doesn't love a head start?

CHAPTER SEVEN

SUPPORTING READING

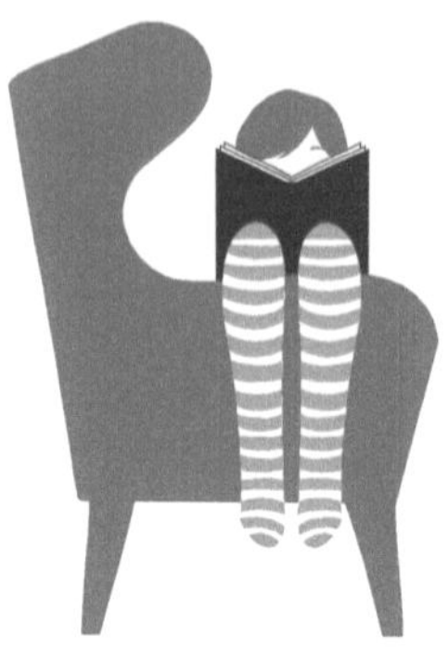

For many parents and educators supporting young people who experience difficulties in learning to read, it can become a daily battle, as can navigating the education system and advocating for a child. (See chapter 2 for what you should be expecting and advocating for.) Whether a young person has a diagnosed learning disability, is struggling with the move into YA reading from middle-grade, is confronted by gender stereotyping in books, or has become a hardcore reluctant reader, it is just plain hard to be the adult watching from the sidelines and feeling helpless.[1]

Diagnosed learning issues are complex and multifaceted and, as many families will know, often where there is one diagnosed condition there can be another, further adding to the complexity.

Young people with learning difficulties may include:

- Students with specific diagnosed learning difficulties, disorders and impairments, such as visual impairments, hearing impairments, physical impairments, intellectual impairments, autism spectrum disorder, speech language impairments, social emotional disorders and processing disorders.

- Students with undiagnosed learning difficulties; literacy, numeracy and/or metacognition.
- Gifted and talented students.
- English as an additional language or dialect (EALD) students.

The Disability Discrimination Act 1992 and the Disability Standards for Education 2005 outline that schools must ensure that all students with disability can access education 'on the same basis' as their peers and are supported with reasonable adjustments to meet their individual needs.

Discussion about reading challenges should include the perspectives of both parent and child. For many years I watched the journey of one particular student and marvelled at the tenacity and devotion of the mother in ensuring her daughter became a reader and knew the joy of story. I often observed her frustration, but I also observed a quiet determination. For many years I silently cheered her on from the sidelines, and also provided support in my role as teacher librarian. I have asked her to share her story.

Raising a 'left-handed' learner reader

My husband and I did all the 'right' activities to help raise a reader and instil a love of literature in our daughter. Stories were read to her daily from the first few months of life; we both read a variety of materials ourselves; we live in a house filled with books; she has her own extensive book collection; we displayed learning charts throughout our house; we sang and pointed to the alphabet song every night before bed and many times throughout the day. You name it, we tried it!

The kindergarten teacher once shared that our daughter always looked at situations, problems, etc, from a unique perspective, differently from most of her classmates. What I now know is that the kindergarten teacher was identifying a left-handed learning style without naming any of the components.

When my daughter was four I initiated an assessment by a speech and language pathologist as I knew something wasn't 'right'. This professional referred us to an occupational therapist and we started therapy for a period of time. Commencing school taught us both to dislike grading of readers (known as reading levels) with an intensity that is hard to articulate politely! From my perspective as a mother of a child with learning difficulties, sight words are the devil in disguise. I'm ashamed to share that there were far too many tears shed and tantrums (plus books) thrown by both child and parent as my daughter tried her best to learn to read. It was a genuinely heartbreaking nightmare. She was also bullied by her peers as she struggled to learn to read.

We had our daughter assessed by no less than five speech therapy services before we met our angel in disguise, a specialist in dyslexia. She diagnosed our daughter's learning style as dyslexia and introduced us to evidence-based interventions delivered with the degree of knowledge, skill, love and compassion possessed by the very best kind of allied health professionals. We worked very hard and our daughter has reaped the rewards of this hard work.

In addition to working with a specialist, we moved our daughter to a different school environment, spent a small fortune on audio books, ebooks and graphic novels, and we kept reading, reading, reading.

This is what I have learnt from my daughter's journey:

- Never, ever give up! Be your child's champion and advocate. If you don't or won't believe in your child, no one else – including themselves – ever will.
- Reading is about understanding. How we access the words, sentences and meaning is less important than the access itself. Eye (conventional), ear (audio) and finger (braille) reading are all equally valid and all involve the brain.
- Do the hard yards as soon as possible. Your child will reap the rewards later on. As my elder sister told me on many occasions, you have to have thick, tough skin to be a parent. I made my daughter do many activities on her

journey to being able to read independently that she wasn't thrilled about.

- Being able to spell doesn't make you a superior human being. It's just spelling, people, get over it! As my husband says, 'That's why we have spellcheck.'

If I had to nominate two interventions that were critical to our daughter becoming an independent reader who loves books, they would be:

1. Finding the right allied health professional who works in the area. We will go to our graves forever loving the specialist we met and all her goodness.
2. Being in a supportive educational setting. Perfect doesn't exist in a school but find the best you can.

My beautiful, brave 'Dyslexian' (how my daughter describes herself) gave me the proudest parent moment when she 'ear' read (that is, listened to an audio book of) Jane Austen's *Pride and Prejudice*. She read this book at the recommendation of a very high-achieving academic superstar peer. I – who loved and excelled in English at school – confess to never having read a Jane Austen book. My heart burst with pride.

This story puts the human heart into what can be a tiring journey. We know that academic success is tied to reading and we, as parents, want our children to achieve their full potential. What I think this story shows is that full potential is reached when parents, educators and specialists work in partnership and the child is valued for the learner they are, and their strengths are both acknowledged and rewarded. It also shows that sometimes tough decisions need to be made in the best interests of the child. The next story is of a student (whom I'll call Abby) I taught for many years, and is similar in that the input of specialists, teachers and parents has been key in Abby reaching her full potential as a reader and learner. I interviewed Abby, with parental permission, for the story that follows.

I first met Abby as a Year One student. She had just changed schools due to the previous one not meeting her needs, mostly in the area of literacy. I had been told before her enrolment that Abby was absolutely terrified of the library as her experience of a school library to date had not been positive. The day she came to her first library lesson with me I curbed my usually over-the-top loud style of welcome and bent down to her level to introduce myself. She didn't want to come into the library that day so one of my staff took a few books out to her and together they sat outside to read.

It took some weeks before Abby was comfortable enough to enter the library and many months before she would talk to me and trust me. I was aware she was sizing me up and working out my style and I did eventually win over this clever and sceptical little person. I am proud to say that, to this day, we are the best of teacher/student mates.

Throughout her early years of primary school, Abby worked hard at learning to read but it was often an exercise that reduced her to tears and heightened her anxiety around written work, assessments and library lessons. In Year Two she was diagnosed with dyslexia and received support and modifications to her learning and assessment, as well as time with specialist staff, but reading and written work were very much things she 'didn't enjoy at all'. Throughout these years she was always comfortable in the library and when I asked her what she liked about our library, despite all the books (she had previously declared, 'Oh there are just *too many* books in this place! They freak me out!'), she said that it was because we 'didn't just do books in the library'.

We had a great makerspace zone and vibe to our library. Abby was highly creative and loved to make and problem-solve – the key skills embraced by the makerspace movement. For many years, Abby spent every lunchtime in the library creating wondrous objects out of paper, wood, fabric and glue. She was a highly valued member of the coding and robotics club and respected by her peers, who could see how creatively gifted she was and who were always keen to 'do the reading and writing bits for her' (her words).

The makerspace opened our library doors wide, welcoming everyone, including students who did not previously see themselves as 'library kids'. Our hope has always been that having spent time in the library making and creating, they will walk out with books. Abby regularly left the library with a book after a session in the makerspace, thanks in part to our placement of book displays on the way to and from the makerspace zone. As teacher librarians we also initiate regular conversations with students about books that might further their interests in a particular area. One day I could see Abby working on a robotic horse and armed her with several non-fiction books on horses so she could ensure hers was anatomically correct, as well as a fictional story about ponies I knew she would be able to read and enjoy.

Reading continued to be a challenge for Abby but she was an incredible storyteller who would write and illustrate lengthy narratives and share them with her friends and teachers. When Readers Cup competitions were held in school, Abby was upfront about the fact that she was not going to even read all of the books, but that she would make up for it with her ability to 'think outside the box'. She was always a valued member of any Readers Cup team.

Abby confessed that she often borrowed library books she never read so it looked like she was keeping up with her peers. But she did enjoy audio books and non-fiction texts and I would always slip a graphic novel into her borrowing pile, or maybe a novel I knew she would be able to read independently. There was regular communication between her parents and me about Abby's reading and what she would enjoy, so we made a great team!

Abby and her mother joined my Year Six Girl Zone Book Club. The set books were at a much higher reading level than what Abby could manage on her own, but the lovely thing about book clubs is that I encourage parents or caregivers to read with or to their child and talk about the story as they go. I believe the book club was essential in making Abby confirm her identity as a reader – she was hanging out with 'the readers' so she must be a reader too, right?

Parents and educators have worked alongside Abby to ensure her success. But to be honest, most of Abby's success is down to the hard work she has put in and an awareness that she loved stories and was determined to access them any way she could, often as audio books or graphic novels.

Like Abby, many young people with reading or learning challenges discover the power of story through graphic novels. Allison Rushby is the award-winning author of several middle-grade novels and adult titles, and she is also an avid reader of graphic novels. I have asked her to talk about why and how she uses graphic novels, as well as her all-time favourite ten.

Allison Rushby

I grew up in a house of readers. As the daughter of a novelist and being a novelist myself, I simply expected my kids would be readers as well. It was clear from very early on that our firstborn, Ivy, was going to have some challenges in life. She was soon diagnosed as having a developmental delay that included a comprehension disorder. Her presentation is unusual and it often takes educators quite some time to understand her learning style. Ivy has good spelling and reading but poor comprehension. Her good spelling and reading stem from her enhanced visual skills, which she has developed because she relies on visual cues to get by in the world. Because her comprehension is poor, standard print novels are confusing for her. Audio books can be a useful tool for people with learning difficulties, but because a comprehension disorder is all-encompassing, audio books are also not much use to us (in fact, they are even harder for Ivy to comprehend as there are no visual cues at all).

I knew that if I wanted Ivy to read and enjoy books, graphic novels were really going to be our only option. I needed to become knowledgeable about them. And fast. So I did. I am constantly on the hunt, ordering in from overseas, looking for what's out in which territories, what's coming out soon and often pre-ordering a year in advance. I think we got very lucky with our timing. In recent years graphic novels have taken off in a big way. In fact, graphic novels are now so popular that Scholastic has developed an entire imprint around them (called Graphix).

I'm constantly surprised at the snobbery that persists around graphic novels – I often hear parents saying things like, 'Oh, but I want my child to read a real novel.' To be honest, I doubt whether this will continue much longer. With graphic novels constantly on *The New York Times* bestseller list, they can no longer be overlooked.

Megan has asked that I submit my top ten graphic novels and I'm ashamed to say I'm going to cheat disgracefully and include series and more than one book per entry. But your child's love of reading will only be enhanced for it so I'm really not that ashamed! Although not top favourites, I have also included a few examples of books you will often find on the curriculum that are available in graphic novel form, as I often find parents aren't aware of their existence and they do make authors like Shakespeare far more accessible.

1. *Smile* and *Sisters* by Raina Telgemeier (Scholastic)
2. Amulet series by Kazu Kibuishi (Scholastic)
3. *El Deafo* by Cece Bell (Abrams Books, 2014)
4. *Shakespeare's A Midsummer Night's Dream: A Graphic Novel* adapted by Steve Barlo and Steve Skidmore, illustrated by Eduard Coll (Hachette, 2022) (Other Classics in Graphics novels are also available)
5. The Baby-Sitter's Club graphic novel series based on the novels of Ann M. Martin, illustrated by various artists (Scholastic)
6. Percy Jackson and the Olympians graphic novel series based on the novels of Rick Riordan, adapted by Robert Venditti, illustrated by Attila Futaki (Puffin)
7. *Awkward* by Svetlana Chmakova (Hachette, 2015)
8. *Roller Girl* by Victoria Jamieson (Puffin, 2024)

9. *Anne of Green Gables: A Graphic Novel* based on the novel by Lucy Maud Montgomery, adapted by Mariah Marsden, illustrated by Brenna Thummler (Simon & Schuster, 2017)
10. *Jane Eyre: The Graphic Novel* based on the novel by Charlotte Brontë, adapted by Amy Corzine, illustrated by John M. Burns (Classical Comics, 2008)

THE GENDER DEBATE

I have worked in both co-ed and single-sex schools and I've heard the gamut of thoughts on 'gendered' books. When I worked as a teacher librarian in a boys' school, I had so many people commenting along the lines of, 'Well, you'll have a hard time getting boys reading!' I found this both infuriating and disappointing and would have loved to have shown these naysayers my library on any given lunch break, filled with young male readers. To be fair, some of those boys were there for the chess, to look at surfing magazines or use the iPads, but they were comfortable in a space of books, and borrowing rates were high. Some of the best conversations about books I ever had were in that library and the requests for new books came in thick and fast. I then worked in an all-girls school library and had similar rates of borrowing and the same sorts of conversations around books. The book choices on the shelves were also largely the same and I always aim to stock my library with books that will appeal to all.

We do our young readers a disservice by making assumptions about what boys will read and what girls will read. I see and acknowledge the differences in bookish taste, but I also see similarities in what all readers will access and enjoy if given the opportunity.

Jacqueline Harvey is one of Australia's most popular authors for children (*The Girl and the Ghost* and a number of series, including Alice-Miranda, Clementine Rose, Willa and Woof, and Kensy and

Max), a teacher and a presenter of talks and workshops at schools and festivals. We have had discussions about book gendering time and time again. Jacqueline has much to say about why the labelling has to stop.

Jacqueline Harvey

If I had a dollar for every time I've heard a parent (or teacher) actively steer their boy away from reading one of my books, sadly I'd have enough money to keep me in expensive coffee for quite some time. It happens at book signings (when the child has clearly been keen to meet me), it happens at schools – it just happens. 'You don't want that, it's got a girl on the cover'; 'Maaate, that's a book for girls'; 'Boys don't read those books' – you get the picture. And I know I'm not alone. I've had this discussion with many of my author friends who write books with girls as the central characters.

As a former teacher I know it doesn't take a huge amount of encouragement to convince a girl to pick up a book with a boy on the cover, but try that in reverse and more often than not it's an insurmountable challenge. If we're not encouraging our boys to read books with girls as the main characters we're doing them a great disservice. What are we telling our boys? That stories about girls are lesser – they don't matter as much – they're not as good as boys? And never mind that many books with girls on the cover include boy characters in the stories – I know mine have loads of them.

Even worse is when during school visits I've been confronted in a co-ed school by a room full of girls. When I've asked where the boys are I've been met with, 'Well, you know, we didn't think they'd enjoy your talk because your books are for girls.' At which point my head is about to explode. I pride myself on being able to entertain and inform all children in my talks – my talks are fun and fabulous and I've had lots of feedback that confirms I'm good at this. To think that boys miss out because the teacher (who in all likelihood hasn't even read my books) has decided that I only write books for girls is not only ludicrous but offensive to me – an educator with over twenty years' experience. I cannot imagine the girls being removed from a talk by a male author who writes about male protagonists – it just wouldn't happen.

Okay, the publishers play a big role in perpetuating the myths. Marketing is often quite gender specific. Books with sparkly, pink rainbow unicorns on the cover probably won't appeal as much to boys as to girls, and I get that boys and girls lean towards different things. But just a girl – a girl who looks like she's going to have an adventure and probably bring down a bad guy or two – why is that still a problem, even if the background cover is purple or, heaven forbid, pink? My covers have a whole palette of colours from blue to green to yellow and inky black as well as pink and purple. Society has come a long way but to think that the gatekeepers still limit the reading choices of our boys by reinforcing gender stereotypes is disappointing to say the least.

I write about strong girls (and boys). They have adventures, they solve mysteries, they're funny and clever and kooky. They travel to different countries and learn new things, they have fun, yet my audience is still probably around 95 per cent female. When I do meet my boy readers, they are passionate. I love asking them why they like Alice-Miranda or Clementine Rose. Here are some of the responses: 'I don't like Alice-Miranda, I love her ...'; 'She feels like my best friend ...'; 'She's brave and funny and she has great adventures ...'; 'Clemmie has a pet pig and she's always getting herself into trouble ...'; 'I love the mysteries ...'

One of my favourite anecdotes about boy readers happened at a major Australian writers' festival a few years ago. I'm not going to name names, but I was on the bill with three of the biggest (male) names in children's literature. During my last signing session three boys in Year Six approached me with books. Their librarian, who was standing beside them, said, 'Tell Jacqueline why you're buying her books.' I was intrigued. One of the boys explained that before they were allowed to come to the event they had to read a book by each of the authors and they all enjoyed mine the most. Did that make me feel awesome? You bet! I asked those boys to go back to school and share their love of Alice-Miranda with their friends. Who knows if they did, but good for them for being brave enough to pick up a book with a girl on the cover and for admitting they enjoyed it.

Unfortunately, those experiences are far too few – and not because I don't think boys will enjoy my books. My Kensy and Max series deals with a boy and girl twin and they're about to find out something amazing about their family. Will boys read it because there is a boy on the cover? Who knows! But I hope so, and I hope they might go back and explore some of my other stories too – once they know for sure that I don't just write books for girls!

KEEPING TWEENS READING

Life commonly gets busy with homework and after-school activities for kids once they hit middle/upper primary school. Research tells us that as students move from primary to secondary school, reading for pleasure declines and even previously keen readers often disengage from literature.[2] The pressure is on to help young people find a balance between reading, social media, socialising, studying and extracurricular pursuits.

It is also a challenging age in terms of book choices as they begin to transition from younger reader books to middle-grade novels and young adult (YA) books. I have plenty of senior primary students at school who get all angsty at my lack of 'adult content' books, but then I also have many who are still happy reading tales of fairies and puppies. I see a huge range of reading maturity and it keeps me on my toes catering for the wide variety of reading ages and stages. As always, conversations with individual children and their parents are the key to success here.

If you feel your child is needing or wanting to make the transition to middle-grade novels, I would encourage you to read alongside them for a while to ensure the process is smooth. As a bonus, I guarantee that you will enjoy many of the middle-grade novels, as much as your child does. Middle-grade is a description of a reading demographic, not a genre type, with these novels being targeted at students in the upper years of primary school and early years of secondary school. They typically clock in at around 40,000 to 50,000 words in length. Tweens are emerging from their childhood years and becoming more aware that the world is a large and sometimes scary place. For this reason, middle-grade novels often feature themes of friendships, family, social issues and community or wider world issues, with relatable central characters who navigate complex situations and try to solve problems. It is common for children to want to read novels with characters who are the same age or slightly older, using the experiences, mistakes and successes of the characters to question how they might face similar realities in their own lives. Tweens and teens want independence and the space to take risks, but also want to receive reassurance both in real life and in their reading choices. Through the vicarious experience offered by reading novels, they have the opportunity to step into other people's shoes and walk with them, developing empathy and understanding.

I overheard a conversation some years ago in my library that has always stayed with me. It was between two eleven-year-olds and one was recommending the other a beautiful middle-grade novel called *Mother's Day* (Anne Brooksbank) saying, 'I think you should read this book. It's got a divorced family and the main character is trying to work out what is happening with her mum. It's a little bit like what happened to Maggie's family and I actually feel like I kind of was in Maggie's head when I was reading it.' I had to walk away because (a) I had tears in my eyes at how amazing this level of bookish understanding was and (b) these students were sharing a special moment and I was not going to step in and ruin it.

Chapter 14, 'Reading the Dark', gives further insights, but the tween years are also the time when parents and educators will notice a distinct shift in the themes explored in literature. Children are more aware of some of the darker themes in life, and literature is often where they will explore the moral and ethical issues around challenging topics. Literature can be a gateway to some really tough conversations, at an age where conversation with adults is often at a minimum. Talking through book characters has certainly been something I have done with my children when talking about the grief and loss we have experienced as a family. Feeding them a book every now and then with a bereaved character has meant we can talk about the character, rather than their own feelings, which can sometimes be hard to articulate. At all times it is imperative to balance the light and the dark in the literature your tweens are reading, but try to not be alarmed by books with darker themes. Quality middle-grade novels manage the big emotions with care: deep friendships but little or no romance; minimal or no violence; depression with hope; grief with moments of light and laughter. On writing middle-grade novels, author Allison Tait states, 'Basically, you don't want to traumatise your readers. You want to evoke emotion and provoke thought, but you have to remember that your ideal reader is a child.'[3]

If you find yourself with a tween or classful of them who have stalled with their reading, I would recommend trying some of the following ideas:

- Sign them up to an online reading challenge like the Premier's Reading Challenges in your state – there is nothing like a bit of pressure to read and the lure of a certificate and/or prizes.
- Offer new books as a reward for tasks done or as end-of-school or end-of-term gifts.
- Read with them. Middle-grade novels are as fabulous for adults as they are for children. This comes back to what I have said earlier about being a reading role model, but it also shows your tween or teen that you value the books they read. It also means you will be present when spontaneous conversations about issues start to flow.
- Read to them. Reading the first chapter or two of a really great middle-grade novel will often pique enough interest for them to pick up the book left lying around.

- Browse blogs, author social media accounts and popular tween magazines, and let your child choose their reading material – a sense of independence is all important. Autonomy in reading choices is crucial at this age.
- Attend book launches, local library events, children's literature festivals and bookshops. There is nothing like meeting an author to inspire reading, and middle-grade authors are some of the coolest people you and your tweens will ever meet.
- Join a book club! Over the years many of my participants have said it's their favourite co-curricular activity and parents have commented that it's been such a good way to bond with their child at what can be a tricky time to remain really connected. See 'How to start a book club' (page 239) for hints.

Some of these ideas might seem forced, even onerous, but if your child connects with some books they adore then they will be off and flying with their reading again.

I have asked Joe Visser to talk about his teen reading journey. His reviews have appeared in *The Sunday Telegraph* and on sites such as *Children's Books Daily* and *Creative Kids Tales*. Now as a young adult he is a singer, songwriter and feature writer for various publications.

Joe Visser (AKA Book Boy)

I've always read widely, including books that I may not be the target audience for, be it books for girls, or books that are sometimes considered 'too old' for someone my age. But reading these books, I believe, furthers a young person's understanding of the world.

The first book I can remember reading by myself was the second Harry Potter book. I read the first one with Mum when I was five or six, and that kind of sparked my love of reading. My mum has been very influential in the kinds of books I read – she recommends a lot of books to me – but more recently, I have heard about books through other people or mediums.

I listen to the *Dear Hank & John* podcast, which has influenced what I read a lot lately, especially in regard to poetry. I also hear about books through friends, and my English teachers have given me some suggestions.

Teenagers, especially boys, generally stop reading or read less when they turn fourteen or fifteen. There are a few possible reasons for this. Often it is around this age that you start to read and analyse books for school so there is less time to read for enjoyment.

Another reason is that young people may wish to start reading more 'grown-up' books and their parents may not let them. I think this is a mistake. I'm not saying that parents should let their children read whatever they want, as there is some material in books that is not appropriate to expose a young person to, but I suggest that parents read the book first, and think about how bad it would really be to let their child read it.

When I turned thirteen I started reading more books that were considered to be for adults, from authors such as Stephen King and books such as *All the Light We Cannot See* by Anthony Doerr. Because my mother had read these before, she knew what they were about and that they posed little or no threat if I were to read them. Books such as *A Game of Thrones* by George R. R. Martin are ones I am not allowed to read yet.

I also read books that are 'for girls' or aimed at girls (or books with girl protagonists) because a good book is a good book, no matter who the target audience is.

SUPPORTING THE MOVE INTO YA READING

Young adult (YA) books are aimed at readers from around the age of thirteen plus, but there is wide variance within the genre. Some are exclusively aimed at readers sixteen plus, so it is important to look at the suitability of each book for your own young readers. YA literature has always been popular but perhaps the rise in social media has meant it has more of a presence now because young people are avid consumers and creators of social media content. The YA literature scene has embraced the trend with enthusiasm.

Like middle-grade, YA is a reading demographic, not a genre, so there are many types of stories exploring a range of topics and styles. Teens are able to find something they like amid sub-genres and series and accompanying online communities. There have always been teenagers who read and share passionately and the growth in social media has made it easier to connect with other passionate readers. Fan-fiction writing and artwork have found spaces online and the opportunities to be validated by others has amplified the interest in YA books.

YA books are popular with both teens and adults because they are relatable and appeal to a wide and diverse audience. Many adults actually prefer reading YA novels to lengthier adult tomes. Authors of quality YA are skilled writers who remove every extraneous word, leaving only the very best and essential, and the true beating heart of the story: all the emotion and tension of an adult novel but punchier. YA authors are often risk-takers (as are their readers!) and don't feel obligated to stick to a formula, often meshing genres together. They often also touch on profoundly important topics such as homelessness (*Because of You* by Pip Harry), the plight of refugees (*The Bone Sparrow* by Zana Fraillon), identity (*Take Three Girls* by Cath Crowley, Simmone Howell and Fiona Wood), sexuality (*The Sidekicks* by Will Kostakis), grief (*The Protected* by Claire Zorn), and LGBTQIA+ communities (*You Know Me Well* by David Levithan and Nina LaCour).

In recent years filmmakers have latched onto series, such as The Hunger Games (Suzanne Collins) and realised how much good YA there is to exploit. It can often be much easier to sell a book to a reluctant reader when there is also a film. Librarians also capitalise on movie tie-ins and while it seems like movies would draw kids away from reading, both mediums benefit the other. I am a massive fan of the YA-book-to-movie phenomenon and have seen just about every incarnation of them over the last ten years – you'll often find keen teacher librarians up the back of the cinema of teen 'book-to-movie' releases.

CHAPTER EIGHT

THE SOCIAL LIFE OF READERS

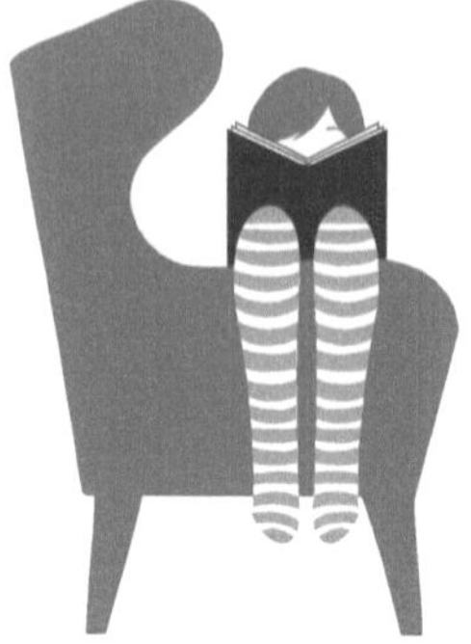

Reading is generally considered a solitary pursuit. Sitting alone in one's personal home library with a cup of tea and a slice of cake, a plate resting on the arm of the plush green velvet reading chair with the perfect pendant light illuminating the pages of a new novel. Well, this is one of my fantasies anyway. When we imagine readers we often picture them alone. Popular media has a tendency to portray 'the reader' in this light and it does reading such a disservice.

Being a librarian draws next-level media stereotyping. I recently got reading glasses for the first time and the full-bearded, waistcoat-wearing hipster optometrist got so excited when he found out I was a librarian. 'Oh my! Imagine being a legit librarian now with your brown cardigans, brogues and glasses.' It wasn't really the look I was going for.

My younger brother, who has just come through his own man-bun, bearded hipster phase, certainly doesn't fit the stereotype of 'the reader'. He is a mad keen surfer, used to be a builder, then completed a Masters in finance, can hold his own in any social situation – and is a voracious reader. He wasn't a reader as a child and my parents despaired. But on a very boring work trip with my parents during his early teens he discovered Harry Potter, and has never looked back.

Readers come in all shapes, sizes and persuasions and the world of reading can be a ridiculously social place. Still, stereotypes exist for a reason and many readers are happy to embrace the solitary reader tag and wear it with pride. I just hope that readers can also be seen as vibrant, highly sociable and excellent conversationalists.

COMPETITIONS FOR READERS

Book-based competitions are the time for readers to shine! A Readers Cup–style competition is a way to have students participate in meaningful and wide reading. I liken Readers Cup to a sporting activity: there are teams to form; training and preparation to do; competitions; and much socialising and solidifying of friendships in 'downtime'. In fact, I wonder if some teams even *read* the books, as so much time seems to be spent chatting, laughing and gossiping about other teams. Readers Cup competitions sometimes even support the creation of uniforms. Ava was once in a team called the 'Reading Ninjas' so they all wore black, had ninja bands and paper ninja stars.

Readers Cup competitions consist of teams of four students who read from a list of approximately six books chosen for their particular competition, be it school, regional or state-based. Team members are encouraged to read all books on their list and 'train' together by discussing the books and asking each other practice questions. In many states of Australia there will be school heats in Term One with the winning team going on to the regional heats in Term Two, and the state finals held in Term Three. Readers Cup exists across Australia, though not all states yet run regional and state heats.

Five ways to ensure you produce an ever-so-sociable reader

1. Advocate for author visits in your school community and ensure the build-up is akin to a rock star visit. Author visits are fun, shared experiences and break down negative stereotypes about 'those who read books'.
2. Sign up to the email lists and social media accounts of local bookshops and festivals and look out for literary events. There are teen book clubs run by bookshops and festivals, story times for younger ones, and craft and writing workshops for all ages. These events attract like-minded parents and children, and I often find the same faces at events around town.
3. Consider your local public library as your friend. My own children are booked into many library activities and they love them. We often take friends along or they will settle in and make some new friends over a two-hour gardening workshop or a mini-party to celebrate the birthday of a book.
4. Join a book club for young people with your child or sign them up to an age-appropriate one. If your school library doesn't have a book club, start one with friends and their children or find one at your local independent bookshop or public library.
5. Follow authors on social media and connect with other readers in the same way. Obviously I'm not advocating for young people on social media, but for teens this has become a way for them to connect with like-minded souls the world over. There are all kinds of reading and writing groups for people to join online and it's amazing how many authors hang out on social media and love to connect with their readers.

If you do not have a Readers Cup or similar competition in your school community and would like to start one up, it's important to first gain the support of your principal and other teaching staff. A Readers Cup competition can be a great learning opportunity, but if a class already has a heavy reading load, teachers will have a hard time encouraging students to read another six books. Many schools hold an interschool Readers Cup in Term Three, forming part of Children's Book Week celebrations and using a shortlisted book as one of the titles to be read. In other schools, set classroom texts are sometimes used as one of the Readers Cup titles or teachers will read one text aloud to their class.

AUTHOR VISITS

Never underestimate the power of author or illustrator visits in schools, kindergartens or public libraries to inspire students and staff. Meeting the creators of books makes the writing and/or illustrating process accessible and can inspire students with their own creative projects.[1] Author and illustrator visits provide unique insights into the process of book creation and bring literature to life for students, giving them a rich understanding of the literary and artistic devices employed by an author or illustrator to construct meaning.

School libraries have shrinking budgets that are often spent on library resources, with author visits seen as the 'icing on the cake' only if money allows. It would be easy to assume that I speak from a position of privilege, as all of the schools I have worked at over the past twenty-five years have allowed me to fund paid author visits. However, in each school, my library team and I have worked hard to ensure the school community understands the value of school author visits.

Author visits are possible in schools of any size and economic sway. It is a matter of advocating, fundraising and working towards your author visit goals. It is so very easy to put author visits in the too-hard basket or justify the lack of them due to poor funding or disinterest from school management. Being glum about a lack of funding or interest is never going to magic up an author visit, but being an enthusiastic advocate will.

Free author visits: promote, promote, promote!

Where funds are limited, schools can take up offers of free visits from local authors or illustrators who are keen to build their audience and promote their work. Occasionally publishers or bookstores will offer free school visits as part of a promotional tour or by arrangement with a charity. Promotion of the author and their books is expected for free visits, and I make sure that I send home promotional flyers and book order forms before the talk. The aim of the author, bookstore or publisher with free visits is to sell copies of books and increase awareness about an author or book. Such visits are a win for all involved *if* the school does a thorough job of promoting the event, and teaching staff and school administration see the value. For these visits I do not expect the presenter to conduct workshops or in-depth writing lessons that form part of the curriculum; rather, I see these sessions as a way to build excitement and fanfare around books and reading within the school community.

Paid author visits: connect with curriculum!

Paid author visits are an entirely different matter and I budget for at least two paid author or illustrator visits each school year. I communicate with speakers agencies or consider my own contacts in the children's book industry to decide who would best meet the needs of the school community. In collaboration with teachers, I work out which areas of the curriculum might be most enhanced by working with or hearing from an author or illustrator. Involving teachers is crucial as they are best situated to facilitate many of the connections between author, students and curriculum. They play a key role in motivating and empowering students to apply the knowledge learnt to their own reading and writing.[2] I also prepare teachers to be involved in author visits as I see these visits as professional development for staff.

For many years I invited Narelle Oliver to do storyboarding workshops with students in Year Three and lino-cutting workshops with Year Six. These workshops, held over several days, connected with several curriculum areas and provided real-life opportunities for students to engage with a masterful teacher, author and artist. Teachers were expected to complete prep work before the visit, which involved reading her books and completing an author study. After the visit many weeks were spent following up on the work begun in workshops.

I was recently chatting with a Year Eleven student about a story she was writing for English and she pulled out of her bag a handmade concertina-fold book which was her story plan. She had learnt this technique of storyboarding in Year Three with Narelle Oliver and was still using it all these years later; these are the moments we live for as teachers.

Over the years I have met a number of adults who vividly recall Narelle Oliver's workshops they participated in twenty years ago at primary school. Not every author visit will connect with every child, but there are moments of pure connection that last a lifetime for some students.

Check out 'How to host an author or illustrator visit' (page 244) for tips on getting the most out of a visit to your school.

Meeting your favourite author or illustrator (a favourite anecdote from when Ava was seven)

As I read Ava her books tonight and she tried to keep her eyes open after a *massive* day at the StoryArts Festival in Ipswich, she pondered her favourite illustrators. 'I think my second favourite illustrators are now Tony Flowers and Peter Carnavas because they were really good teachers today and Tony Flowers said it was okay to make your illustrations fart.' When I asked who her *favourite* illustrator was she looked at me incredulously: 'Me, of *course*!' These two generous illustrators inspired her to believe that she is also an illustrator.

Earlier in the day I had overheard her talking with her friend and listing the authors she had met at the festival and her friend asked in a hushed tone, 'What about Nikki Gemmell? Did you meet her?' to which Ava replied, 'Well, she's not at this festival, but I'm meeting her *really* soon' and they both squealed, jumped and hugged. She's actually not meeting Nikki Gemmell anytime that I know of and perhaps I should discuss the importance of telling the truth, but it was very cool to witness young people discussing authors like famous pop stars.

LITERARY AND BOOK-RELATED EVENTS

Some families go to sporting events, some travel to the beach or the bush each weekend, and some like to watch movies together. My family seems to lean towards literary events – probably something you can't escape when several members of the family are librarians. Literary pursuits, fuelled by excellent coffee for the adults, are what we *do* and some of our best family memories are of book launches and other bookish events around town.

In an age where our young people spend more and more time glued to screens, there is something a bit special and fabulous about a trip to your local library, bookstore, theatre or gallery to discover some reading gems and engage with creative activities. Literary events fire up young minds and if a young person connects with the ideas presented in a workshop or production, they will be busy for days afterwards honing new skills. When books come to life in the form of a literary event, children fully immerse themselves in the story and experience it with all their senses.

Finding out about literary events

Pretty much every week I check in with the social media and email lists of my favourite local independent bookstores, council library, our state library and our magnificent art gallery to see what upcoming events they have planned. Many of these events are free or low cost; the hardest part is finding out about them and booking a spot.

Public libraries

Public libraries are simply the *best* places to visit with young people and they almost always have a fabulous calendar of free events.

Workshops are run by artists, authors, gardeners and performers and they are, without a doubt, some of the best my children and I have ever attended. They are creative, suit all ages and genders, and encourage engagement in the community – wins all round, I say. With the recent focus on makerspaces and robotics in libraries there are also a wide range of activities on these topics. Library workshops generally aim to 'increase engagement with the collection', so whether you have an avid reader or a reluctant reader, these workshops will always see you walking away with armfuls of borrowed books.

Bookstores

Bookstores have become extremely events-driven and this has been a wonderful bonus for those of us who love nothing more than a great literary event. I cannot understand why more parents have not cottoned on to the wonders of a Sunday morning bookshop trip: breakfast, multiple coffees, author workshops or signings, and some retail therapy. Our local bookstore has a dedicated children's bookstore next door and if I had all the time in the world I could book my children into an event most weeks. My friends and I also spend time at bookstore events in the evenings, enjoying a glass of wine, some cheese and a talk by our latest author love. Some bookstores host book clubs for young people, which are invaluable in connecting like-minded little souls.

At around nine years old, Murray and I took Sam and a friend of his to an event at a local bookstore with author/illustrator Remy Lai, based around her book *Pawcasso*. The boys met Remy's dog, participated in a drawing workshop and genuinely enjoyed a few hours spent in the company of other young people, chatting all things reading, writing and illustrating. The boys both got a signed copy of one of her books and as we ate ice cream afterwards, they read their books. I'm always so keen to promote bookstore events to friends and the local community, as they are such an enjoyable experience in which the whole family can be involved. It also provides a balance to other extracurricular pursuits. If you have a local bookstore, support them and their events and share event details with those around you.

State libraries

I am immensely fond of the various state libraries around Australia. We once attended a brilliant community day where Georgia sat entranced as all the instruments in the orchestra were introduced to her and Ava had books read to her by one of the coolest authors around, Anita Heiss. We attended a fabulous 'create a character' workshop with author/illustrator Leigh Hobbs and spent several hours relaxing, reading, storytelling and crafting. And it was all free!

For older children, many of the state libraries run subsidised writing programs or digital media courses. There are so many young people out there who want to write, illustrate and meet the creators of books and these sorts of opportunities are priceless. Sign up to the email list of your state library, their children's and adult programming is worth keeping an eye on.

Meeting authors and illustrators is awesome!

At a Jacqueline Harvey high tea event I once hosted, Jacqueline enthralled the audience with her talk and with her genuine warmth and enthusiasm. She spent several hours signing books and posters for young fans, her smile never once fading. Ava's last words before bed that night were, 'She hugged me, Mummy! Jacqueline Harvey wrote Clementine Rose and she HUGGED me!' Never underestimate the impact a brilliant author visit can have on a child.

Theatre and live performance events

There is nothing better than a book or story transformed into a stage production, ballet, play-based experience, dance class, digital experience or visual art workshop. Literary outings extend the book reading experience, adding another dimension to the story and allowing young readers and young viewers to experience it in a different format. We attend many theatre productions that have a literary bent – they allow you to prepare young children by reading the book or telling the story beforehand, so that they will have a better idea of the narrative structure of the work before they attend.

There are fabulous theatre and ballet companies as well as festivals that are using books as the basis for their productions. We saw *The Peasant Prince*, a play based on the wonderful book of the same name by Li Cunxin and Anne Spudvilas. The adaptation of *The Peasant Prince* absolutely brought this book to life for myself and my children, and I spent much of the performance with goosebumps watching this amazing story leap from the pages onto the stage.

Literature festivals

Literature festivals have long existed and if you are a reader yourself, you have probably enjoyed hanging out at adult literature festivals over the years, absorbing stories and engaging with thoughtful, mediated conversations and intellectual literary, political and cultural debates, as well as adding books to your to-be-read pile.

Many years ago, I spent so long chatting to someone in the Jasper Fforde signing line that we ended up exchanging numbers to continue our conversation, and I now call this person a friend. Literature festivals are excellent places to meet like-minded souls, and celebrate the importance of art and culture in communities. Some literature festivals have a children's and young adult program as part of their offerings, meaning that all ages of readers can attend. I love a major literature festival, but I love a dedicated children's literature festival even more. As an educator and a children's author myself, it can feel that the programming for children's and young adult events is an add-on to the main event – lovely to offer but perhaps not as important as adult literature and conversation. The children's programming for festivals is often the least funded, least recognised and gets the least space in the program. Many children's authors and illustrators feel relegated to the 'kids' table at the wedding' and yet it is the 'kids' table' that we should be paying attention to. Young people are our future readers, our future festival attendees and our future authors and illustrators – and leaders.

I am fortunate that my parents took me along to the Brisbane Writers Festival from a young age and I well remember the excitement of meeting a 'for real life' author. Attending literature festivals was something I took as a given throughout my life and I have rarely missed a year at my local literature festival. I took Murray to his first festival in his mid-forties and I carefully chose sessions on the adult program that I thought a commercial beekeeper with a love of politics, war history and the Australian landscape would enjoy. I was introducing him to something I really valued, and was anxious he somewhat enjoy the experience.

I need not have been concerned. He was like a kid in a lolly shop – excited by all he saw, rushing to purchase books after sessions and asking enthusiastic questions in sessions. The following day he took our three youngest children out of school to attend the children's program; I have long been an advocate for skipping school to attend literature festivals if your school does not take their students. I also advise sending an email to your school about how much your children gained from the experience and encourage future participation.

At the children's program that day, the kids attended a number of sessions, including one by rock star author Nat Amoore, an outstanding presenter who engages young people in reading with her high-octane energy and humour. Nat commented to me later that, over the laughter of the children in her session, she could hear the deep, delighted belly laughter of Murray. After seeing her present, he was just as excited to meet her as the kids were, and her books have become firm favourites in our house.

Children's literature festivals play a role in shaping future generations' perceptions of the power of words and they strengthen a community's relationships with words, ideas and with each other. In urban and regional areas alike, children's literature festivals serve social, arts and educational functions and they can become a cornerstone of the community.

I have been involved in children's literature festivals, as a volunteer, program curator, presenter and as a parent attendee over many years. Most recently I have become involved in Somerset Storyfest, which has been on quite the journey over its thirty-year history.

Somerset Storyfest has grown from a singular annual event hosted at Somerset College on the Gold Coast to a year-round calendar of events, its signature Gold Coast festival and several regional children's literature festivals. The aim of these regional festivals is to expand on Storyfest's mission, 'share stories, build better lives', and to bring a love of storytelling and the benefits of books to as many regional areas as possible. Somerset Storyfest takes a proactive and engaging approach to children's literature and creates events which allow young people to connect with authors, illustrators, creatives and educators who inspire and delight. The festival events bring books and stories to life – something we want all young people to experience and have access to. For more information see www.storyfest.com.au.

BOOK CLUBS

Hosting book clubs will always be my favourite extracurricular activity. Some teachers love nothing better than coaching soccer or blowing a whistle on a netball court, but my skills do not extend to such pursuits. I've pretty much been banned from involvement in school sport following some 'incidents' which are best left unmentioned but which have provided much laughter in the staffroom at my expense. Let's say no more! My book clubs are for *all* young people – I want the keen readers and the reluctant readers alike. I want the proficient readers who churn through books quickly, I want the readers who read differently (audio, dyslexic-friendly font) and the readers who really labour over each word but persist anyway. Often my wording on the flyer or in a newsletter will say:

Are you a reader?
Do you kind of want to be a reader?
Do you like talking?
Hanging out with others?
You should probably join our Book Club.

Book clubs are for the readers and also for the talkers because ideas in books need discussion and robust debate. Book clubs are about the joy of reading for pleasure and encouraging reading as a social activity. They help us to:

- connect with others through a shared love of literature;
- discuss the big ideas and messages in literature;
- personally connect with a story or character.

If your school library doesn't have a book club but you would like your young reader to join one, start one up with friends and their children or find one at your local independent bookshop or public library. A book club can be as informal or formal as you choose. Make the decision based on the needs of your members, but remember that it is all about getting your readers enthusiastic about books – it is not a study group!

Some of the following questions and ideas are great to use as a starting point for guiding discussion. Do keep in mind that these are a guide only and will not suit each book you read. I have these printed out on laminated cards and small groups discuss several questions before reporting back to the whole book club group.

- Does the title 'fit' the book?
- Do the characters seem real and believable? To what extent do they remind you of yourself or someone you know?
- Is the focus on a single character or on several whose lives are intertwined?
- What is the point of view from which the story is told?
- Is the reader expected to identify with the characters or observe them?
- Think about the pacing. Are the characters and plot quickly revealed or slowly unveiled?

- Did any songs spring to mind as you read this book? As a group could you create a playlist to go with your book? Many authors now share a book playlist.
- Is there a linear plot or are there multiple plotlines, flashbacks or alternating chapters related from different points of view?
- Does the story emphasise people or does it highlight situations and events?
- What message do you think the author is trying to convey?
- What are the major themes of the book and do you feel they are relevant today?
- Does this book fit into or fight against a literary genre? How does the author use (science fiction, humour, tragedy, romance) to effect in the novel?
- How is humour (or another applicable emotion) explored in the language, ideas and characters of the book?
- Would this book make a good movie? Why?
- Who would you recommend this book to and why?
- Have you discovered anything about yourself as a reader as you read this book? Perhaps you've always avoided (insert the applicable genre) but found you really enjoyed this novel?

BOOK LAUNCHES

I have been taking my children to book launches from birth and they are often events you can happily take even very young children to – just be guided by the age range of the book as to what age child the launch may be aimed at. Book launches are mostly short events with 30 to 40 minutes' worth of formalities and a book reading before signings and festivities. Many authors will organise activities for young fans to be involved in, and there is often food, at least a celebratory cake, for hungry little people.

One of my favourite book launches remains the launch of Narelle Oliver's *Don't Let a Spoonbill in the Kitchen!* It was an afternoon of true book celebration and a riot of music, art activities, book buying and indulging in wonderful cupcakes that looked like they had leapt from the pages of the book. The then Governor-General of Australia, Quentin Bryce, launched the book and she spoke with immense warmth and sincerity about the power of books in the life of a child and the honour of being able to meet the creators of picture books. Narelle took the audience through the process of creating the rhyming text and the vibrant illustrations with many an anecdote thrown in about problems encountered along the way, all relayed with her self-deprecating drawl and twist of humour. This book launch was an affair to remember and many years later Ava still takes *Don't Let a Spoonbill in the Kitchen!* off the bookshelf. For her this story now has a story behind it and will always hold a special place in her literary heart.

Five reasons to attend children's book launches

1. To meet the authors and illustrators behind the books.
2. To celebrate the birth of another story with cake, clapping and much merriment.
3. For a little glimpse into how a book came to life.
4. For the ritual of a launch – listening to the various speakers, a lovely book reading and the signing and dedicating of books.
5. For the conversations that follow.

CHAPTER NINE

A BALANCED LITERARY DIET – A FEAST OF GENRES

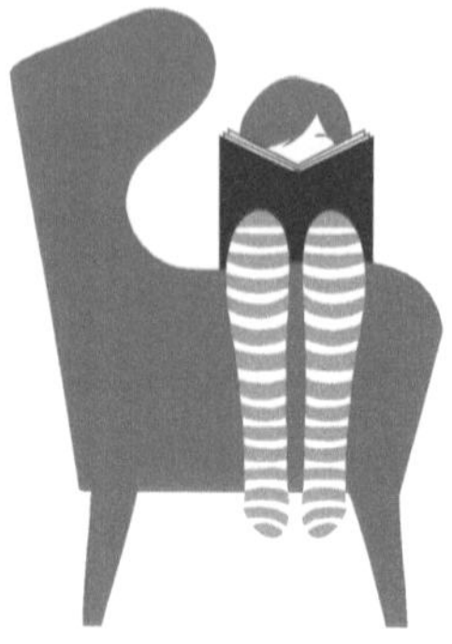

Giving young people choice in what they read is crucial to them developing a love of reading. Teacher librarians and school libraries are all about self-selected reading. I've long been a vocal advocate for 'let them read what they want, when they want', including what I like to refer to as the 'marginalised genres' such as vampire stories, chick lit, horror, toilet humour and romance. However, I confess that, as a parent, I'm sometimes a little concerned by the reading choices my children make.

Ava went through a stage of reading only short, mass-produced books full of toilet humour. But when I say a 'stage', it went on for six months and she would read nothing else and could spot a toilet humour book from the front entrance of a bookstore or library. I'd be lying if I said I wasn't frustrated. I once added a 'worthy' text to her pile of fart books on the counter of our favourite local children's bookstore, mainly to cover said pile of fart books. Afterwards I gave myself a stern talking to about being grateful that my children were choosing to read and that the fart book phase would pass. It did, although she still loves a good poo joke.

The power of reading for pleasure means that, as parents and educators, we need to put aside our own thoughts on what children *should* be reading. Kids enjoy reading the most when they can escape into a book with no expectations, when they don't have to worry about analysing themes or other literary devices a parent or teacher may want them to learn from the book.

To get a better understanding of what your own child or your students enjoy about free-choice reading, it is helpful to ask some of the following questions. Do keep in mind that this will just be a snapshot of their reading at this particular point in time.

- What has been your favourite book recently?
- What do you think is the purpose of reading? Why do you think we need to read?
- If you could read any type of book at all what would you choose to read?
- Have you had times when you have read like a demon? Explain in your own words.
- Have you had times when you've read very little? Explain in your own words.
- What book was your favourite when you were really little?
- Have you ever become obsessed by a particular series? What do you think you liked most about this series?
- How do you choose books to read?
- How do you share what you read with your friends and what do you tell them about it?
- Do you re-read favourite books?

It may seem odd to move from a discussion on self-selected reading to a section on reading widely. However, I believe the two ideas can sit side by side and even play nicely without whacking each other over the head, trying to prove who is more important.

I like to compare a balanced reading diet to a balanced food diet and ask children what might happen if they decided to eat only pineapple for the rest of their life. As much as they may love pineapple, it wouldn't be healthy because we need to eat a range of foods from the various food groups to grow healthy and strong. And so it is with reading. We might *think* we will enjoy living on a diet of adventure novels, but eventually our brain will cry out for something more, something different. Like our body, our brain needs variety in order to grow.

Encouraging young people to read widely and enjoy a balanced reading diet can add immeasurably to their enjoyment of recreational reading. Think about your own reading tastes. Sometimes you may yearn for dark, intense crime and other times you want nothing more than a light, fluffy romance. Being made aware of a genre you didn't even know existed can open reading doorways and lead to all manner of literary adventures.

Below I've outlined a range of book genres and explored the benefits young readers may gain by engaging with them. For each genre I've included a list of recommended books suitable for the eight- to fourteen-year-old age group. These lists are by no means prescriptive and are merely springboards for you to find your own favourites. Please check the appropriateness of a book for each individual reader.

HUMOUR

Too often adults dismiss humorous books as not as worthy as 'highbrow' literary choices. Engaging young people, particularly reluctant readers, with books they adore is how we create readers. Writers like Andy Griffiths, Terry Denton, Kate and Jol Temple, Tim Harris, Adrian Beck, R. A. Spratt and Matt Stanton have all used their wit and sense of humour to entertain, heal, educate and instil a love of reading in young people.

Why encourage the reading of humour?

- Humour engages children as they are naturally playful and generally laugh far more than adults. Humorous literature harnesses the exuberance and wonder of youth with words and ideas.
- Young people interact and foster friendships through humorous literature, sharing the laughs with their peers.
- Humorous books reflect reality, which is a mixture of sad and funny, joy and pain, highs and lows.
- Far from being an 'easy option', humorous literature encourages critical reading as young people learn to read between the lines and develop an awareness of subtlety and sarcasm, right and wrong.

Humorous Book Recommendations

Brock the Croc series by Adrian Beck, illustrated by Dean Rankine (Larrikin House)

Dog Man series by Dav Pilkey (Scholastic)

Fluff series by Matt Stanton (HarperCollins)

Frog Squad series by Kate and Jol Temple, illustrated by Shiloh Gordon (HarperCollins)

Funny Kid series by Matt Stanton (HarperCollins)

Hello Twigs series by Andrew McDonald, illustrated by Ben Wood (Hardie Grant)

Nanny Piggins series by R. A. Spratt (Random House)

Ratbags series by Tim Harris, illustrated by Shiloh Gordon (Puffin)

Samurai vs Ninja series by Nick Falk, illustrated by Tony Flowers (Random House)

Sharkman and Blowfish: World Domination by David Woodland (Berbay Publishing, 2024)

Shower Land series by Nat Amoore, illustrated by James Hart (Puffin)

MYSTERY

I was never into mystery stories as a child and it wasn't until my mid-twenties when my mother introduced me to Agatha Christie's most popular sleuth, Hercule Poirot, and Donna Leon's Commissario Guido Brunetti that I became an avid reader of mystery. There is something mildly addictive about figuring out what will happen next and putting all the pieces of a puzzle together. For many young readers, mysteries contain the excitement of a life far removed from their own suburban existence. Young protagonists who lead investigations, collect and study the evidence, and solve mysteries are inspiring to the would-be detectives of tomorrow or simply those who have a curious mind and sense of adventure.

Not only are they fun and usually fast-paced page turners, but mystery novels help young readers to read critically, consider cause and effect, logical deduction, and how vital information and facts may be collected.

I've asked bestselling author R. A. Spratt to share the elements she includes in her Friday Barnes, Nanny Piggins and Peski Kids series to create stories with tension and intrigue.

R. A. Spratt

I don't know how I create tension and intrigue to hook young readers in. I really have no idea what I'm doing and I haven't done for twenty years now. I believe that storytelling is a magical art and you can't explain magic.

I'm not speaking figuratively. I literally mean magical. My ideas start out as nothing more than electrical energy passing between the neurons in my brain. This electricity conjures up images, voices and motivations in my mind which I blend together in a web of ideas. I take the twenty-six squiggles that are the letters in the Roman alphabet and transcribe them into a computer. This is printed up and sold to thousands of children and libraries. Then the squiggles are decoded into the mind of the reader. Between my neurons and their neurons an entire world is created full of characters we care for much more than we do the living breathing characters we live alongside in real life. A reader's heart will race, they'll laugh, they'll shed a tear as they go on a journey with my characters. To me this is pure magic, or at the very least a miracle of neuroscience and biochemistry.

As to intrigue and tension – I'll start with intrigue. I once heard a radio interview with an acclaimed novelist (I can't remember who) and she said that from reading Dickens she had learnt that the trick to storytelling was figuring out the story you wanted to tell and then telling it very slowly (I think she said this in a much cleverer way, but I heard this interview decades ago so I can't remember her exact words).

I always think of storytelling as laying a trail of breadcrumbs to lead someone along a path. Which is actually a terrible misuse of an analogy because Hansel and Gretel laid breadcrumbs to lead themselves back, not to lead someone else forward ... in any case, storytelling is entirely linear. The line can go in circles and double back, but you write out the ideas one sentence after another, always moving forward (except if you write pick-a-path books, which might explain why those books are emotionally unsatisfying). To make a story intriguing, the trick is to not lay down an entire loaf of bread at the beginning of the path. If you put down a whole loaf the birds eat the bread until they are full and then they fly away. You've got to lay out one crumb at a time if you want the bird to follow you.

To write a mystery novel you, as the author, know the whole plot in your head but you've got to deal this information out one piece at a time. To keep the story moving forward, every sentence you write should progress the plot or develop character or both. But in mystery, it is good to deal out misinformation as well. It makes the characters more interesting and it gives the reader more to think about.

Tension comes from the readers caring about the characters or the resolution of the plot. They usually care more about the characters so if you can make the problem of the plot intertwine with the problems of your characters, you double-down on tension.

Mystery Recommendations

Azaria: A True History by Maree Coote (Melbournestyle, 2020)

Danger Road by A.L. Tait (Scholastic, 2025)

Detective Beans and the Case of the Missing Hat by Li Chen (Penguin, 2024)

Eleanor Jones Can't Keep A Secret by Amy Doak (Penguin, 2024) (teen readers)

Enola Holmes: The Graphic Novels series by Serena Blasco, illustrated by Tanya Gold (Andrews McMeel Publishing)

Fozia and the Quest of Prince Zal by Rosanne Hawke (UQP, 2021)

Friday Barnes series by R. A. Spratt (Puffin)

Paradise Sands: A Story of Enchantment by Levi Pinfold (Walker Books, 2022)

PD McPem's Agency for Mysterious Mysteries series by Anna Battese, illustrated by Ruth-Mary Smith (Riveted Press)

Scar Town by Tristan Bancks (Puffin, 2023)

Sherlock Bones series by Renée Treml (Allen & Unwin)

Stella Montgomery series by Judith Rossell (HarperCollins)

The Underdogs series by Kate and Jol Temple, illustrated by Shiloh Gordon (Hardie Grant)

The Wolves of Greycoat Hall series by Lucinda Gifford (Walker Books)

Urban Legend Hunters series by Joel McKerrow, illustrated by Wayne Bryant (Larrikin House)

HISTORICAL FICTION

A good historical novel leads the reader through adventures of the past, bringing real historical events to life. I personally have learnt more about Australian history through reading Jackie French's and Pamela Rushby's novels, than I did in all my years of history lessons at school. Learning about the past helps us to understand the world today and perhaps even prepare for the future by recognising mistakes which must not be repeated. Historical fiction personalises accounts of past atrocities, which helps us to develop greater empathy than if we were to read a strictly factual account of the same historical event.

Historical fiction books are set in vastly different eras, from ancient Egypt and medieval Italy to colonial Australia, so young readers may need help understanding the specific context. They should also be encouraged to read a few chapters before deciding to abandon a book. It can take longer than usual for a reader to find their groove in a historical fiction book, but the effort required is worth it when you see your child fall through the cracks of history and into a fabulous tale.

Historical Fiction Recommendations

All the Beautiful Things by Katrina Nannestad (HarperCollins, 2024)
Courage Be My Friend: The Vivian Bullwinkel Story by Jenny Davis (Fremantle Press, 2024)
Elsewhere Girls by Emily Gale and Nova Weetman (Text Publishing, 2021)
History Hunter series by Mark Greenwood (Fremantle Press)
Hitler's Daughter by Jackie French (HarperCollins, 1999)
Interned by Pamela Rushby (Walker Books, 2022)
Outlaw Girls by Emily Gale and Nova Weetman (Text Publishing, 2024)
Ruby Road series by Charlotte Barkla (Walker Books)
Silver Linings by Katrina Nannestad (HarperCollins, 2023)
The Blue Cat by Ursula Dubosarsky (Allen & Unwin, 2017)

The Girls Who Changed the World series by Jackie French (HarperCollins)
The Great Gallipoli Escape by Jackie French (HarperCollins, 2024)
The Mud Puddlers by Pamela Rushby (Walker Books, 2023)
The Ratcatcher's Daughter by Pamela Rushby (HarperCollins, 2014)
The River Charm by Belinda Murrell (Random House, 2013)
The War that Saved My Life by Kimberly Brubaker Bradley (Text Publishing, 2016)
The Year the Maps Changed by Danielle Binks (Hachette, 2020)
Tulips for Breakfast by Catherine Bauer (Ford Street Publishing, 2022)

REALISTIC FICTION

Contemporary realistic fiction are stories that are believable and set in the modern world. These works of fiction explore plausible conflicts and contain characters who seem real and identifiable. What puts the 'real' in realistic fiction are the themes – they touch on all that is wonderful and confronting about being a human today. Common contemporary themes explore family situations, peer relationships, growth and maturity, and cultural differences.

These stories have so much to offer. They help children address their own physical, social and emotional changes, and provide role models who are facing tough situations. They can also help children discover that their problems and desires are not unique – that they are not alone in experiencing certain feelings and situations.

On the other hand, realistic fiction may also provide a gateway for kids to experience someone else's 'real' life – the life of another young person, perhaps on the other side of the world. They can see that societies are not all the same and that different communities hold diverse values and customs. In effect, realistic fiction can help children to develop an awareness of how there are many different perspectives in this world whilst, at the same time, fostering an appreciation for all that we have in common.

Belinda Murrell is the author of many award-winning novels for children and teens and writes across a large range of genres from fantasy to historical fiction and realistic fiction. Her series Pippa's Island is a fine example of realistic fiction writing and she has shared her thoughts on the genre here.

Belinda Murrell

I grew up in a book-mad family and as well as devouring piles of books every week I adored writing my own stories. When I had my children, I began writing stories for them, very much inspired by what my kids loved to read. And although my first stories – both as a child and as an author – were full of magic and adventure, such as The Sun Sword Trilogy and historical time-slip novels and mysteries, my most recent stories have been about friends, families and animal adventures.

My aim with Pippa's Island was to write sparkling books set in a realistic world about a fun-loving girl and her friends. I wanted to celebrate the joyful, inspiring, funny, kind, creative, caring, sassy girls I know.

On one level the stories are about everyday life at school, hanging out on weekends, embarrassing yourself in dance class, dealing with stage fright at the school talent quest or going away on your first school camp. The series also deals with issues such as making friends, the importance of community, finding courage, standing up for what's right and coping with change.

One of my key aims was to create quirky characters who were inspiring role models for readers. The main characters are realistic in their emotions – sometimes cranky, jealous, prickly or anxious, but also kind, brave and compassionate. The girls all have their own aspirations – whether it is to become a vet, an artist or an engineer, to save wildlife or travel the world. Likewise, the older women in their lives have interesting careers such as a stockbroker, fashion designer, musician, marine biologist and graphic designer.

Stories about real life are like a mirror, helping children to understand how to navigate human relationships and solve everyday problems of friendship, families, sibling rivalry, school, sport and emotions.

On the other hand, realistic books can also provide a window into the lives of others, giving children the opportunity to walk around in someone else's shoes. To understand how different people might think and feel. For this reason, I ensure my books portray diverse and imperfect families, and characters from different social and cultural backgrounds.

Research has shown that reading fiction helps children to build emotional intelligence and to develop empathy for other people by exploring others' thoughts, perspectives and experiences. As well as building compassion for others, reading realistic books helps them to realise that their own personal problems and fears are not unique. They are not alone in the world.

Realistic fiction helps young readers realise that life is a constant rollercoaster of ups and downs, and not always easy. But while there are disappointments and difficulties along the way, there is always joy and hope, a theme celebrated in all my books.

Realistic Fiction Recommendations

Are You There, Buddha? by Pip Harry (Hachette, 2021)

Cora Seen and Heard by Zanni Louise (Walker Books, 2024)

Everything I've Never Said by Samantha Wheeler (UQP, 2018)

Freddie Spector, Fact Collector series by Ashleigh Barton, illustrated by Peter Cheong (Hachette)

Howzat Pat! series by Pat Cummins and Dave Hartley, illustrated by Serena Geddes (HarperCollins)

Indigo in the Storm by Kate Gordon (Riveted Press, 2023)

Juno Jones series by Kate Gordon, illustrated by Sandy Flett (Riveted Press)

Kelpie Chaos by Deb Fitzpatrick (Fremantle Press, 2024)

Leo and Ralph by Peter Carnavas (UQP, 2024)

My Brother Ben by Peter Carnavas (UQP, 2021)

Paws by Kate Foster (Walker Books, 2021)

Queenie in Seven Moves by Zanni Louise (Walker Books, 2023)
The Bravest Word by Kate Foster (Walker Books, 2022)
The First Summer of Callie McGee by A. L. Tait (Scholastic, 2023)
The Right Way to Rock by Nat Amoore (Puffin, 2021)
The Secrets We Keep by Nova Weetman (UQP, 2016)
Through My Eyes series by various authors (Allen & Unwin)
Ultra Violet: Down to Business by Cristy Burne, illustrated by Rebel Challenger (Larrikin House, 2024)
Willa and Woof series by Jacqueline Harvey (Puffin)

FANTASY

It's impossible to overstate the powerful and positive effect Nevermoor had on children's publishing, particularly the fantasy genre. Its popularity allowed other authors to venture down their own magical paths and create worthy young heroes who battle evil, usually with the support of a mentor and a collection of friends. The beauty of fantasy lies with its capacity for variation and unexpected wonder.Some authors incorporate magical elements into our ordinary existence, others place their characters (and their readers) into a fantastical realm.

Just as adults like to escape from the monotony of real life, children also need to indulge in escapism. Fantasy can be that space, whether it's imagining being friends with a witch, hunting down demon robot dogs, or protecting innocent unicorns. Reading fantasy and imagining the worlds within helps fire up creative processes. It can also enhance critical thinking skills, particularly in books where the depicted political and socioeconomic systems are complex and mirror our own. Young people can advance their knowledge of government and explore social issues. So fantasy is not just about escaping the real world, but also gaining a more sophisticated understanding of it and hopefully becoming mature and thoughtful citizens of the world.

Fantasy Recommendations

18,000 Holes in the Universe series by Adam Wallace and Lisa Foley, illustrated by James Hart (HarperCollins)

A Glasshouse of Stars by Shirley Marr (Puffin, 2021)

Bravepaw series by L. M. Wilkinson, illustrated by Lavanya Naidu (Allen & Unwin)

Chronicles of Whetherwhy series by Anna James, illustrated by David Wyatt (HarperCollins, 2024)

Deltora Quest series by Emily Rodda (Scholastic)

Dragonkeeper series by Carole Wilkinson (Black Dog Books)

Impossible Creatures by Katherine Rundell (Bloomsbury, 2023)

Isaac Turner Investigates series by Sam Sedgman (Bloomsbury)

Kingdoms and Empires series by Jaclyn Moriarty, illustrated by Kelly Canby (Allen & Unwin)

Losing the Plot by Annaleise Byrd (Walker Books, 2024)

Ophelia and the Marvellous Boy by Karen Foxlee (Yearling Books, 2014)

Ranger's Apprentice series by John Flanagan (Random House)

Rowan of Rin series by Emily Rodda (Scholastic)

Seven Wherewithal Way series by Samantha-Ellen Bound (Affirm Press)

Starfell series by Dominique Valente, illustrated by Sarah Warburton (HarperCollins)

Talismans of Fate series by Melanie La'Brooy (UQP)

The Ateban Cipher series by A. L. Tait (Hachette)

The Garden of Empress Cassia by Gabrielle Wang (Puffin, 2002)

The Grandest Bookshop in the World series by Amelia Mellor (Affirm Press)

The Mapmaker Chronicles series by A. L. Tait (Hachette)

The Secret of the Stone by Kathryn Lefroy (Fremantle Press, 2024)

The 113th Assistant Librarian by Stuart Wilson (Penguin, 2024)

Wednesday Weeks series by Denis Knight and Cristy Burne (Hachette)

SCIENCE FICTION

Science fiction (sci-fi) has traditionally been associated with futuristic space novels where alien life and other planets featured heavily. Technology has also been a major component of this genre. But sci-fi actually incorporates many different sub-categories and, over the past two decades, authors have been mashing these up to create new and original genres. For example, writers have merged history with technology to create steampunk or placed apocalypse survivors into dictatorial environments to make dystopian sci-fi. The prevalence of innovation within the genre means it remains highly sought-after for young readers. Science fiction can be defined by its setting and technological content, but within these boundaries there is so much scope to explore – an artificially intelligent detective turns sci-fi into a crime thriller, a boy from one planet falling in love with a girl from an opposing species produces a *Romeo and Juliet* equivalent, and an intergalactic broadcast of celebrities fighting on a reality TV program makes a biting satire on fame. And for younger readers, authors can still promote messages of kindness, friendship and acceptance through a speculative lens. Humorous alien-life stories are very popular, but even when they are less so, there will always be the curious reader who gazes out beyond the air pollution to imagine what's up there among the stars.

Science Fiction Recommendations

Aquatica by Lance Balchin (Hardie Grant, 2018)

Blossom by Tamsin Janu (Scholastic, 2017)

E-Boy series by Anh Do, illustrated by Chris Wahl (Allen & Unwin)

Grimsdon by Deborah Abela (Puffin, 2019)

In the Dark Spaces by Cally Black (Hardie Grant, 2017) (teen readers)

Mechanica by Lance Balchin (Five Mile Press, 2016)

The Callers series by Kiah Thomas (HarperCollins)

The City of Ember series by Jeanne DuPrau (Yearling Books)

The Red Wind by Isobelle Carmody (Puffin, 2011)

The Unexplainable Disappearance of Mars Patel by Sheela Chari (Walker Books, 2020)

The Wild Robot series by Peter Brown (Allen & Unwin)

When You Reach Me by Rebecca Stead (Yearling Books, 2010)

DYSTOPIAN FICTION

Dystopian novels have existed as long as writers have questioned political systems and the extent to which they control our lives. Just as Jules Verne, H. G. Wells and Jonathan Swift challenged readers of their time with their ideologies, so too did George Orwell and Aldous Huxley, Lois Lowry and Margaret Atwood. But it was really Suzanne Collins's Hunger Games series that made the genre once again on trend in children's and YA literature.

The opposite of utopia, dystopia is the idea that society is controlled by beings in power and people are devoid of free will. It is an idea that fascinates us all, even young people, and perhaps especially today when our world seems to be more divided than ever. Placing protagonists into an uncertain future is another way for readers to ponder the calamities of their own time. Allowing young people to ask serious questions about how they want the world to develop encourages problem-solving, a strong desire for compassion and critical thinking skills.

These books are long lasting and remain relevant over time. Orwell's doublespeak seems to be around us everywhere and unless we open a dialogue with our children about some of the troubling things happening, we are perhaps doomed to repeat the mistakes of the past.

A sub-genre within the dystopian category is the post-apocalyptic novel, which sees the breakdown of society. Instead of a controlling regime, ordered and secretive, we have total chaos and devastation. Sometimes it's due to natural weather events, a deadly pandemic virus or overloaded computer systems causing technological annihilation. In these novels children are exposed to survival efforts that can be vicious and scary, or collaborative and positive, as communities band together to benefit all. Often the latter are presented as adventure stories with the emphasis less on social commentary and more on the action, so they are gripping and engaging.

Dystopian Fiction Recommendations

After the Lights Go Out by Lili Wilkinson (Allen & Unwin, 2018) (teen readers)
A Single Stone by Meg McKinlay (Walker Books, 2015)
Divergent series by Veronica Roth (HarperCollins) (teen readers)
Hive by A. J. Betts (Pan Macmillan, 2018) (teen readers)
How to Bee by Bren MacDibble (Allen & Unwin, 2017)
The Apprentice Witnesser by Bren MacDibble (Allen & Unwin, 2024)
The Giver by Lois Lowry (Houghton Mifflin, 1993) (teen readers)
The Inheritance by Armin Greder (Allen & Unwin, 2021)
The Maze Runner series by James Dashner (Delacorte Press)
The Sky So Heavy by Claire Zorn (UQP, 2013) (teen readers)
The Tribe series by Ambelin Kwaymullina (Walker Books) (teen readers)
The Winter Trilogy by Mark Smith (Text Publishing) (teen readers)
Uglies series by Scott Westerfeld (Simon & Schuster) (teen readers)

MYTHS, LEGENDS AND FAIRYTALES

Though separate genres, in a sense, myths, legends and fairytales fall under the umbrella term of 'traditional tales'. They come in and out of favour and well-meaning censors can be critical of messages sent to, say, young girls who may feel they need saving by a Prince Charming. But I think they offer us an escape from reality and a framework to consider our place in the world. Sophie Masson is a multiple award-winning French–Australian author of over fifty books, many of which are based on myths, legends and fairytales. There is simply no other person more qualified to comment on traditional tales and, as she said to me recently, 'they are absolutely essential for the development of children's reading, ideas and imagination'.

Sophie Masson

As a child I adored the myths of Greek and Celtic heroes, Norse gods, Chinese star-crossed lovers; the legends of King Arthur and Robin Hood; the fairytales of Perrault, Grimm and Hans Christian Andersen. I returned again and again to my favourites and was drawn to novels that used elements from these stories, such as Nicholas Stuart Gray's superb *The Stone Cage*, which is a glorious riff on the fairytale of 'Rapunzel'. (Why it is out of print beats me, especially as it has been cited as a huge influence by many well-known fantasy writers, including Neil Gaiman.) Without even being aware of it, through all this reading I was absorbing all kinds of things that would stand me in good stead later as a writer. Myths, legends and fairytales are different genres yet they form part of a great human inheritance that is very often anonymous, at least in its sources, and yet distinctly individual. They offer questions and potential, not answers and certainties – despite the censors' claims, they are not prescriptive, even though they can certainly seem arbitrary. And for a writer they offer multiple creative interpretations and possibilities: for instance, going back to 'Cinderella', I never saw it as girl-saved-by-Prince-Charming (who in fact, in the fairytale, is a cipher, and the really important characters are all female, both the good and the bad). Instead, for me it is a story of a neglected, abused child, who, through the kindness of a stranger, is finally given an opportunity to escape into a different, happier life. That is certainly how I interpreted it in my novel *Moonlight and Ashes*.

Introducing these stories to children is easy; there are multiple retellings of the great myths, legends and fairytales around, aimed at different ages and reading levels, from lavishly illustrated picture books to graphic novels to compilations such as Roger Lancelyn Green's classic *Tales of the Greek Heroes*. Countless well-known contemporary authors have tackled retellings, including Ursula Dubosarsky (*Two Tales of Twins from Ancient Greece and Rome*), John Heffernan (*Two Tales of Brothers from Ancient Mesopotamia*) and Anthony Horowitz (*The Kingfisher Book of Myths and Legends*). These tales, drawn from around the world, with their adventures, magic and fantastical creatures, are also really well-suited to lively storytelling sessions. Later, young readers can be introduced to fantastic novels that use these traditional tales as inspiration: for instance, Rick Riordan's Percy Jackson and the Olympians series, *Ella Enchanted* by Gail Carson Levine, *I Was a Rat!* by Philip Pullman, T. H. White's *The Once and Future King*, Lloyd Alexander's The Chronicles of Prydain and many others too numerous to mention. Young adult readers are also well served with lots of great novels based on myth, legend and fairytale. And you can keep reading in these genres well into adulthood – in fact, all of your life. They will never get stale – their very magic and wonder have kept them alive for thousands of years and I think they are every child's inheritance.

Myth, Legend and Fairytale Recommendations

A First Book of Myths: Uncover Tales of Gods and Monsters by Mary Hoffman (Dorling Kindersley, 2024)

Atua: Māori Gods and Heroes by Gavin Bishop (Puffin, 2021)

Norse Myths: Tales of Odin, Thor and Loki by Kevin Crossley-Holland, illustrated by Jeffrey Alan Love (Walker Studio, 2024)

The Great Deeds of Superheroes by Maurice Saxby, illustrated by Robert Ingpen (Millennium Books, 1989)

Two Selkie Stories from Scotland retold by Kate Forsyth, illustrated by Fiona McDonald (Christmas Press, 2014)

Two Tales of Twins from Ancient Greece and Rome retold by Ursula Dubosarsky, illustrated by David Allan (Christmas Press, 2014)

Two Tengu Tales from Japan retold by Duncan Ball, illustrated by David Allan (Christmas Press, 2015)

Two Trickster Tales from Russia retold by Sophie Masson, illustrated by David Allan (Christmas Press, 2013)

THE CLASSICS

The debate about whether or not the 'classics' are still relevant for young readers is one that pops up repeatedly. It is a debate that often emerges in response to the changing state and national school curriculums, but also because so much quality and 'edgy' contemporary literature is available now. It is a constant challenge to find a balance between material that young people will immediately engage with and respond to, and introducing them to something that might taste a bit strange at first but will ultimately be quite satisfying. Seeing readers 'get' Shakespeare or Austen or Orwell is a magical moment.

The 'classics' are great stories. They are classics because they are the milestones of literary tradition, originally breaking away from established ideas or challenging the status quo of the time. They are classics because they are still the best at what they 'do' and are part of a literary history that influences the work of contemporary writers. Having some knowledge or understanding of the classics makes the references in contemporary fiction have a deeper meaning and engagement.

At least once in a student's secondary schooling they will be asked to read a modern classic – maybe *Lord of the Flies* (William Golding), *To Kill a Mockingbird* (Harper Lee) or *The Outsiders* (S. E. Hinton). Usually these books contain a different style of writing, an increasingly disappearing vocabulary and a perspective that may be verging on political incorrectness. Exposing children to some of these texts outside the classroom means they will have some knowledge when they are confronted with them on school reading lists.

Reading modern classics is a satisfying way to access history. Take *The Catcher in the Rye* (J. D. Salinger) as an example. It has captured the first glimpse of the concept of the adolescent. Before the creation of the character Holden Caulfield, we were children and then we were adults. The teenage years in a person's life were pretty much ignored. This novel also coincided with the beginnings of an economic boom, the start of popular culture, increased leisure time, greater equality for women and the birth of rock 'n' roll. To bring these days alive so vividly to young people and ask them to reflect on what has changed and what hasn't is a sure way to engage them in their own history and culture. Australian modern classics from *Picnic at Hanging Rock* (Joan Lindsay) to *The Fringe Dwellers* (Nene Gare) depict our past, unique landscape and cultural identity and capture how important it is to tell our own stories.

Recommended Classics

45+47 Stella Street and Everything That Happened by Elizabeth Honey (Allen & Unwin, 1995)

Bamboozled (30th Anniversary Edition) by David Legge (Scholastic, 2024)

Hating Alison Ashley by Robin Klein (Puffin, 1984)

Little Brother by Allan Baillie (Puffin, 2004)

Looking for Alibrandi by Melina Marchetta (Puffin, 1992)

Magic Beach (35th Anniversary Edition) by Alison Lester (Allen & Unwin, 2025)

Midnite by Randolph Stow (Puffin, 2004)

My Sister Sif by Ruth Park (Puffin, 1997)

Playing Beatie Bow by Ruth Park (Puffin, 1982)

Storm Boy by Colin Thiele (Rigby, 1963)

Swashbuckler by James Moloney (UQP, 1995)
The Best-Kept Secret by Emily Rodda (HarperCollins, 2017)
The Listmaker by Robin Klein (Puffin, 2016)
The Nargun and the Stars by Patricia Wrightson (UQP, 2008)
Thunderwith by Libby Hathorn (Hachette, 1999)

NON-FICTION

There are children who love nothing more than reading every non-fiction book in the library. These children crack me up with their encyclopaedic knowledge of sharks, deserts, the body or whatever their current obsession is, and I really enjoy having a natter to them.

Modern non-fiction books rely heavily on good design with eye-catching graphics and varied typography and layout, which are intended to make complex concepts more easily accessible and interesting. These design features encourage non-linear reading and mimic the interactive nature of browsing online. Readers can dip in and out of non-fiction books, making them perfect for reading in small chunks. They also don't require a sustained level of attention, so wriggly or reluctant readers are often kept engaged.

Non-fiction books expand our knowledge in a diverse range of subjects and help build up a solid foundation of general knowledge in younger readers. In the various areas of interest and study, not only is knowledge expanded but vocabulary is too. We read non-fiction to learn how to navigate information effectively – in both print and digital form. The best non-fiction books contain a contents page, index and glossary, to help children find areas of interest quickly and to develop an understanding of how information is organised in headings or subject areas. Non-fiction books also expose children to a variety of text types and visual aids like diagrams, graphs, captions, lists, headings, subheadings and labels.

Non-fiction Recommendations

Alight: A Story of Fire and Nature by Sam Lloyd, illustrated by Samantha Metcalfe (CSIRO Publishing, 2023)

Always Was, Always Will Be by Aunty Fay Muir, illustrated by Sue Lawson (Magabala Books, 2024)

Australia: Country of Colour by Jess Racklyeft (Affirm Press, 2023)

Bonkers About Beetles by Owen Davey (Flying Eye Books, 2018)

Country Town by Isolde Martyn and Robyn Ridgeway, illustrated by Louise Hogan (Ford Street Publishing, 2023)

Democracy! by Philip Bunting (Hardie Grant, 2023)

Fabulous Frogs by Katrina Germein, illustrated by Suzanne Houghton (CSIRO Publishing, 2024)

Fauna: Australia's Most Curious Creatures by Tania McCartney (National Library of Australia, 2019)

Flora: Australia's Most Curious Plants by Tania McCartney (National Library of Australia, 2024)

Phasmid: Saving the Lord Howe Island Stick Insect by Rohan Cleave, illustrated by Coral Tulloch (CSIRO Publishing, 2015)

Songlines: First Knowledges for Younger Readers by Margo Neale and Lynne Kelly, illustrated by Blak Douglas (Thames & Hudson, 2023)

Tamarra: A Story of Termites on Gurindji Country by Violet Wadrill (Hardie Grant, 2023)

Taronga Big Book of Animals by the Taronga Conservation Society Australia (Penguin, 2024)

The Illustrated Encyclopaedia of Peculiar Pairs in Nature by Sami Bayly (Hachette, 2021)

The Trees: Learning Tree Knowledge with Uncle Kuu by Victor Steffensen, illustrated by Sandra Steffensen (Hardie Grant, 2023)

This Book Thinks Ya Deadly! by Corey Tutt, illustrated by Molly Hunt (Hardie Grant, 2023)

This Is Not a Sad Book (But It's OK to Feel Sad) by Elizabeth Vercoe with Kerry Abromowski, illustrated by Grace Fraraccio (Affirm Press, 2024)

Universal Guide to the Night Sky by Lisa Harvey-Smith, illustrated by Sophie Beer (Thames & Hudson, 2023)

Wonderful Wasps by Katrina Germein, illustrated by Suzanne Houghton (CSIRO Publishing, 2022)

You Can Do Hard Things by Jess Sanders, illustrated by Martina Stuhlberger (Affirm Press, 2024)

NARRATIVE NON-FICTION

Narrative non-fiction is a genre that blends the factual, informative nature of non-fiction with the storytelling techniques of fiction. In the realm of children's literature, narrative non-fiction has become an increasingly popular genre in school and home libraries. Narrative non-fiction presents factual information about real events, people or places, but embeds it within a narrative plot structure. An example might by the telling of a story about a historical figure, a scientific discovery, an environmental issue or cultural phenomenon, which also incorporates the elements that make traditional fiction so appealing: character development, setting, conflict and resolution.

Narrative non-fiction is distinguished from pure non-fiction by its approach. While traditional non-fiction might focus on presenting facts and figures in a straightforward manner, narrative non-fiction seeks to weave these facts into a compelling story. It often includes dialogue, descriptive settings and action that propel the narrative forward. Additionally, it may offer a perspective or emotional angle, making the facts more relatable.

Narrative non-fiction is particularly well-suited for children because it taps into their natural curiosity and love for stories and it can make complex subjects more accessible. Topics such as space exploration, social justice movements or the history of ancient civilisations can feel distant and hard to grasp; when presented as a story, however, these topics become personal and relatable. This human connection allows young readers to grasp the significance of these topics in a way that a traditional textbook might not.

My own narrative non-fiction text, *The Beehive* (illustrated by Max Hamilton) wove my love of native Australian bees in school settings with information about how to create habitats for native bees and the importance of pollinators in our environment. The story is told through the eyes of Willow, a young student who is excitedly waiting to receive a hive split from her school's native bee hives. Each page contains non-fiction information, which is related to, but separated from, the narrative. The story can be read with or without reading the non-fiction information.

Narrative Non-fiction Recommendations

Albert Namatjira by Vincent Namatjira (Magabala Books, 2021)

Great White Shark by Claire Saxby, illustrated by Cindy Lane (Walker Books, 2021)

Iceberg by Claire Saxby, illustrated by Jess Racklyeft (Allen & Unwin, 2021)

Little Lon by Andrew Kelly, illustrated by Heather Potter and Mark Jackson (Wild Dog Books, 2020)

Mamie by Tania McCartney (HarperCollins, 2019)

Meet ... Sidney Nolan by Yvonne Mes, illustrated by Sandra Eterović (Penguin Random House, 2015)

Night Watch by Jodi Toering, illustrated by Tannya Harricks (Walker Books, 2024)

Peregrines in the City by Andrew Kelly and Sue Lawson, illustrated by Dean A. Jones (Wild Dog Books, 2022)

Platypus by Sue Whiting, illustrated by Mark Jackson (Walker Books, 2015)

Seed to Sky: Life in the Daintree by Pamela Freeman, illustrated by Liz Anelli (Walker Books, 2024)

The Beehive by Megan Daley, illustrated by Max Hamilton (Walker Books, 2024)

The Echidna Near My Place by Sue Whiting, illustrated by Cate James (Walker Books, 2022)

The Opal Dinosaur by Yvonne Mes, illustrated by Sylvia Morris (CSIRO Publishing, 2024)

To See Clearly: A Portrait of David Hockney by Evan Turk (Abrams Books, 2023)

BIOGRAPHIES AND AUTOBIOGRAPHIES

For young readers who choose to read non-fiction almost exclusively, biographies and autobiographies can be a soft introduction to the power of story while still sticking with facts. Reading biographical works introduces young readers to iconic personalities. Many biographical works are available in 'younger reader' formats, and compendiums of famous or inspiring individuals are really popular too.

It is fascinating to take a look at someone's life and gain a better understanding of the ideas and motivations that helped them to succeed or overcome adversity. The stories can be truly awe-inspiring, and I am a big fan of using books to help young people to see life through a different lens.

History often comes alive for children when they read personal accounts and real-life stories. Biographical works are a great way for children to see the chronology and significance of historical events, including how the past impacts the present.

Biography and Autobiography Recommendations

Born to Run: My Story by Cathy Freeman (Puffin, 2007)

Boy: Tales of Childhood by Roald Dahl (Penguin, 2012)

Chinese Cinderella by Adeline Yen Mah (Penguin, 1999)

Enchanted Air: Two Cultures, Two Wings by Margarita Engle (Atheneum, 2015)

Father of the Lost Boys (younger reader edition) by Yuot A. Alaak (Fremantle Press, 2024)

Finding Nevo: How I Confused Everyone by Nevo Zisin (Black Dog Books, 2017) (teen readers)

Jandamarra by Mark Greenwood, illustrated by Terry Denton (Allen & Unwin, 2013)

Last Man Out by Louise Park (Wild Dog Books, 2023)

On Two Feet and Wings by Abbas Kazerooni (Allen & Unwin, 2012)

Say Hello by Carly Findlay (HarperCollins, 2019) (teen readers)

Ugly (younger reader edition) by Robert Hoge (Hachette, 2015)

Unmasked (YA edition) by Turia Pitt and Bryce Corbett (Random House, 2018)

PLAYS AND FILM SCRIPTS

We all know *the* rule. The rule of all rules. You should never, *ever* see a movie before you have read the book. It is a rule many of us live and die by. Yet for some strange reason we all seem to think that you shouldn't *read* a play or film script; you should go see the play or film. Just as you would miss out by not reading that book before heading to the cinema, there is a lot to be lost by not considering plays and scripts as a form of literature.

The white space between the dialogue and stage directions is simply filled with potential. Readers are invited to work hard to imagine what these moments might look and sound like. Scripts inspire us to use our mind's eye and visualise the characters' world as if it were appearing before us, almost hologram-like. We are not given lengthy descriptions and internal monologues with which to make sense of what is happening, but, instead, must use inference and deduction – two incredibly important skills required to be a strong reader.

Plays, given that they are essentially transcriptions of speech, often focus on the dynamics and relationships between characters –

the drama, conflict, actions, reactions and resolutions. There is rarely a narrator and limited authorial intrusion so readers can get up close and personal and really see how meaning is made without lengthy exposition. They can become intimate with the text by observing what the characters say and do.

Reading plays and scripts also exposes young people to language that is often poetic and rhythmic. The playwright and scriptwriter must be economical in the way they craft their story and consider how their words will sound spoken aloud on stage. By reading plays and scripts, younger readers gain a greater appreciation of the power of deliberate language choices and the fun that can be had with words.

Of course, we also want to introduce our children to the joy and wonder of seeing live theatre or beautifully produced films, but there is something to be said for reading plays and scripts and encouraging our young readers to perform those words in their own heads, in their own voices, before seeing them interpreted by another on the stage or screen.

Recommended Plays and Film Scripts

Boy Overboard: The Play by Patricia Cornelius (based on the novel by Morris Gleitzman) (Currency Press, 2007)

Hating Alison Ashley: The Play by Richard Tulloch (based on the novel by Robin Klein) (Puffin, 1988)

Jasper Jones: The Play by Kate Mulvany (based on the novel by Craig Silvey) (Currency Press, 2017)

Stage Fright!: Four Wacky Plays by Richard Tulloch (based on the stories of Paul Jennings) (Puffin, 1996)

Two Weeks with the Queen: The Play by Mary Morris (based on the novel by Morris Gleitzman) (Currency Press, 2011)

SHORT STORIES

The short story is an underrated form. To be able to create a story, complete yet concise and satisfying, is a highly demanding exercise. Writers such as Roald Dahl and Ray Bradbury perfected this art with much practise and talent. Children are very lucky that some of the best authors including David Malouf, Tim Winton and Peter Carey started out in short story writing and have many offerings for them to study.

Short stories are also valuable for young people who struggle to get through a novel. It allows them to achieve a sense of completion without too much frustration or fear of failure. Short stories come in a range of genres, so it's easy to find something that a child might like – whether it be humour, adventure or mystery. By understanding the conventions of the format, young people will be more confident and capable with their own narrative writing.

Short Story Recommendations

Begin, End, Begin: A #LoveOzYA Anthology edited by Danielle Binks (HarperCollins, 2017) (teen readers)

Borderlands: Riding the Slipstream edited by Paul Collins (Ford Street Publishing, 2024)

Bush and Beyond: Stories from Country by Tjalaminu Mia, Jessica Lister, Cheryl Kickett-Tucker and Jaylon Tucker (Fremantle Press, 2018)

Funny Stories: And Other Funny Stories by Morris Gleitzman (Puffin, 2018)

Give Peas a Chance by Morris Gleitzman (Puffin, 2007)

I Am the Mau and Other Stories by Chemutai Glasheen (Fremantle Press, 2023)

Meet Me at the Intersection edited by Rebecca Lim and Ambelin Kwaymullina (Fremantle Press, 2018) (teen readers)

Rich and Rare edited by Paul Collins (Ford Street Publishing, 2015)

The Book of Horses and Unicorns by Jackie French (HarperCollins, 2014)

The Hush Treasure Book by Hush Foundation (Allen & Unwin, 2015)

Total Quack Up! edited by Sally Rippin and Adrian Beck, illustrated by James Foley (Puffin, 2018)

Town by James Roy (UQP, 2007) (teen readers)

Unreal! The Ultimate Collection by Paul Jennings (Viking, 2015)

POETRY

There is something hardwired into the human brain that, independent of culture or upbringing, responds to rhyme, rhythm and words that can be memorised and chanted. Before adults overthink and panic about poetry, they should pause and recognise that it is very often the first form of text or story that we share with a young child, be it through songs or nursery rhyme.

Natalie Jane Prior is a multiple award-winning author and now a friend, and not just because she thought to include me as the image of the librarian in *Lucy's Book*, illustrated by Cheryl Orsini! *A Boat of Stars*, a poetry anthology she edited with Margaret Connelly, is a beautiful collection of accessible poems to share with the young. Natalie is the perfect person to tell us how and why to share poetry with readers young and old.

Natalie Jane Prior

Like prayer and music, poetry is primal. It's language operating simultaneously at its most fundamental and sophisticated levels. Nothing enriches a child's understanding of how language works more than poetry. Reading it teaches children to think outside the square, to see things from unexpected angles. In our modern world this skill is becoming essential. Don't think of poetry as an optional extra: think of it as a weapon in your children's arsenal for life.

Even if it's not something you're naturally drawn to yourself, teaching your children to love poetry is not as daunting as you might think. Start off by making sure that your new baby has one good quality book of nursery rhymes and one anthology of poems aimed at early childhood, and read one or two as part of the nightly bedtime routine. You'll soon find which ones are the favourites. Encourage your children to learn these by heart and recite them with you and, as they move further into the pre-reading stage, point out the rhyming words on the page so that they can associate the sounds with the letters. Move your bodies in time with the rhythm of the words as you read or recite: march and clap and bounce, and find ways of making every favourite poem your very own. Many picture books aimed at the very young are also written in verse. Some are better than others, but ALL good picture book texts depend for their success on rhythm and cadence – something that is worth playing up to when you read them aloud.

Finally, don't be afraid to experiment. When my daughter, Elizabeth, was small, a poem we read over and over again was 'The Night Mail' by W. H. Auden, which was written for a 1936 documentary film for adults, about sorting mail. What was it about this poem that made it special for us? It was the rhythm of the words, mimicking the train rattling over the tracks as it sped from London to Scotland, picking up mail of all different kinds along the way. Is there a poem you are particularly fond of? If so, share it. Chances are, your children will like it too.

Poetry Recommendations

A Boat of Stars: Modern Australian poems to inspire and enchant edited by Margaret Connelly and Natalie Jane Prior (HarperCollins, 2018)

A Ute Picnic and Other Australian Poems by Lorraine Marwood (Walker Books, 2010)

Can You Keep a Secret?: Timeless rhymes to share and treasure (10th anniversary edition) edited by Mark Carthew, illustrated by Jobi Murphy (Leaping Lizards Press, 2020)

Guinea Pig Town and Other Animal Poems by Lorraine Marwood (Walker Books, 2013)

It's the Sound of the Thing: 100 new poems for young people by Maxine Beneba Clarke (Hardie Grant, 2023)

Limelight by Solli Raphael (Puffin, 2018)

Love Poems and Leg Spinners by Steven Herrick (UQP, 2001)

Note on the Door: And other poems about family life by Lorraine Marwood (Walker Books, 2011)

Right Way Down and Other Poems edited by Sally Murphy and Rebecca M. Newman, illustrated by Briony Stewart (Fremantle Press, 2024)

Spotlight by Solli Raphael (Puffin, 2020)

Starlight by Solli Raphael (Puffin, 2025)

Untangling Spaghetti: Selected poems by Steven Herrick (UQP, 2009)

100 Australian Poems for Children edited by Clare Scott-Mitchell and Kathlyn Griffith, illustrated by Gregory Rogers (Random House, 2002)

VERSE NOVELS

Verse novels are narratives told in verse. They may be written in rhyme or free verse – or include a variety of poetic forms. Some verse novels are made up of short, individual poems; others are longer, chapter-length poems. But always they tell a story: the bare bones and heart of the story without being weighed down by flesh and fat. Kat Apel is an expert verse novelist and her books are never on the shelves of my primary school library – they are constantly in the hands of young readers and as soon as they are returned they are borrowed by someone else! Kat talks here about the weight of words.

Kathryn Apel

I have often thought that a poet is a combination of bodybuilder, topiary artist and clown, and that's especially true when writing verse novels. Every word is weighted. For each word on the page, a multitude of words has been pruned out. Yet verse novels surprise and delight with wordplay and poetic twists. They are eloquent – words seem to have more resonance. Verse novels deal with issues that have a lot of heart. They have humour and laughter too, but I think the raw emotions are key. Because they're often written in first person and because they're distilled words, you climb right inside the characters' hearts – both as writer and reader. Their heartaches become your tears, their insecurities become your introspections, their achievements become your joy.

In terms of reader engagement I would say that verse novels are a paradox; they appeal to kids who struggle with words on the page, but also to sophisticated readers. There is often more white space than words and that makes for a clean, clear read, while the layout helps pace the poem and enhance meaning. Being more about emotions than details, verse novels move the story along at a swift pace. They are often very visual – in a sense, the words are the illustrations – and that opens up a whole new realm of visual literacy, with hidden layers to the text. (Kids love to discover little tricks scattered through the pages.) So they're enabling, while also being engaging.

However, I don't think I can write about verse novels without acknowledging that kids might initially be reluctant to read them. When they pick up a book and flick through it for themselves they see poems and are often hesitant to read further. (I suspect frequent analysis of poetry within the education system makes it seem arduous – when really poetry is so much fun!) So the first time your child encounters a verse novel, it might be necessary to introduce it with a shared reading: maybe lightly discuss word placement on the page, look for pictures in words, talk about rule-breakers, or how the book is making them feel. When they're engaged, you can step back and let them take over the reading – or continue reading together.

I always envisaged *Bully on the Bus* as a shared reading experience between a young child and their parent or caregiver, to give young children words and open up discussions about situations where they might not feel safe. Often kids will say to me they 'forget' a book is a verse novel and are just swept away by the story. Sometimes they just can't turn the pages fast enough! Other times they want to dwell in the words on a page; walk away and savour the feelings they create. Again, that paradox – verse novels could be read quickly, but might need to be read slowly.

To me, verse novels are a treasure hunt in book form. That's something we can all enjoy!

Verse Novel Recommendations

Bindi by Kirli Saunders, illustrated by Dub Leffler (Magabala Books, 2020)

Bully on the Bus by Kathryn Apel (UQP, 2014)

Grace Notes by Karen Comer (Hachette, 2023) (teen readers)

Inside Out and Back Again by Thanhhà Lại (UQP, 2012)

Leave Taking by Lorraine Marwood (UQP, 2018)

Little Bones by Sandy Bigna, illustrated by Tamlyn Teow (UQP, 2025)

Mina and the Whole Wide World by Sherryl Clark, illustrated by Briony Stewart (UQP, 2021)

Pearl Verses the World by Sally Murphy, illustrated by Heather Potter (Walker Books, 2009)

Pookie Aleera Is Not My Boyfriend by Steven Herrick (UQP, 2012)

Queen Narelle by Sally Murphy, illustrated by Simon O'Carrigan (Walker Books, 2023)

Roses Are Blue by Sally Murphy, illustrated by Gabriel Evans (Walker Books, 2014)

Sister Heart by Sally Morgan (Fremantle Press, 2015)

Song of a Thousand Seas by Zana Fraillon, illustrated by Aviva Reed (UQP, 2025)

Sunshine on Vinegar Street by Karen Comer (Allen & Unwin, 2023)

The Kindness Project by Deborah Abela (Puffin, 2024)

The Little Wave by Pip Harry (UQP, 2019)

The Only Branch on the Family Tree by Sherryl Clark, illustrated by Astred Hicks (UQP, 2025)

The Spangled Drongo by Steven Herrick (UQP, 1999)

The Way of Dog by Zana Fraillon (UQP, 2022)

Tom Jones Saves the World by Steven Herrick (UQP, 2002)

Too Many Friends by Kathryn Apel (UQP, 2017)

Toppling by Sally Murphy, illustrated by Rhian Nest James (Walker Books, 2010)

What Snail Knows by Kathryn Apel, illustrated by Mandy Foot (UQP, 2022)

Where the Heart Should Be by Sarah Crossan (Bloomsbury, 2024) (teen readers)

Zoe, Max and the Bicycle Bus by Steven Herrick (UQP, 2020)

COMICS, GRAPHIC NOVELS AND MANGA

Comics and graphic novels tell stories in both visual and written form. Comics are serialised stories that are told over many editions and often many years. We get to know the characters slowly and we see different 'snapshots' of their lives. Graphic novels, on the other hand, are a single work in one book – a story from beginning to end.

Young people rely heavily on visual media for their information and entertainment. They don't read instructions these days; instead they find someone demonstrating it on YouTube. Graphic novels often fulfil this visual need in their reading too. Graphic novels are sophisticated and it takes a certain maturity and ability to decode the words and pictures simultaneously to construct meaning and follow the narrative. Japanese manga has another layer again – a cultural awareness and appreciation for the artistic design and genre itself. Children of all ages love graphic novels and there is a steady diet of Marvel, DC, manga and novel-adapted illustrated books to suit every taste.

I met the author Stephen Axelsen at the StoryArts Festival many moons ago. Stephen has a wicked sense of humour and I love seeing this sparkle come through in his writing and illustrations. I've asked Stephen to talk about graphic novels as I reckon he has created some of the best in the country for young people.

Stephen Axelsen

'Sequential art', 'graphic novel', 'bande dessinée' and 'comic strip' are all interchangeable descriptors for the format, to some degree. 'Sequential art' sounds technical and prissy, 'graphic novel' ponderous, and 'comic strip' or 'comic book' inaccurate because so many publications are not comedic at all. Presently, I prefer the French term 'bande dessinée' (drawn strip), both for the straightforward description of the medium and because it is French.

I love the making of strip stories as much as I do reading them – more probably. There is such a sweet marrying of picture and word, especially when doing both the writing and the illustrating. There is a kind of perpetual cross-pollination. A neat graphic idea in a single frame might shift the course of a narrative, for a page or for the whole story. One bright phrase might require the scrapping of a double spread of art. Now that I think of it, some pollination instances can be quite cross-making!

The construction of a framed art page is like cutting a jigsaw puzzle with a blunt jigsaw. It requires much shuffling and shaving, squeezing and stretching. Two millimetres are cut here and pasted there, to make space for an important extra word in a slightly bigger balloon. I love it when a page falls into place and the final frame leads seamlessly to the next page. The 'turn of page', especially at the end of a double spread, is critical. The graphic novel provides the scope for a lot of story in a limited space. There is room for a plot and subplots for character development, for action and drama and quiet spells. There is room for a novel.

Why read graphic novels? For kids who think books are a waste of time, or who find streams of uninterrupted book words scary, a graphic novel is a good option. A few words with a picture can be read in manageable bite-sized pieces. These few words are read and understood with the help of their supporting image. Each digested speech balloon is a small victory. Slowly, bigger balloons are managed. The balloons drag and lift the nine-year-old child up and away, away to Dostoyevsky or some such. I have met a professional writer who taught himself to read because he absolutely had to understand what The Phantom was saying inside those balloons.

Perhaps a graphic novel does too much of the visual imagineering for the reader/watcher. Does this inhibit the development of a young person's imaginative capabilities? I don't know. This is a question for the neuropsychologists. But I strongly suspect that the exposure to really good imagery intertwined with compelling stories can only be nourishing. It still is for me. I continue to look, absorb and expand my own perceptions, skills and ambitions.

The graphic novel is not just beneficial to the reluctant reader, nor just for the adult socially inept 'geek'. At their best, the graphic novel is an art form with its own rich aesthetics. There are many and various ways the illustrations can tell a story, often with a sparse amount of text. There is a wealth of visual tools to aid in the evocation of mood and tone, pathos and drama, humour and discordance: the spacing, placing and shaping, overlapping or even absence of frames, use of colour, texture, line style (bold, broken, tremulous). In fact, the elements of any two-dimensional visual art can be employed and structured for effect in the sequence of frames.

A graphic novel can be an almost filmic experience, like seeing a movie with 90 per cent of the frames removed. But unlike a movie, the story and the art can be absorbed at leisure, re-read in bits, the illustrations lingered over. Just as the reader of an unillustrated book can admire the word craft of a fine writer, a graphic novel reader can revel and delight in the drawing and colour skills of a fine illustrator, and the wonderful innovative ways that ideas, sometimes difficult or abstract, are rendered visually. The illustrator is not an embellisher or embroiderer of words. The good illustrator is an enhancer and an augmenter (and another word that I can't think of!).

Recommended Comics, Graphic Novels and Manga

Amulet series by Kazu Kibuishi (Scholastic)

Enola Holmes: The Graphic Novels series by Serena Blasco and Tanya Gold (Andrews McMeel Publishing)

Frog Squad series by Kate and Jol Temple, illustrated by Shiloh Gordon (HarperCollins)

Keeper of the Lost Cities: The Graphic Novel series by Shannon Messenger, adapted by Celina Frenn, illustrated by Gabriella Chianello (Simon & Schuster)

KidGlovz by Julie Hunt, illustrated by Dale Newman (Allen & Unwin, 2015)

Pablo and Splash series by Sheena Dempsey (Bloomsbury)

Pawcasso by Remy Lai (Allen & Unwin, 2021)

Roller Girl by Victoria Jamieson (Puffin, 2024)

Sherlock Bones series by Renée Treml (Allen & Unwin)

The Adventures of Nelly Nolan 1: The Nelly Gang by Stephen Axelsen (Walker Books, 2013)

The Greatest Thing by Sarah Winifred Searle (Allen & Unwin, 2022) (teen readers)

The Underdogs series by Kate and Jol Temple, illustrated by Shiloh Gordon (Hardie Grant)

Urban Legend Hunters series by Joel McKerrow and Wayne Bryant (Larrikin House)

CHAPTER TEN

MULTIMODAL READING

There is an element of apprehension among parents and educators about reading in the digital age. The overwhelming perception is that young people are choosing technology over reading and online games over the worlds in books. The advent of ebooks, apps and the rise in the use of personal devices has caused waves of concern, and there is good reason to be mindful of both screen time and digital reading. However, the clock cannot be turned back to a time before technology – nor would we want it to be – so the challenge is to embrace the wonders of reading in a digital age.

Technology means we are now more connected than ever before to the stories of others, both worldwide and in our local community. In fact, we have the opportunity to expand the literary experiences of young readers beyond traditional print texts and into this digital age of reading. Rather than screen time eroding literacy rates, it could actually instigate the 'golden age of reading'. We have the opportunity to consider new ways of thinking and doing in literacy learning if we acknowledge the richness of the digital activities in which our young people are engaged. And for those who despair the decline of 'the book' as we know it? We are now some way into the digital book revolution and it seems clear that traditional print books will happily sit alongside ebooks and other digital reading opportunities.

Changes to the way we teach literacy are also occurring in classrooms, in response to ever-evolving digital technologies. The challenge for educators is to embed new ways of reading and writing into classroom planning and teaching, while holding onto the richness of experience gained from traditional print-based texts. Likewise, as parents now have access to multiple digital options with which to equip and entertain their children, many families struggle to find the right balance of screen time. They too are looking for answers as to how the various forms of reading may co-exist in a technologically complex world.

Multimodal literacy is a way of articulating the increasingly diverse forms of communicating information. Modes of reading (such as images, words, sounds, movement, tactile and spatial) may be used in combination, to make meaning when reading, comprehending and responding to various multimedia and digital texts, and in the planning, writing and producing of multimedia and digital texts.[1]

Multimodal texts include picture books, graphic novels, ebooks and visuals, such as posters, where meaning is made by combining visual images, text and spatial modes. Digital multimodal texts include web pages, social media, apps, animations, films, podcasts and some ebooks and online gaming tools, where meaning is made through spoken language, visual (still and moving), audio, gestural, written and spatial modes. And finally, 'real-life' multimodal text experiences include performance, song, storytelling, some online gaming tools and dance. Modes such as images, words, sounds and movement in a text may be processed by the reader simultaneously or one mode may dominate. For example, the reading of a picture book will be dominated by the visual mode and in listening to an audio book the mode of sound will be dominant.

Digital technologies have enabled rapid changes in the way young people learn to read and become literate, hence the focus on multiple ways of reading or 'multimodal reading'. This chapter will examine ways of incorporating multimodal reading into your homes and classrooms. It will give you the tools to embrace, or at least work with, new and ever-evolving digital technologies.

TURN THEM INTO EXPERTS FIRST!

Familiarise your young reader with their technology and have them develop their expertise so they are not reliant on adults to use their digital device or online reading mode of choice. This may seem ridiculous in a world where teachers and parents often bemoan the fact that 'the young people' navigate new technologies with seeming ease and grace. However, often their level of expertise is related to what results in the fastest outcome for them, not necessarily how to use the technology for maximum academic or social benefit. In schools many units of work around digital technologies often start with skill development, whether it be for a particular app, a new brand of robotics equipment or a 'new to them' program. It is important to find the balance between playful independent exploration of technology and planned, sequential and specific skill development. As an example, when introducing ebooks to students, I demonstrate basic skills, such as using the dictionary, adding notes, highlighting and inserting bookmarks. We look at and brainstorm reasons why customised reading in an ebook may be of benefit, changing the font size, background colours, text-to-audio function and page layout.

Computers touch our lives in so many ways, from movies to medicine, education to entertainment, gaming to government, construction to commerce. It was just a few centuries ago when only the elite and religious could communicate through writing and reading. With computers dominating nearly every aspect of our lives, it is vital we have students who can create and instruct these digital technologies using coding skills. This 'new literacy' of coding enables students to not just use digital technologies, but to read, comprehend and create them.

EBOOKS

Nothing can replace the tactile nature of a print book and the importance of young children learning to turn a page and work out what is the front cover, back cover, spine and endpapers. Equally, there is something to be said for the persistence it takes for a newly confident reader to sustain reading from start to finish of a book without hyperlinking out, clicking on pop-ups or swiping from side to side.

However, digital devices for reading have much to offer. Good literary apps and worthy ebooks do an amazing job engaging readers, particularly those who are unable to sustain attention for an entire print book or those who need to 'read' while moving (hello toddlers, sporty types and fidgeters of all ages), and can remove barriers to reading and learning for those with print disability. They also allow slightly older readers to delve deeper into a book – clicking on an author bio, navigating to the dictionary to find out the meaning of an unknown word, or immediately downloading the next book in a series to keep up reading momentum.

While ebooks tend to replicate a print-text reading experience, for some readers, they open up the world of story in a way that was not possible before, through varied font and screen size options, page-turning features and general layout, as well as many tools and settings (including audio narration and alternate text for images) that allow for a wide range of individualised reading experiences.[2]

Family friends have a ten-year-old daughter who was gifted an e-reading device for her birthday, along with gift cards for the purchasing of ebooks. Her reading rate and fluency have increased exponentially, and it has given her a sense of autonomy and responsibility in her choices, as she can now access books at the touch of a button wherever she is. She has become incredibly adept at leaving succinct yet insightful reviews on titles she has purchased and she now requests further gift cards for ebooks as presents or pocket money. I see this as a gentle introduction (always monitored by parents) to the world of digital technologies and the responsibilities that go along with such a privilege. Book choices need to be responsible, safety measures need to be considered when commenting on or reviewing books, pop-ups need to be read with a critical eye, and a budget for books needs to be considered with transactions that occur digitally. Well before your child enters the world of social media, ebook reading can provide a sense of 'dipping your toe' into the puddle that is the internet.

AUDIO BOOKS

Children's books in audio form are a great way for kids to experience stories in an aural mode. Audio books have similar benefits to being read aloud to, with audio books considered an important tool in literacy development.[3] Some people view audio books as the 'easy' option for young people, but as part of a balanced literary diet they greatly enrich the reading experience, and many of the skills and strategies used are comparable to reading a visual text. They also help to develop attention and listening skills and many children who are unable to make it through a long children's book will make it through the same story in audio, carried along by the sound effects, accompanying music, and expressive voices of actors and storytellers.

Audio books can also help to introduce children to text which is above their reading level, particularly when a child is following along with the print version and is hearing the words while seeing the shape of them on the page. The expressive voices of the professional narrator provides a fluid reading of a text which presents proper use of punctuation and cadence.[4]

Like ebooks, audio books also remove barriers to story, particularly for those with print disability. Taking away the mechanics of reading texts can help children to focus on understanding the story, and also enables children to visualise the story, the setting and the characters in their head. A love of reading can be sparked when a child finds an audio book they love and the print copy of the book is introduced when they are ready.

For me, the wonder of audio books is how portable they are with one digital device providing countless hours of story. Commuting to sport, school, holiday destinations or the shops can be made so much more enjoyable with a great audio book and the entire family can engage simultaneously and discuss it at length.

When Murray and I met, our children bonded quickly over their mutual love of audio books. With four kids in the back seat on long car rides to school and various activities, we have listened to all kinds of children's books, YA fiction and adult fiction and non-fiction. While some members of the family may dip in and out, depending on their interests, audio books inevitably create a sense of family harmony (read: silence). One day, all four kids were so engrossed in a book that we just kept driving. And driving. Everyone was so content, it seemed a shame to go back to the chaos of home and wrangling bags and wet swimmers out of the car!

As a commercial beekeeper, Murray has been a devotee of audio books for a long time. Many of the areas of Australia to which he commutes have little to no wi-fi, and even radio can become difficult to find. So he is in the habit of downloading podcasts and audio books to listen to. During the pandemic he was commuting regularly between Queensland and Victoria, in order to pollinate almond crops in Mildura. These roadtrips were long, so he decided to re-engage with the work of Jane Austen, which he had loved in his twenties. Upon his return from this period of intense driving, and after some weeks of listening to Austen novels, he took up conversing in Austen-esque language and offering parenting and relationship advice to me and the children. I recommend varying ones audio book diet for this reason.

ONLINE STORYBOOK READINGS

There are a number of online streaming services that are subscription-based and these are often available for free through council libraries. Story readings by professional actors or expert readers connect children with literature through the complementary mode of film, creating a multimodal reading experience. I do not advocate readings of books on YouTube by individuals, as they do not credit or pay the original creators of the book, and can often result in poor-quality recordings of loved stories.

I recommend a subscription-based service called StoryBox Hub, at home and in the classroom. For the past few years I have made good use of it in the lead-up to Anzac Day, because it has a beautiful collection of Anzac Day stories exquisitely read aloud. While I love reading aloud to my own children and to my students at school, StoryBox Hub's readings offer students a variety of voices and storytelling techniques. I cannot watch *I Was Only Nineteen* read by John Schumann (illustrated by Craig Smith) without ending up in tears. The warmth with which John reads this powerful book is heartfelt and he introduces it standing in front of Melbourne's Shrine of Remembrance – not something I can re-create in real life. Likewise, I will never be able to read a book like *One Minute's Silence* by David Metzenthen (illustrated by Michael Camilleri) as emotively as actor Shane Jacobson. The reading by Tiffany Speight of *Anzac Biscuits* by Phil Cummings (illustrated by Owen Swan) provides students with a context for the story which I cannot replicate in a school library. Tiffany is seated in a country kitchen and the filming switches between the book and the kitchen where Anzac biscuits are being made. The visuals invite young viewers into the setting of the story from the comfort of their library or home and add a whole other dimension to the book.

GAMING

Gaming is widespread among tweens and teens and many parents and educators despair at the hours that can be lost in online worlds. However, for many young people, gaming is a space in which they experience success, sustained and pleasurable entertainment, and a sense of control and independence over their environment. Online gaming can also serve as a rich source of storytelling and story-creating, imaginative growth and connectedness with peers, both online and offline.

Gaming requires high levels of literacy and comprehension: the ability to follow complex narratives; the skills to synthesise multiple modes of reading; the need to read deeply and think critically to solve complex problems; and the mechanical literacy to navigate a gaming environment, make quick decisions under pressure, and skim, scan and decode fast-moving text and images. Online gaming also often requires a high level of written ability through responding to comments from other players, coding avatars, and contributing hacks and critiques to gaming sites. Our challenge is to harness these positives and engage young people in meaningful ways with other forms of literacy learning. If young people are motivated to read the complex text of a game, we can transfer that motivation to a book through careful text selection: the right book at the right time for the right child.

Spin-off books from popular games are common and, if the text is of a high standard and employs the same tone as the game on which it is based, these books may engage young people in reading. Seeking out a series with similar concepts to favourite games, such as those with complex physical challenges, good versus evil plotlines, or stories of survival of the fittest, can hook keen gamers in traditional print books.

Popular fantasy series often have fan sites similar to gaming sites. Many readers greatly enjoy the sense of connectedness they feel from finding people who love similar books, and gamers are familiar with interacting on fan sites. Many gaming worlds are complex places and the sense of setting is key to engaging players and keeping them 'in' the world. Seek books with complex worlds, maps and a strong sense of place. Follow online interests and use comparative texts to write critiques or innovate on a text/game by adding new characters or changing endings. Reflect on the ethical dilemmas faced in games and seek books with similarly complex ethical issues, such as The Hunger Games series (Suzanne Collins), Deltora Quest series (Emily Rodda) or The Mortal Instruments series (Cassandra Clare).

PODCASTS

Podcasts (both listening to and creating) offer a unique way to engage children with multimodal texts, integrating audio storytelling with literacy, critical thinking and digital skills development. Podcasts combine storytelling, factual narration and auditory cues to make content interesting and accessible. They encourage young children to interpret tone, pace, sound effects and voice inflection, enhancing their comprehension skills in ways that extend beyond written text.

For older children, podcasts are a way of engaging with a serialised story or theme-based content and, like audio books, they can be something a family can enjoy together.

The podcast *Bedtime Stories with R. A. Spratt*, produced by Rachel Spratt, is a regular soundtrack in our house. Despite their varying ages, all four children go to sleep at night listening to one of their favourite children's authors telling them stories, some written for the podcast and some read from her back catalogue of books, including *The Adventures of Nanny Piggins* and *Friday Barnes, Girl Detective*. It is not uncommon that Murray or I will be shocked awake by the sound of Spratt's bugle blaring the theme music to the podcast in the middle of the night.

What I particularly love about *Bedtime Stories with R. A. Spratt* is the way fans of the podcast will slip seamlessly between listening in the podcast and reading her print books, both forms of storytelling supporting one another. James has collected each of the books that have come out of the podcast, including *Shockingly Good Stories* and *Astonishingly Good Stories* and he regularly swaps between the books and the podcasts.

For younger children, podcasts help build auditory processing skills and introduce them to storytelling structures. Programs featuring songs, rhymes or interactive activities can be especially engaging. There are a huge variety of podcasts which cater to early childhood listeners that are also entertaining for grown-ups.

Podcasts aimed at older children and teens often include more complex narratives, fact-based shows, debate-focused shows, interviews, or introduce new ideas in science or history. Many of them mirror adult podcast formats, such as true crime. The award-winning podcast *The Unexplainable Disappearance of Mars Patel* is a scripted serial mystery for middle-grade listeners. It is performed by children and there is a spin-off book series too. Perhaps your young reader might be inspired to create their own podcast.

Podcast Recommendations

Bedtime Stories with R. A. Spratt (R. A. Spratt)

Bust or Trust: A Kids' Mystery Podcast (Small Wardour)

Dino Dome (ABC Kids Listen)

Fierce Girls (ABC Listen)

Imagine This (ABC Kids Listen)

Maddie's Sound Explorers (Magic Star)

Sherlock & Co. (Goalhanger) (older listeners from teen years)

Short & Curly (ABC Listen)

Smash Boom Best (APM Studios)

Story Salad (ABC Kids Listen)

Squiz Kids (The Squiz)

Tai Asks Why (CBC) (older listeners from teen years)

The Fact Detectives (Kinderling Kids)

The Unexplainable Disappearance of Mars Patel (GZM Shows)

Wow in the World (Wondery Kids)

Creating podcasts

Young people may also create podcasts as a multimodal text type, either for school purposes or as a form of artistic expression. Podcasts can provide new ways to engage with stories, current events, science, ethics and more. They offer an excellent opportunity to meet curriculum goals while developing essential listening, literacy and digital skills. The steps below provide a kid-friendly guide to creating a podcast.

1. **Choose a topic.** Have your child or students pick a topic they are passionate about. It could be related to their favourite hobby, an area of study, or even an imaginary story.

2. **Plan and script.** Look at the way podcasts are structured and create a simple outline or script. Encourage them to think about the story structure and main points they want to share.

3. **Record and edit.** Here you can go as simple or high tech as you like. For the podcast I co-host, we use a very simple recording program and plug-in microphones. There are plenty of free editing tools, like Audacity or GarageBand, that make it easy to refine recordings.

4. **Add sound elements.** Sound effects, music and even silences can enhance storytelling. Free resources such as the BBC Sound Effects library can be used for this purpose.

5. **Encourage teamwork.** Work in pairs or in small groups to foster collaboration. Assigning roles, such as host, interviewer or sound engineer, can help children understand the different aspects of production.

6. **Share.** Once the podcast is complete, have children share it with the class or with close family and friends, noting privacy policies at all times.

CRITICAL LITERACY SKILLS

At the start of this chapter I talked about the importance of up-skilling students in the use of devices. Equally as important is equipping them with skills to critically analyse a multimodal text by evaluating:

- the credibility/quality of the texts (that is, who is producing them?);
- the commercialisation that comes with accessing multimodal texts online (for example, advertising, hyperlinking to promote

other texts, in-app purchases, etc);

- the appropriate ways to use content in the creation of their own multimodal texts. For example, copyright laws – how many times do we teachers need to talk to students about using copyright-free images and music (bangs head against classroom wall)?

There is no doubt that technology-infused experiences of literacy are reshaping learning environments and the contemporary reading practices of children. Older generations did not have to contend with the constant movement between modes and media that children now need to efficiently manage to create meaning from texts.

What is clear, is that in order for students to tap into the advantages of digital reading, they need new skills and strategies to successfully use and adapt to rapidly changing information and communication technologies. Digital literacy is ever-evolving, and the challenge for educators, parents and carers is to transform reading instruction and experiences in response to emerging technologies and harness new possibilities for communication and collaboration.

CHAPTER ELEVEN

READING FOR THE FUTURE – SUSTAINABILITY AND NATURE

Connecting sustainable futures and nature with reading books makes common sense if we want our young people to be engaged and receive a well-rounded education. There are few things better than seeing children get grubby in the garden, enjoying the natural world around them and learning about how to care for the earth. Observing bees, collecting leaves, inspecting insects and making mud pies is an essential part of childhood and I have very rarely encountered a child who does not enjoy pottering around in nature. Likewise, I have rarely (ever?) encountered a child who does not enjoy a quality book that is the right fit for them. While not all children have equal access to beautiful natural environments, a keen interest in sustainability and nature can be piqued early in a child's life with the right books and experiences.

Life on earth is at a critical period and there is increasing concern that we are not living within the capacity of our planet's resources. Quality books can help to put the issues in context and be a catalyst for positive change in ourselves and our young readers. Books can provide a sense of hope and joy about the environment and our ability to 'make a difference'. The importance of being in, learning about and having fun in nature is not a new concept, but the word 'sustainability' is a reasonably modern term. A simple definition for sustainability might be 'enough for all, forever'. I like this way of thinking about sustainability because it includes the idea that we need to look after the planet and its resources for future generations and share it with all people in the world. It also suggests that we need to live our lives with a sense of social justice and fairness.

More broadly, our society relies upon the natural environment – therefore sustainability is ultimately about supporting nature to provide us with what we need. It is about changing our behaviour to better manage resources and environmental services, so they can be sustained into the future. This may not be immediately obvious, but sustainability is also about creating an awareness of the link between the resources and environmental services we use and the natural systems that support them. These are big concepts for young children (and for adults) but kids understand about sharing, and research tells us that they are very capable of taking action for sustainability.

So when is the right time to introduce young children to environmental concerns and the concept of living sustainably? I have seen firsthand that even the youngest of children are able to grasp principles of sustainability: being mindful to dispose waste responsibly, understanding that their fruit scraps can be composted or given to the worms and knowing that insects should be returned to their habitat after inspecting them. Many young children will also have overheard discussions in the house or on the television about the effects of droughts, floods, pollution, poverty, conflict or other real-world environmental and social issues. Educating children with the help of age-appropriate books about the environmental and social challenges facing the planet need not be doom and gloom; rather, it can be a joyous way to empower young people to become problem-solvers and action-takers in looking after our planet. There are books on nature and sustainability aimed at children from birth, and embedding these books into all stages of childhood and into classrooms is common sense. An educational community that thrives is one where parents, students and staff work towards common goals for the good of the students and improved learning outcomes. There can be no greater goal than a school going slowly and steadily down the path to more sustainable and socially-just practices that create a learning environment that is clean, green, innovative, community-focused and inspires a lifelong love of the environment.

There are many fact books specifically on environmental issues and while these are useful, I believe there is much to be gained from stories and non-fiction texts where sustainability and nature themes are woven through a broader narrative: Like honey, stories are sticky and their concepts tend to get stuck in your mind more than isolated facts. Few children (or adults) are going to fall in love with a book that lists information about household recycling, but when a favourite character is on a 'fraught with challenges' mission to make her mother recycle the milk cartons, that story and the emotional journey will stick in the minds of young and old alike.

In Australia, the Environment Award for Children's Literature is a good place to start when developing a collection of books that supports sustainability. The Wilderness Society manages this award because they see that children's books can have a profound effect on young people in shaping the adults they become. They seek to award books that promote a love of nature, a sense of caring for the world and a curiosity in children. Similarly, the Commonwealth Scientific and Industrial Research Organisation (CSIRO), an independent Australian government agency responsible for scientific research, has a well-respected publishing program that includes children's books with a focus on environmental science, aquatic science, plant and animal sciences and natural history.

Dr Lyndal O'Gorman is a senior lecturer in the School of Early Childhood and Inclusive Education at the Queensland University of Technology in Brisbane. Her university teaching focuses on arts and sustainability education in early childhood and primary school contexts, and her research and writing also explores these topics. Lyndal worked as an early childhood teacher in urban and remote schools for thirteen years prior to her academic career and she has a strong personal commitment to the arts, as well as environmental and social sustainability.

Dr Lyndal O'Gorman

For thousands of years, the arts have played an important role in highlighting social and environmental issues. The first Australians painted and carved images of their world at least 40,000 years ago. In 1937, Picasso's painting *Guernica* brought the horrors of the Spanish civil war to the world's consciousness and the work has since become a symbol of peace. Contemporary American artist Chris Jordan's website presents dozens of mind-blowing and confronting images that challenge us to consider humanity's impact on the planet. Mysterious British street artist Banksy's images pop up all over the world on city walls, challenging viewers to explore tough questions about social justice. The saying 'a picture paints a thousand words' communicates how powerfully art can change the ways in which we see the world. And now, more than ever, the world needs us to change the way we see it and live in it and advocate for it.

It's vital that adults who live and work with young children consider their own attitudes and preconceived ideas about sustainability. Is sustainability going to be just an interesting topic to explore and a chance to learn a little about the birds and the bees (and the worms!) or are we willing to challenge ourselves to think about what 'enough for all, forever' might really mean for our own patterns of behaviour? If we are passionate about leaving the planet in better shape for future generations, we need to live consciously now and advocate for the natural world of which we are a part, and then children will catch that passion too.

Artwork in galleries, picture books and even on the street can help children to learn about the social and natural world and the challenge of living sustainably. These days it's all but impossible for even very young children to avoid seeing confronting images. The news is full of footage of children living in poverty, or in their war-ravaged homes far away, or of wildlife and natural places that are affected by pollution and other forms of human activity. Children can use their own art to make their learning about sustainability visible to those around them. They often know more than we think they know! And art can be a language for children to use to express their thoughts and feelings about big ideas. When adults give children time and space for conversations about big issues, to engage with literature that explores those ideas, and opportunities to make their learning visible through talk and artmaking, I believe amazing things can happen.

For example, if a child has time to look at a leaf and to draw that leaf from observation, she learns to appreciate it. Appreciating the leaf leads to love, and love leads to a desire to protect – the leaf ... the tree ... the forest. I believe that sustainability is not something one 'does' for 30 minutes on a Wednesday afternoon. When we spend meaningful time with children we are in the privileged position of helping them to see the world differently – whether the world is a leaf, or a compost bin or a community in another part of the world, far from view. Children's literature can be a fabulous starting point for conversations about sustainability and social justice because literature helps us to see the world from another perspective, and therefore to see the world in new ways. These new perspectives can lead to a desire in even young children to take action so that there might be enough, for all, forever.

The amazing thing about sustainability education is that as we are helping children to see the world differently, we see the world differently too. This knowledge can change us forever – in ways that make the planet a better place for us and for those who are to come.

READING TO SUPPORT SUSTAINABILITY

Stories are the best way I know to engage children in learning and encourage behavioural change – there is nothing like having your four-year-old tell you sternly that you have not put the yoghurt container in the recycling bin! This is what nearly all sustainability and nature themed books aspire to do: to engage the reader in a particular topic so that they learn something new and/or change their behaviour, and ideally the behaviour of those around them. Many a government has tried (and failed at times) to elicit behavioural change at huge economic cost and whilst recycling may largely be a succcss story, we have many more challenges and opportunities for further changing how we sustain and live with the natural world. This is where literature and reading are of invaluable importance. For our children they provide inspiration, adventure in wild places and new ideas, but for our local communities and society more broadly they provide critical thinking of how we live.

When we combine real-life experiences with literature, we see great outcomes and learning in action, something we strive for in educational settings. A few years ago, our Junior School Earth Angels team introduced two native stingless beehives to the campus as part of our long-term School Sustainability in Action Plan. As part of the budgeting and fundraising for this project, we sourced a number of books for the library on bees and beekeeping – ranging from non-fiction books aimed at professional beekeepers to picture books and non-fiction texts for the very young, and fiction stories for middle-grade readers where bees were either central characters or central to the plotline. Our aim was to provide resources that would not only further learning but also create a sense of story around our bees, spark curiosity and hopefully fire up little imaginations as to what may be happening inside our hives and in the lives of individual bees. One such title was *How to Bee* by Bren MacDibble, which has been awarded a number of literary awards and is aimed at a reading audience of approximately 10 plus. *How to Bee* is set in future earth at a time when humans have polluted the world to the point that bees are almost extinct. Dystopian in nature, this book has been hugely popular as a middle-grade book club choice and set text. MacDibble has cleverly woven issues of sustainability and nature into a gripping, often edge-of-your-seat storyline, and for those who have read it, bees will never be looked at in the same way again! My own narrative non-fiction title *The Beehive* (illustrated by Max Hamilton) was in part inspired by *How to Bee*, along with my lifelong love of bees and a passion for introducing native stingless bees into schools.

There is incredible beauty in the quiet of a book, as there is in the relaxation of tending to gardens or just being in nature. Promoting a love of nature and an interest in sustainability in children is a critical element in building a society that respects and protects our world, and books that celebrate all these themes are crucial in starting and continuing the journey.

CHAPTER TWELVE

READING MINDFULLY

Mindfulness is something of a buzzword but it is one trend I am happy to support – there simply *has* to be an antidote to the fast-paced society which most of us find ourselves a part of today. At times it can feel like our lives are just spinning around and spluttering ahead, without the option to take a moment and just *be*; to focus our awareness on the here and now and calmly accept our thoughts and feelings as they come and go. I first heard about mindfulness from my father, who has been espousing the virtues of training your brain for as long as I can remember. What I find most interesting about Dad's passion for mindfulness is that his job is as a professor in policing, security and terrorism, specialising in violent extremism. For someone who spends much of his life researching a terribly negative aspect of the world, he's an exceptionally calm person, which I can only put down to his mindfulness practice. So forget the buzzword and go with the ideas that underpin it.

For me, mindfulness is a way to improve my concentration and ability to be present. I know I am often in a state of mindfulness or 'flow' when I am engaged with and deeply 'inside' a beautiful book.

It provides a time of calm in an otherwise busy day. On a wider level, mindfulness has been shown to have a strong relationship to improved attentional functioning, including sustained, selective and executive attention, and the ability to improve working memory and brain function.[1] Mindfulness practices are used in the treatment of young people with attention difficulties and more recent studies have conducted research on the potential benefits for students with reading difficulties.[2] It is logical that employing mindfulness techniques when reading would improve our ability to cope with sustained reading and reduce reading errors, as we are slowing down and following a straight path through a text.

Readers require sustained concentration to read and make meaning from literature. They need time to reflect and appreciate the nuances in language; we might call this deep reading, slow reading or mindful reading. Mindful reading is not skimming and scanning a text, highlighting or adding notes, reading while multitasking or becoming side-tracked by social media or your to-do list. Rather, reading mindfully requires the ability to be in the present moment, just you and the book, aware but without judgement of all that is occurring around you and inside you.

READING AS FLOW

Many keen readers have experienced times when they suddenly realise they have lost many hours in a good book having been in a state of 'flow'. Based on Dr Csikszentmihalyi's Flow Theory, flow is characterised by a feeling of complete absorption in an activity. In a flow state, one is completely focused, involved and enjoying the process of performing an activity. We are not self-conscious or concerned by failure because there is oneness with the activity: the reader is with their book; the pianist is with their piano; the gardener is with the earth.

Georgina Manning, director of Wellbeing for Kids, is a mindfulness educator and I trained under her to become accredited as a Peaceful Kids facilitator. Her knowledge of the research behind mindfulness is extraordinary and here she unpacks some of the ideas around mindfulness and reading.

Georgina Manning

Ever read a page of a book and realised that you took in none of what you have just read? Your mind is filled with the day's ups and downs, and you end up going back and forth between past and present. Our minds are not focusing on the present and our body is on autopilot. We are there physically, with our eyes reading the text, but we are not processing the words, comprehending it or relating it to our lives. We can live each day on autopilot, going about our daily tasks, but not engaging our mind.

When we can bring our full awareness to what we are doing, we allow our minds to rest and be wholly attentive of the present moment and the joy this often brings. 'I can't wait to go on holidays and "get lost" in my book' is a phrase we often hear. It's interesting we wait until the holidays to allow ourselves to be lost in the moment, almost as though we need permission to stop and engage in a nurturing activity. In our fast-paced multitasking world, the process of getting lost in a book, reading, is almost seen as a luxury, only to be indulged in when everything else is done.

What takes us away from being mindful and allowing ourselves to be fully immersed in a good story? Is our fast-paced multitasking world so overwhelming to the mind that we have forgotten the art of just being? When we are in the 'being' as opposed to the 'doing' mode, we allow ourselves to be immersed in our present moment. If we are constantly up in our heads, going through our to-do lists, we are not allowing our minds to fully rest and rejuvenate.

Reading is one of the easiest ways to practise entering the 'being' mode. Reading brings us into the present moment and takes us away from our to-do lists and worries, which often activate our body's stress response. When we are engaged mindfully in a deeply relaxing and nourishing activity such as reading, this usually switches off our stress response and allows both our minds and our bodies to rest and have a calm awareness. As we experience that sense of calm by being present, we are training our brain to develop new neuropathways that help our brain to naturally become more mindful during our other day-to-day activities. The more we practise being mindful informally, the more we are naturally mindful at other times of the day.

Reading before we sleep has also become a lost art. The increase in screen time before bed is becoming an epidemic that is having catastrophic effects on the brain. As children's brains are growing, they particularly need time each day to rest and just play. They also need wind-down activities every night to help them to drift off into a deep, nourishing sleep. Going from screens straight to bed is extremely disruptive to children's sleep patterns and quality of sleep. If we don't allow our brains to slowly wind down from the day and immerse ourselves in a relaxing activity such as reading, we are still wired even in our sleep. Reading is one of the most powerful activities we can do for our brains before sleep. As an experiment, for two weeks, try switching off all screens at least an hour before bed, spend at least 30 minutes reading before turning out the lights and feel the benefits for yourself.

Practise reading mindfully

If you would like to practise reading mindfully, or encourage your children to, try the following: choose a time when you can focus on your reading for an extended period without distractions. Pick a book that engages you but will not exhaust you mentally. A print book will be a better choice than an ebook which comes with a suite of options and distractions, and the physicality of a print book can help you to focus. Pay attention to the book itself – the weight of it in your hands, the colour of the paper, the size of the font and how the font runs across the page. Read and stay present for as long as you can.

Like everything that is worth doing, mindfulness takes practise and I am certainly no expert. But rather than worry that mindfulness is just one more thing to fit in, I continue to read about it and share books on mindfulness with my own children and the children in my school. I keep it in the front of my mind and in doing so I am aware it is there for me to fall back on when time and life circumstances shift and change, as they invariably do.

At one school I incorporated times of 'mindful reading' for students from kindergarten to Year Ten. Library lessons had a focus on the art of reading mindfully and the skills one needed to develop to do this. We looked at the research and science behind mindfulness and shared beautiful picture books with mindfulness theories. This is not something which sits outside of the realms of the school curriculum.

Practising mindfulness can support the development of skills in self-management, self-awareness, social management and social awareness, which are four key ideas outlined in the Personal and Social Capability learning continuum in the Australian Curriculum.[3]

Along with looking at literature, lessons ended with students spending quality time reading as mindfully as they could in the library, outside near our native stingless bees or under a tree in the playground. These lessons lay the groundwork for individual students and families to incorporate these concepts and practices at home. With the support of school management this can be a beneficial way to implement a whole-school approach to mindfulness and wellbeing.

BOOKS ENCOURAGING MINDFUL PRACTICES

The following books are suitable for introducing language and principles around mindfulness. They should start conversations with children about how they might be able to practise being mindful.

A Handful of Quiet: Happiness in Four Pebbles by Thich Nhat Hanh (Plum Blossom Books, 2012)

A Quiet Girl by Peter Carnavas (UQP, 2019)

I Am Peace: A Book of Mindfulness by Susan Verde, illustrated by Peter H. Reynolds (Abrams Books, 2017)

Is Nothing Something?: Kids' Questions and Zen Answers About Life, Death, Family, Friendship, and Everything in Between by Thich Nhat Hanh, illustrated by Jessica McClure (Parallax Press, 2014)

Making Mindful Magic by Lea McKnoulty (Tien Wah Press, 2015)

Silence by Lemniscates (Magination Press, 2012)

Sitting Still Like a Frog by Eline Snel (Shambhala Publications, 2013)

Slow Down World by Tai Snaith (Thames & Hudson, 2017)

Take the Time: Mindfulness for Kids by Maud Roegiers (Magination Press, 2010)

CHAPTER THIRTEEN

CELEBRATING AND REPRESENTING DIVERSITY

Representing and reflecting diversity in literature is an important consideration for so many reasons, but there are two main ones and they dovetail perfectly into this book's broader themes. Children who read about lives different from their own develop more empathy for other individuals, and children are inclined to read more if they can see themselves in stories.

Every young person deserves to see themselves and their experience of the world in a book. Initiatives such as We Need Diverse Books and The Diversity in Australia and Aotearoa New Zealand (DANZ) Children's Book Award have pushed for essential change in the publishing industry to produce and promote diverse children's books. But, while the landscape is rapidly changing, there is still a long way to go. Diverse books are those that authentically represent diverse and marginalised people and communities – disability, LGBTQIA+, gender diversity, class, race, culture and religion.

Early reading experiences should include books that, like a mirror, offer kids the opportunity for self-reflection and provide windows into the lives of a range of characters to help them build an understanding of the diversity that exists in the world. It is encouraging to see books that contain stories and images of diverse families, like *Come Over to My House* by Sally Rippin and Eliza Hull (illustrated by Daniel Gray-Barnett), being used extensively in home and school libraries.

Middle-grade readers are also being afforded a broader range of reading material. Stories of refugees and immigrants, disabled people and those from different religious backgrounds are increasing within the age group category that has predominantly leaned towards humour and adventure.

Diverse texts also play a crucial role in allowing readers to see their own lives reflected in story. Children from other countries, wrangling a new language and culture, should be able to see a face similar to their own smiling out from the pages of a picture book. Young readers with a disability need to see that their stories are worthy. Older teens figuring out sexual orientation or experiencing racism or bullying deserve books which portray them in positive ways. The importance of authenticity in representation is key. Having diverse writers speak to an audience from a published position gives those voices credibility.

The work of authors and advocates, such as Kate Foster, Carly Findlay, Randa Abdel-Fattah, Will Kostakis, Anita Heiss, Cheryl Leavy, Trevor Fourmile, Maxine Beneba Clarke and Eliza Hull, cannot be underestimated. Advocacy work is emotionally draining and comes at personal cost as the divide between work and home life can become blurred. It is a job for us *all* to share the load in continuing to advocate and keep a close eye on diversity and the representation of diversity in children's literature, in all literature. The narrative is changing, and this is cause for celebration, but we still see book bans and challenges which predominantly target diverse books and authors. Diverse creators need to be supported and mentored to tell their stories, and caregivers, teachers and librarians need financial and managerial support to keep diverse books on their shelves. Books are powerful tools in smashing stereotypes and harmful tropes, in building connections and understandings, and in allowing young people to walk in the footsteps of others.

FIRST NATIONS VOICES AND REPRESENTATION

Throughout my teaching career, I've been privileged to know Des Crump, a proud Gamilaroi man and Indigenous linguistics academic, and Michelle Witheyman-Crump, both of whom have a deep passion for First Nations children's literature. First Nations stories, woven with cultural depth and unique perspectives, give young people an authentic lens into Australia's rich Indigenous heritage, fostering a deeper understanding and respect for the First Nations' history, values and worldviews.

Incorporating First Nations voices into children's literature is vital for all young readers. By celebrating First Nations narratives, we offer all children a chance to learn from a wealth of knowledge and storytelling traditions that are integral to Australia's history and future.

Des Crump and Michelle Witheyman-Crump

Australian children's literature has embraced Aboriginal and Torres Strait Islander culture; though, one could argue that many of those stories reaffirm the idea of 'other' and 'different' rather than 'valid' and 'worthy'. Creation stories and depictions of remote community life have filled the literary landscape for years. Urban Indigenous voices are also becoming stronger and clearly recognised.[1] There is a clear shift in First Nations storytelling to more authentic depictions of lives and worldviews of the diversity of Aboriginal and Torres Strait Islander young people and their families. Language diversity is also explored in this new mode of stories with traditional languages, contact languages and urban language woven into the storytelling process.

The main reason for having Aboriginal and Torres Strait Islander books in schools and having non-Indigenous children reading them is that Australia has a shared history. Unfortunately, this history is more often told by non-Indigenous voices. It is now the time, not to mention proper and reasonable, that Aboriginal and Torres Strait Islander people are the storytellers of their own histories. Author and advocate Anita Heiss, and others, have raised awareness of the range of Aboriginal and Torres Strait Islander authors, and organisations such as BlackWords and the Indigenous Literacy Foundation have also played an important part in this process.[2]

Exposing young people to Aboriginal and Torres Strait Islander authors is not just about diversity, it is about providing authenticity to their worldview and allowing readers a glimpse of lives beyond their own. Aboriginal and Torres Strait Islander lives and stories are constantly changing and reflecting the world around them. Stories need to go beyond the stereotypes and historical moments that are stuck in time.

Storytelling is a personal process, particularly for Aboriginal and Torres Strait Islander writers whose lives and identity have been determined by a history of government policies and media stereotypes. Yarning Strong is a series that seeks to answer the question 'What's it like to be a young Aboriginal or Torres Strait Islander person in Australia today?' Stories written by Aboriginal and Torres Strait Islander authors unpack this question and provide the background content for teachers to bring it to life in the classroom.[3]

Respected author, academic and activist Tony Birch has also highlighted the critical need for non-Indigenous writers to create more authentic Indigenous characters, not 'stock' representations, advising authors to 'read, watch, look and listen to everything you can to engage with Indigenous issues'. Birch adds that experience with Aboriginal and Torres Strait Islander people and their daily lives can help create more rounded, nuanced Indigenous characters.[4] Author Gayle Kennedy, winner of the 2006 David Unaipon Award, and acclaimed author for children and adults Anita Heiss both reinforce the notion that Aboriginal and Torres Strait Islander literature should not be homogenised nor seen as a niche, but as part of the rich literary diversity Australia has to offer.[5]

BOOKS THAT SUPPORT FIRST NATIONS VOICES AND REPRESENTATION

Afloat by Kirli Saunders, illustrated by Freya Blackwood (Hardie Grant, 2024)

Backyard Footy by Carl Merrison, illustrated by Samantha Campbell (Hachette, 2024)

Borderland by Graham Akhurst (UWA Publishing, 2023) (teen readers)

Burn by Melanie Saward (Affirm Press, 2023) (teen readers)

Come Together: Things Every Aussie Kid Should Know about the First Peoples by Isaiah Firebrace, illustrated by Jaelyn Biumaiwai (Hardie Grant, 2022)

Come Together Again: A Celebration of First Nations Music, Song and Dance by Isaiah Firebrace, illustrated by Jaelyn Biumaiwai (Hardie Grant, 2024)

Cunning Crow by Gregg Dreise (Magabala Books, 2019)

Day Break by Amy McQuire, illustrated by Matt Chun (Hardie Grant, 2021)

Djinang Bonar: Seeing Seasons by Ebony Froome, illustrated by Leanne Zilm (Fremantle Press, 2024)

Dream Little One, Dream by Sally Morgan and Ambelin Kwaymullina (Puffin, 2020)

Finding Our Heart: A Story about the Uluru Statement for Young Australians by Thomas Mayo, illustrated by Blak Douglas (Hardie Grant, 2020)

Giinagay Juluum, Hello Mountains by Melissa Greenwood (HarperCollins, 2024)

Growing up Wiradjuri edited by Anita Heiss (Magabala Books, 2022) (teen readers)

Gurril, Storm Bird by Trevor Fourmile, illustrated by Jingalu (Magabala Books, 2023)

Koori Princess by Anita Heiss (Magabala Books, 2022)

My Place by Nadia Wheatley, illustrated by Donna Rawlins (Walker Books, 1987)

Same, But Little Bit Diff'rent by Kylie Dunstan (Windy Hollow Books, 2012)

Sorry Day by Coral Vass, illustrated by Dub Leffler (National Library of Australia, 2019)

Sorry Sorry by Anne Kerr (Boolarong Press, 2014)

Stolen Girl by Trina Saffioti, illustrated by Norma MacDonald (Magabala Books, 2011)

The Boy from the Mish by Gary Lonesborough (Allen & Unwin, 2021) (teen readers)

The Silverleaf Chronicles series by Ambelin Kwaymullina (Text Publishing) (teen readers)

The Skin I'm In by Steph Tisdell (MacMillan, 2024) (teen readers)

The Upwelling by Lystra Rose (Hachette, 2022) (teen readers)

Three Dresses by Wanda Gibson (UQP, 2024)

Took the Children Away: The Iconic Song of the Stolen Generations by Archie Roach, illustrated by Ruby Hunter (Simon & Schuster, 2020)

Welcome to Country by Aunty Joy Murphy, illustrated by Lisa Kennedy (Walker Books, 2023)

Wurtoo: The Wombat Who Fell in Love with the Sky by Tylissa Elisara, illustrated by Dylan Finney (Hachette, 2024)

Wylah the Koorie Warrior series by Jordan Gould and Richard Pritchard (Allen & Unwin)

LGBTQIA+ VOICES AND REPRESENTATION

I first met Will Kostakis many years ago when he was a visiting author at my school. He captivated audiences then, as he does now, with his disarming honesty, dry humour and genuine warmth. He has won legions of teen (and teacher librarian!) fans with novels including *The First Third*, *Loathing Lola*, *The Sidekicks* and *Monuments*. His multiple award-winning novel *We Could Be Something* also won the Prime Minister's Literary Awards Young Adult Literature Prize in 2024.

Through characters who reflect varied identities and orientations, LGBTQIA+ stories broaden perspectives, foster empathy and understanding, and encourage all readers to embrace diversity in identity and love. As authors like Kostakis continue to create authentic narratives, they offer valuable insights and celebrate the unique strength of every individual's journey, supporting the creation of compassionate, inclusive communities within schools and beyond.

Will Kostakis

When it comes to embracing diversity in literature – be it the author's identity and experiences, or those of the characters on the page – we are trending in the right direction. I say trending, when I really wish we were striding, leaping or … already there.

We, perhaps without realising it, rank diverse identities in terms of acceptability. For instance, the same people who would insist I talk less about growing up gay when speaking to teens – 'The focus should be on the text and the craft!' – are the same people who will ask me to reflect on my experiences growing up as a Greek–Australian. Both my sexuality and my heritage have shaped me as a person and, in turn, the texts I produce. But, depending on who I am talking to, one part of my identity may be more palatable than another.

A few years ago, I was invited to discuss my YA novel *The First Third* with a class of Year Ten girls who had recently finished a text study. As I entered the room, the teacher quietly cautioned me not to mention the gay character, Sticks. It was a request that took me by surprise, but I honoured it. I removed all mentions of one of the book's most prominent characters in my discussion of it. As a closeted gay man, the act of excising Sticks from my presentation was me diminishing the value of my own experiences to preserve my career.

At the talk's conclusion, I asked the students who their favourite character was, expecting them to name Yiayia, the character modelled after my own grandmother. Instead, one student preferred the character Sticks. I tried to steer the conversation back to unforbidden territory by asking the girls about their favourite scene. The same student raised her hand. She named the scene where Sticks explained losing his virginity to another boy. The girls around her nodded in agreement.

This fascinated me. I didn't comprehend why a group of – I assumed – heterosexual teen girls connected with a scene about a gay boy grappling with his sexuality. The answer shouldn't have been surprising.

'It helped me understand my friend Sam a little bit better.'

We talk about diversity in literature as if it only affects the people now seeing themselves on the page. I mean, it does, the impact is incredible. I remember the only gay content I encountered in high-school English – William Shakespeare's 'Sonnet 20' felt like a revelation to my Year Nine self, not because it reflected my own experience exactly, but because if Shakespeare could write about gay stuff, then maybe it was okay for me to live a life of … gay stuff. But reading that poem did not just allow the – it later turned out – three gay kids in that class to see themselves, it also helped the other twenty or so boys understand them a little bit better.

Diverse texts foster empathy. And young readers are curious. They crave that understanding of others. Whatever the misgivings of their gatekeepers, young readers will seek out the content that satisfies their curiosity. If they do not find it in their homes or libraries, they will search for it online.

Coming out as gay eight years into my career gave me an insight into the importance of supporting #ownvoices creators. The content of my work was mostly celebrated, particularly its diverse representations, but when I came out, my writing was viewed differently. We are, it seems, more comfortable with assumed-straight men writing gay characters than gay men writing them.

Straight Will was asked to speak at schools, and occasionally asked to steer clear of discussing gay characters. Gay Will's books were no longer appropriate for high-school students. They were 'how-to' manuals for deviant behaviour, perceived as political … but they were the same books.

As a straight man, the professional costs for reflecting the world's diversity were near zero, but reflecting that same diversity when I was more open about my identity became a high-wire act.

In a reading community where there are no consequences to coming out, sure, initiatives like #ownvoices might not be as important. Anyone can write anything so long as it is well-crafted, well-researched and well-intentioned. But that community does not exist, not yet anyway.

We're … trending towards it.

BOOKS THAT SUPPORT LGBTQIA+ VOICES AND REPRESENTATION

A Child's Introduction to Pride: The Inspirational History and Culture of the LGBTQIA+ Community by Sarah Prager, illustrated by Caitlin O'Dwyer (Black Dog and Leventhal, 2023)

An Unexpected Party edited by Seth Malacari (Fremantle Press, 2023) (teen readers)

Avast!: Pirate Stories from transgender authors edited by Michael Earp and Alison Evans (Fremantle Press, 2024) (teen readers)

Different for Boys by Patrick Ness, illustrated by Tea Bendix (Walker Books, 2023) (teen readers)

Everything Under the Moon: Fairy tales in a queerer light edited by Michael Earp, illustrated by Kit Fox (Affirm Press, 2023) (teen readers)

I'm Not Really Here by Gary Lonesborough (Allen & Unwin, 2024) (teen readers)

Introducing Teddy: A gentle story about gender and friendship by Jessica Walton, illustrated by Dougal MacPherson (Bloomsbury, 2016)

Julián is a Mermaid by Jessica Love (Walker Books, 2019)

Love Makes a Family by Sophie Beer (Hardie Grant, 2018)

My Shadow is Purple by Scott Stuart (Larrikin House, 2022)

Take Three Girls by Cath Crowley, Simmone Howell and Fiona Wood (Pan Macmillian, 2017)

The Henna Wars by Adiba Jaigirdar (Hachette, 2021) (teen readers)

The Sidekicks by Will Kostakis (Penguin, 2016) (teen readers)

We Could Be Something by Will Kostakis (Allen & Unwin, 2023) (teen readers)

Who Are You?: The kid's guide to gender identity by Brook Pressin-Whedbee (Jessica Kingsley Publishers, 2017)

Who's Your Real Mum? by Bernadette Green, illustrated by Anna Zobel (Scribble, 2020)

Wrong Answers Only by Tobias Madden (Penguin, 2024) (teen readers)

DISABLED VOICES AND REPRESENTATION

Kate Foster was in my orbit for some years in kidlit circles before I realised she was the author of some of my favourite middle-grade titles, including *Paws* and *The Bravest Word*. In fact, Kate does quietly go about her work with little fuss and fanfare but her writing is hard not to notice and her advocacy work in the diversity space deserves to be recognised. She is the founder of the DANZ awards and passionate about encouraging and teaching a wider understanding of autism and mental illness through a positive approach and representation in her books as well as her presentations and talks.

Kate Foster

The children's publishing industry is making strides and awareness is growing when it comes to the representation of marginalised and minority people in books for young readers, but disability representation continues to lag, and not just a little bit, but by an awful lot. I find this odd, disappointing, and rather surprising for many reasons. Here are a few statistics that stand out to me:

- According to their website, the World Health Organization estimates that approximately 16 per cent of the world's population is disabled.[6]
- A 2024 media release by the Australian Bureau of Statistics suggested there are 5.5 million disabled people in Australia.[7]
- It was estimated using data from the 2015 SDAC that around 7.4 per cent (or 329,000) of Australian children aged 0–14 had some level of disability.[8]

With the aged population living longer and improvement and advancement in diagnosis criteria, these numbers are increasing and will continue to do so.

We must also acknowledge the family, friends, teachers, healthcare workers, carers and others who love, support and work with disabled people on a regular basis. It's important to consider how much these percentages increase when we include the wider disability community.

When we look at disabled characters in the books published over the past ten to twenty, years, the first glaring problem is that there aren't many, not when we compare this to the total number of books published. According to a study in 2019 by the Cooperative Children's Book Center, only 3.4 per cent of children's books had disabled main characters.[9]

To make matters worse, when we dig into the books that are published, and then those that receive awards or make recommended reading lists, a whole host of different and more worrying issues are uncovered. One of these is how, time and again, the same harmful and offensive tropes continue to appear in literature. These can include stories in which:

- the disabled person wants or sets out to be cured or accepted;
- the disabled person has a power or strength related directly to their disability;
- the disabled person changes somehow to fit in;
- the disabled person is there to teach other characters, and the reader, about kindness and acceptance;
- a deformity marks a character as being evil or an outcast;
- the disabled character's struggles and trauma are the main focus of the story.

Often, 'recommended' books that feature disabled characters are not written by disabled people, but instead by abled white people from middle-class backgrounds who are writing from an outsider's perspective. By this, we mean their knowledge and research is not from a personal lived experience but gathered from articles and mainstream media, which notoriously only covers the negative aspects of a disability – they are representing the story from the outside looking in as opposed to the inside looking out.

If we analyse the reasoning behind this and think about what message we're passing on to readers, both disabled and otherwise, we'll see a pattern of imposed thinking and expectation that ultimately perpetuates harm. Australian research suggests that children with intellectual disabilities and mental and behavioural problems have a greater risk of experiencing maltreatment than children without disability.[10] As noted in a 2019 article in the *Sociological Review*: 'The way disability is represented in children's literature has the potential to affect non-disabled young readers' views of disabled people in real life and also to reflect disabled readers' lived experiences back to them from the page ... stereotypical representations that portray disabled characters as objects of pity who have a deficit, for example, have the potential to do real harm to disabled people.'[11]

Surely disabled kids have the same right as abled kids to see themselves in fun stories, adventures and fantasy and science fiction, starring as a mermaid or a knight or a princess or a monster slayer. Surely abled kids should be shown that disabled kids, with the right support and accommodations, can be the hero, the comedian, the leader, and the sword-wielding warrior, rather than the sidekick whose purpose is to teach about acceptance or create heroes out of everyone else.

Surely disabled kids can be more than their disability, with them being able to showcase their personalities, strengths and, well, their ordinariness. And it seems more than fair for abled kids to see disabled kids as equal, as ordinary people with the same hopes and dreams and goals as them, whilst acknowledging their disability at the same time. I'd like to think that anyone with even a hint of a moral code and sense of justice would agree with this.

I've received many letters and messages since *Paws* was first published – from parents, teachers and children themselves – to express their gratitude and relief. My books have offered insight and deeper understanding and, as a result, connection. They've allowed neurodivergent children to no longer feel invisible or, worse, like nothing more than the neurodivergent child. The natural and thoughtful treatment of my neurodivergent character by the supporting characters has shown readers how easy it is to make accommodations and include everyone.

There's still such a stigma attached to autism, with adults keen to avoid the negativity often associated with labelling their children. I get it, truly I do. But positively labelling a child, and with the correct label, is empowering, providing self-acceptance; it provides an explanation and not an excuse.

Looking back, as I was growing up, I was called 'too sensitive' and 'too fussy', 'difficult' and 'odd'. I regularly felt like I was either too much or not enough. All of these were labels, incorrect ones, that were both hurtful and harmful and convinced me that I was broken in some way and needed to change. It's hard to describe the extent of how this impacts a person's mental health and their potential. My books, along with so many others written by neurodivergent authors, have helped people start to recognise this passive damage and how words like 'disabled', 'autism' and 'ADHD' are not bad.

We talk a lot about authors writing from the perspective of a character with a diverse background that they don't personally share, and how to do this sensitively and as authentically as possible. It's a common debate these days, especially with publishers wanting, and perhaps feeling pressured, to add diverse books to their lists. This isn't necessarily a bad thing, but rushing to fill these spaces and ticking the boxes only deepens the issue and could in turn cause greater harm.

I've thought long and hard about a solution, and I wonder if it's helpful to switch the approach of the discussion to focus on better understanding the importance of the right representation and the powerful and long-lasting effect it has on young readers.

I was once asked if I would ever write a book that didn't star an anxious and/or autistic child. I immediately said no, thinking that, as an autistic person myself, I'm driven to offer valuable neurodivergent representation in my books. I want neurodivergent children to feel seen and accepted, and I want neurotypical children to have that deeper insight and connection to the neurodivergent people they encounter in life. But then I paused and reframed the question: *Could* I write a story from the perspective of a person who wasn't either autistic or anxious?

The answer is probably not, no matter how hard I researched. I have lived for over forty years as a socially anxious autistic person, seen the world through autistic eyes, interacted and navigated social society with an autistic brain. I can mask, camouflage myself so I appear the same as everyone else. I can mimic and take on behaviours to ensure I fit in. But, despite working hard to ensure everyone around me remains comfortable and not be troubled by my discomfort, on the inside I'm still anxious and I'm still autistic, and I'm experiencing every moment through this finely tuned lens.

I don't expect everyone to fully comprehend this, and so much is difficult to explain or describe in a way a neurotypical person might understand. It is simply my way of surviving and living. Yes, every human is different and negotiates the world in their own unique way, with many of their experiences and struggles overlapping, but this will never make us all 'a little bit autistic' and prove that we're all having the same hard time. I hear this far too often, and it does nothing but erase and downplay my distress. Neurodivergent people are some of the most resilient because they have no choice. Their survival toolbox is bigger than most people's!

By telling stories my way, through my eyes, I'm able to give a fresh perspective on what my autistic experience is really like. I can invite people in, show them ways to include me, challenge their preconceived notions of me, display my strengths and value, and prove that I can do more than society has told me. None of this storytelling is didactic or far-fetched, nor is it without balance.

Studies have shown that authentic representation can be a powerful motivator in engaging children to read, particularly in minority and lower socioeconomic communities.[12] Furthermore, an Edith Cowan University study concludes that the three major barriers to children developing a love of reading are access, opportunity and under-representation in books.[13]

I can only conclude by saying that until the publishing industry creates more and equal opportunities for disabled creatives to tell their own stories, employs more disabled people, and acquires books that are not trope-heavy or trauma focused, then it is up to teachers, librarians, booksellers, families and carers to do the hard work. Each of us must purposely add and stock books with the right kind of disability representation to bookshelves everywhere, hand these books to all children and, most of all, listen and be informed by the disability community about which books are the right books to recommend.

BOOKS THAT SUPPORT DISABLED VOICES AND REPRESENTATION

ABC Disability by Sarah Rose and Alley Pascoe, illustrated by Rebecca Feiner (Hachette, 2024)

A Kind of Spark by Elle McNicoll, illustrated by Kay Wilson (Walker Books, 2023)

Boy by Phil Cummings, illustrated by Shane Devries (Scholastic, 2018)

Come Over to My House by Eliza Hull and Sally Rippin, illustrated by Daniel Gray-Barnett (Hardie Grant, 2022)

Craig Shanahan: Cooking up a storm by John Dickson, illustrated by Claudia Frittitta (Vision Australia, 2023)

Different, Not Less: A neurodivergent's guide to embracing your true self and finding your happily ever after by Chloé Hayden (Murdoch Books, 2022)

Everything I've Never Said by Samantha Wheeler (UQP, 2018)

Fish in a Tree by Lynda Mullaly Hunt (Nancy Paulsen Books, 2015)

Matt Formston: Surfing in the dark by John Dickson, illustrated by Philip Bunting (Vision Australia, 2023)

Nikki Hind: Dressed for success by John Dickson, illustrated by Chantel de Sousa (Vision Australia, 2023)

No Words by Maryam Master (Pan Macmillan, 2022)

Remarkable Remy by Melanie Heyworth, illustrated by Nathaniel Eckstrom (Hardie Grant, 2023)

Small Acts by Kate Gordon and Kate Foster (Walker Books, 2024)

Social Queue by Kay Kerr (Text Publishing, 2021) (teen readers)

Stars in Their Eyes by Jessica Walton and Aśka (Fremantle Press, 2021) (teen readers)

The Unlikely Heroes Club by Kate Foster (Walker Books, 2023)

Thunderhead by Sophie Beer (Allen & Unwin, 2024)

We Are Giants by Amber Lee Dodd (Hachette, 2016)

White Noise by Raelke Grimmer (UWA Publishing, 2024) (teen readers)

MULTICULTURAL VOICES AND REPRESENTATION

Growing up surrounded by a multicultural community has deeply shaped my understanding of the importance of diverse voices, particularly in children's literature. My parents' long-standing commitment to supporting refugee families allowed me to witness firsthand the challenges and triumphs of these communities. As a child and then as a teen, I remember noticing, and seeking out, books that reflected varied cultural experiences. Surrounded as I was by families from Persian, African and Asian descent, I was acutely aware that many of the books in our home did not contain characters or experiences that represented my friends and community.

When young people see characters who share their heritage, culture and experiences, it validates their identity and fosters self-worth. Similarly, books that depict characters from different backgrounds help build empathy, respect and curiosity in children unfamiliar with those cultures.

Multicultural representation in children's books counters stereotypes and broadens perspectives. Rather than confining children to narrow views, these stories reveal that, though backgrounds may vary, the human experience is universal.

In today's classrooms, the presence of multicultural voices in books is not just an enhancement – it is essential. Through these stories, children are reminded that they are part of a world that celebrates diversity, and they're given the tools to build a future grounded in understanding and unity.

Lotte ten Hacken is an experienced educator and teacher. Her PhD research explores the use of picture books as a stimulus for dialogue in order to foster intercultural understanding. She is a dual Dutch/Australian citizen who emigrated from the Netherlands with her family as a child.

Lotte ten Hacken

'Why do I need to give money and say sorry, Mama?' asked my then six-year-old son as we walked home from school with his sister.

His class had been asked to donate a gold coin on National Sorry Day, an event held annually in Australia to commemorate the Stolen Generations. In class, the teacher had read a book called *Sorry Sorry* by Anne Kerr.

It was a good effort from the teachers, but how to explain systemic racism and intergenerational trauma to a six-year-old? As a parent, navigating these complicated questions can be difficult, especially if the answers are not always clear-cut. As a teacher librarian, I spent the next week or so reading books that touch on the Stolen Generations. I gathered a range of books that offered as many perspectives as I could find.

Together, we read *Sorry Sorry* again, as well as *Sorry Day* by Coral Vass (illustrated by Dub Leffler). We also read *Day Break* by Amy McQuire (illustrated by Matt Chun), which looks at the complexities and pain felt by many First Nations people on 26 January. To lighten things up a bit and provide different perspectives, I added in *Same, But Little Bit Diff'rent* by Kylie Dunstan and *My Place* by Nadia Wheatley (illustrated by Donna Rawlins), both of which give varied perspectives of First Nations characters.

In short, I chose a wide range of books to broaden the understanding my children had about the lives of First Nations people. It is important to note that one First Nations character does not represent all First Nations people – it is a trap many of us fall into when we talk about members of minority groups. It is important not to perpetuate the idea that majority/white equals normal and everyone else is 'other'.

In terms of my young children understanding Sorry Day, they concluded that it was important to say sorry for bad things that had happened, because the people at the time didn't care or say sorry and we now want everyone to realise that how First Nations people were treated wasn't okay. I took that as a parenting win!

There are increasingly more great books by First Nations creators that provide an important opportunity for us to hear their diverse perspectives firsthand. These books are not necessarily ones that are just for entertainment (though some are), but many of them are age-appropriate and provide carers (and teachers) some relief from having to provide all of the answers, all of the time. Books can be great discussion starters, and can help plant a seed of curiosity to broaden a child's background knowledge and develop a greater understanding in the future.

As a teacher librarian I have had similar experiences at school where a student has asked a tricky question and I have responded by whipping out a related book, and away we would go with a discussion about what we all thought. Phew! I have been saved by picture books so many times.

It's important to note, however, that not all picture books are created equal. There are literally thousands of picture books and not all of them are high-quality or useful. In fact, some are factually incorrect, perpetuating damaging stereotypes and narrow-minded ideas about cultural diversity (and other topics). It's important to consider the content with a critical eye when choosing texts to share with young people. The notion of books as 'mirrors' (reflecting the reader), 'windows' (showing alternative realities) and 'sliding doors' (prompting active participation beyond the pages) is a super helpful idea to consider when choosing texts to read with our children and students.[14]

One of the first times I saw the power of picture books in my teaching career was when a new student from Pakistan started in my Year Three class (in a predominantly white school). We'll call her Amara (not her real name). Quite a few of the students had never met a person with dark skin before and some children struggled with how to act. Their response was not malicious, although there was some whispering that went on. Some students were over-the-top nice to Amara, but didn't realise they were treating her like a baby rather than an intelligent peer of the same age. Amara had very limited English to begin with, and it understandably took a little while for her to make friends and settle in, but many other students took a similar amount of time to adjust to someone who they saw as 'different'.

Of course, I very quickly turned to my usual solution – picture books! Research shows that books are a great way for children (and adults) to develop empathy,[15] so I gathered a range of mostly Australian picture books that included culturally diverse characters. The picture books we explored in my classroom at that time included *I'm Australian Too* by Mem Fox and illustrated by Ronojoy Ghosh, which highlights all the different places (and reasons) 'Australians' may emigrate. We engaged in interesting discussions about *The Proudest Blue* by Ibtihaj Muhammad and S. K. Ali and illustrated by Hatem Aly, which explores a girl choosing to wear a hijab for the first time. We also read *The Boy Who Tried to Shrink His Name* and *Amma's Sari* by Sandhya Parappukkaran and illustrated by Michelle Pereira, both of which highlight the experiences and discomfort that people who have cultural differences may feel. These all acted as important windows for many of the students in my class.

Finally, we read and explored a dual language (English/Dari) copy of *My Two Blankets* by Irena Kobald and illustrated by Freya Blackwood. In the story a young refugee girl, who has come from a war-torn country, moves to Australia and is welcomed by a kind girl who plays with her and helps her feel as though she belongs. Our new girl in class, Amara, was thrilled, not only because it was in a language she understood but because many of the plot elements of the story acted as a 'mirror' for her.

These culturally diverse books also acted as a 'window' and helped many of the children in my class realise how difficult it would be to come to a new country and not know the language. They started to realise that their experience of going to the shops or to the park was likely quite different for children from different cultures. These books also acted as 'sliding doors', providing a connection to the characters – children were able to apply this to their own life and actions. Unsurprisingly, the students in my class showed much more empathy to Amara after engaging with these culturally diverse books and quickly realised that although she may need some help learning English, she was their equal.

Tackling racism through talk

In my experience, many white students in Australian classrooms have never really thought much about how people with a different skin colour, who wear different clothes or have a different name, may be treated differently. This is such an important first step in developing understanding and educating children about racism. It also helps develop capabilities of intercultural understanding, which is part of Australian education policy – The Alice Springs (Mparntwe) Education Declaration as well as the Australian curriculum. Before students can come to appreciate other cultures, they must first recognise that they have their own culture and there is no one 'normal' or 'right' cultural group.

The normalisation of the idea that 'white' culture is at the top of the racial hierarchy and non-white people are 'other' is called white normativity and research shows it is often perpetuated by well-meaning teachers (and parents).[16] Exploring cultural diversity exclusively through the five f's (food, flags, festivals, folklore and famous people/landmarks) is an example of this approach. Colour-blindness (essentially minimising difference) and silencing (ignoring/shutting down talk about cultural difference altogether) are also common aspects of racism that are often inadvertently perpetuated in many Australian classrooms (and families).

Many people believe that highlighting the similarities and minimising or avoiding talk about difference is desirable, as it is assumed that it encourages social acceptance and cohesion. I know I personally believed that this was the right thing to do and often spoke like this with my students and my own children. I certainly had not previously considered the potential negatives, but I now know that research shows that colour-blindness and silencing can have negative impacts on people from minority groups. When you think about it, ignoring people's differences discounts their lived experiences and overlooks the existence of racism, which is not going to promote positive change.

Unfortunately, there are many picture books that perpetuate a colour-blind view, representing cultural difference only through stereotypes, and not acknowledging the vastly different experiences of minority groups. As I said previously, not all picture books are created equal and it's important to actively think about what message each book might be sending. As a general rule, books that include culturally diverse characters as part of the story (and perhaps experience difficulty because of their difference) are likely to be more beneficial than books where each page is 'celebrating' a child from a different country and there is no real plot.[17]

Despite the commonly held view that children don't see race, there is a body of research that suggests children see racial difference from a very young age (babies even!). Unfortunately, school is the place where children are most likely to experience racism. On the upside, research also shows that education can challenge stereotypes and reduce bias, especially in children under the age of twelve. This is what essentially inspired me to start my doctoral research, exploring how teachers (and carers) can use picture books to foster intercultural understanding. I strongly believe that reading, reflecting and talking about social issues, such as racism, helps to make the world a better place. Although some adults don't seem to believe it, there are studies that show that children from a very young age are more than capable of understanding and discussing race, culture and social justice, and are willing to do so with a trusted adult or peer. Children should be given the opportunity to explore their own culture and the difference in the experiences of white and non-white children in order to challenge stereotypes and prejudice.[18]

Exploring characters and settings

The literature review I embarked on as part of my doctoral research also brought up some other interesting things that I hadn't really considered in depth before. Psychology research with children has found that books with realistic content are more conducive to learning transfer.[19] Some studies have shown children can apply story suggestions and themes more readily to real life if the characters are human (rather than animals/fictional creatures). For example, in one research study,[20] participants were read one of two versions of the same story about the importance of sharing; one version had human characters and the other had animal characters (with human characteristics). Directly after reading they were given multiple stickers and asked if they would like to share some with children who didn't have any. The kids that had read the story with human characters were far more willing to share their stickers. Fascinating, right?

For my own research I chose to use books based on this assumption that children are more likely to apply pro-social behaviours to their own lives if the setting and characters are human and relatable. Don't get me wrong, there are so many great books with anthropomorphised characters (where animals take on human characteristics) and there is absolutely nothing wrong with these stories, especially for recreational reading. But if you're wanting to delve a little deeper into tricky topics such as cultural diversity, refugees, homelessness, disability, even sustainability, the research suggests that human characters and realistic settings are probably the way to go.

Gathering sets of texts and making connections

Another aspect that came up in my literature review was the importance of reading beyond a 'single story' to get as many different perspectives as possible.[21] 'Text sets' are a great way to make sure you are covering as many different perspectives about the same group of people (or issue) as possible. If you're not sure where to start, head to your school (or local) library and talk to the people who work there. Book people always love researching and recommending great books!

The other great thing about exploring related texts is the value it adds to comprehension. It's so lovely seeing kids having lightbulb moments as they remember something from another book that is similar. The official name for this aspect of comprehension is 'making connections' and in schools we encourage text-to-self connections (where it relates to something in their own lives), text-to-text connections (books, movies, TV shows) and text-to-world connections (where it relates to something happening in the real world). There are many research studies showing that children who make these connections have greater reading comprehension, which in turn has significant educational benefits.

During my research, one thing I noticed is that connections are what draw students in but *dis*connections stimulate the most animated class discussions. Disconnections occur when students are curious, confused or even outraged by the situation or the treatment of a character in a story. During these debates I often remind students (and my own children) that being open-minded and learning how to respectfully disagree is a very important life skill that we all need to practise.

Considering critical literacy

Critical literacy involves understanding that texts are created by a person who has particular beliefs and views and who has likely written the text for a specific purpose; no book (or any text) is neutral. This is an important realisation, especially in this information age. Critical literacy often involves looking beyond the literal meanings within a text and considering what is present as well as what might be missing. Analysing and evaluating the meaning of texts helps readers better understand issues related to fairness and equity; in education settings it's often associated with taking action for social justice.

Critical literacy can start with very young children. For example, we can encourage young readers to think about why an author wrote a book. The first steps to critical literacy are realising that authors and illustrators are regular people who have made particular choices. Part of this involves looking at what the characters are like, what words are used and especially the way the images have been put together. As mentioned in an earlier chapter, visual literacy is an important part of reading picture books. For example, consider how aspects such as angles might make someone look more or less powerful, or how distance may either position the reader as an observer or invite us into a scene.

How to: Picture book talks

So, you may be thinking, 'How do I make the magic happen?' The culmination of my PhD research was the creation of a teaching model (or guide) that encapsulates all I have learnt. Through a deep dive into existing research and adding what I discovered through my own real-world research project, I came up with 'Picture book talks'.

1. **Gather books.** The first step is to gather a collection of books about a particular theme (the topic you want to develop greater understanding about). Talk to the 'book people' at your school or public library or your friendly independent bookseller for recommendations.
2. **Read together (aloud).** When reading a book for the first time I always like to read through the whole book in one go without stopping too much, to make sure everyone is getting the flow of the story and they know what's

going on. After reading it through once, I always like to ask if any parts of the story require further explanation. Next, I ask if there are any pages children would like to revisit. There might be pages they just want to look at again because they're unusual or beautiful or sad or funny or weird. Explore all these requests! Every book is different, and every child has a different personality, interests and schema (prior experience and knowledge) so not every book is going to have the same impact.

3. **Read/view/listen independently (multiple times if possible).** The third step is individual exploration of the book. Let them 'read' (pictures and/or words) on their own or possibly with a partner. Encourage the reader to consider what they feel and notice and think about any questions that surface as they read. Encourage them to write or draw these reflections in a book or even on sticky notes stuck to the relevant pages. At school I have students take photos and record these reflections in a digital journal. My PhD research included multiple readings of the same book over a two-week period because research shows us that deeper understanding and reflection come from time and repetition. In a school setting this may involve independent reading in small groups using multiple copies of a text or a digital version of the text. In a home setting this may mean leaving the book strategically placed at the breakfast table or on a bedside table a few times across a few weeks. Or having a bit of a rotation of bedtime stories going at bedtime/morning-tea/whenever-you-read-time.
4. **Talk together.** The final (and most important) step is to talk about the book! Read it again and talk about all the things it made you/them wonder, think, feel, question, etc. Ask them about any connections they made and what they noticed about the words and illustrations. After engaging with it multiple times there are likely to be new things that weren't noticed on the first reading. For some books this may be a full-on discussion and for others it may just be a few minutes. Don't force it! Some books will stimulate more discussion than others. Don't be tempted to skip the other steps and go straight to the talking … the book needs to marinate a little in the child's mind for the best results!

Note. It won't always work. Most of the picture books I have chosen have stimulated animated discussion and I have been excited about the new understanding, empathy and development of intercultural understanding. There was one particular book (which I won't name as there is nothing at all wrong with it) that just fell flat. I had to drag responses out of the students, and it was certainly not a free-flowing discussion. Upon reflection, the book was slightly too young for the group (character age is often a good indicator) and the setting was abstract. It seemed the students could not relate to the content. It was not enough to introduce them to something unfamiliar or (what I deemed) interesting – readers also need buy-in and this only happens when students make connections to the text in the first instance. If it doesn't work the first time, try again.

BOOKS THAT SUPPORT MULTICULTURAL VOICES AND REPRESENTATION

Alone Like Me by Rebecca Evans (Random House, 2022)

Amma's Sari by Sandhya Parappukkaran, illustrated by Michelle Pereira (Hardie Grant, 2022)

Be Careful, Xiao Xin! by Alice Pung, illustrated by Sher Rill Ng (Working Title Press, 2022)

I'm Australian Too by Mem Fox, illustrated by Ronojoy Ghosh (Scholastic, 2017)

My Two Blankets by Irena Kobald, illustrated by Freya Blackwood (Hardie Grant, 2017)

Our Stories series by various authors (Pan Macmillan)

Stay for Dinner by Sandhya Parappukkaran, illustrated by Michelle Pereira (Hardie Grant, 2023)

Swimming on the Lawn by Yasmin Hamid (Fremantle Press, 2017)

Tayta's Secret Ingredient by Amal Abu-Eid, illustrated by Cara King (MidnightSun Publishing, 2024)

The Boy Who Tried to Shrink His Name by Sandhya Parappukkaran, illustrated by Michelle Pereira (Hardie Grant, 2021)

The Month That Makes the Year by Inda Ahmad Zahri (Allen & Unwin, 2023)

The Proudest Blue by Ibtihaj Muhammad and S. K. Ali, illustrated by Hatem Aly (Walker Books, 2020)

Through My Eyes series edited by Lyn White (Allen & Unwin)

CHAPTER FOURTEEN

READING THE DARK

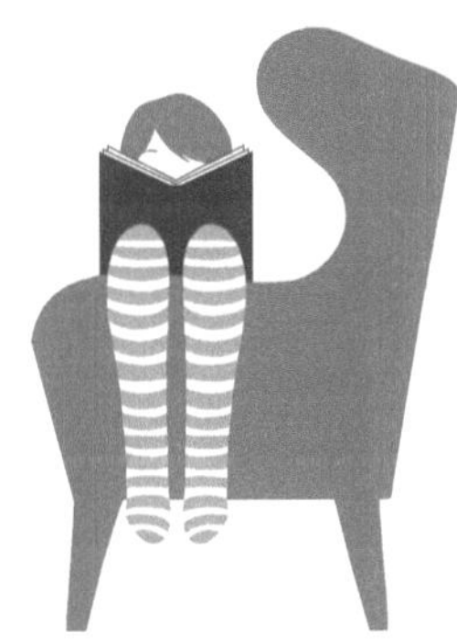

My family and I have experienced 'the dark' many times over. We have dealt with some really awful and quite scary health issues and we are intimately acquainted with grief. The death of my wild-spirited, huge-hearted little brother in 2012 shook our lives until we no longer knew which way was up and which way was down. In 2017, my beautiful and incredibly talented aunt passed away and then, mere weeks later, my husband, Dan, suffered a catastrophic heart attack in his sleep. Our girls, Ava and Georgia, woke to the news that their beloved daddy had died and I had lost the other half of myself. My family and I are extremely close and we are fortunate that we have each other and a village of people who keep us afloat, but 'the dark' is still a journey that is mostly faced alone; no other person can ever comprehend the incredible minutiae of emotions that overwhelm your soul when you lose someone you love.

My beautiful sons, Sam and James, came into our lives some years after their much adored mother died. These boys with dark hair and eyelashes gained older sisters in Ava and Georgia, and while blended families are 'a journey' to say the least, we relish the chaos and the love. Now, as a family, we all have love and loss living deep within us. Grief seeps into your bones and every fibre of your being. At times, grief is exhausting, confusing and painful, but it is an honour to have loved so deeply that you miss acutely. Along with therapy and surrounding ourselves with our village, books dealing with grief and emotions have been very important to our family, and I believe books of this nature are important for *all* young people in helping to develop empathy, understanding, compassion and kindness.

Our house is full of laughter, shrieks of joy and screams of excitement over bodily function jokes, and we read the most ridiculously funny books. But we also read ones about feelings, about children living in poverty or war zones, and about grief. These books are an important part of our day-to-day reading. The light and the dark co-exist in life, as they do in literature, and we do our young people a disservice if we do not allow them to experience the full gamut of human emotions and experiences through carefully written, age-appropriate books.

The books I remember most from my childhood and early teens are *Charlotte's Web* (E. B. White, illustrated by Garth Williams), *Dicey's Song* (Cynthia Voigt), *When Hitler Stole Pink Rabbit* (Judith Kerr) and *Beginnings and Endings with Lifetimes in Between* (Bryan Mellonie, illustrated by Robert Ingpen), and reading the blurbs of any of these books is still enough to reduce me to tears. My mother provided me with stories that would make me cry myself to sleep at night. I can still remember the physicality of the feelings I experienced reading *So Much to Tell You* (John Marsden) and I desperately wanted to bring the main character, Marina, home with me for the weekend from her boarding school. At the time I had many school friends who were boarders and Marina leapt out of the pages and into my life. It was the first book I read many times over.

By Year Five, and especially Year Six and Seven, students ask library staff for 'books which will make me cry'. Just the other day, a new student in Year Six quietly asked me if I could show her where the section for sad books was in the library. After explaining that no such section existed, I pointed her towards my personal favourites – stories of bravery in the face of adversity and tales of families who survive despite the odds. From about the age of nine or ten, young people want to explore complex emotions and become more socially aware, and books are the perfect safe place to do this. A well-crafted story can transport the young reader into a situation they may never face in real life, and soften and shape their thoughts around issues of humanity, justice and the world in which we live.

And yet, many parents would prefer their children continue to only read tales of wonder, magic and joy; that the books their children read reflect only the light in life. I completely understand and I'd love if it could be this way, but quality literature explores a range of experiences. I've had many long, sometimes tricky conversations with parents about books which explore dark themes. I've had complaints and concerns about books that deal with war, mental health, death and illnesses, such as cancer. Many of these books are aimed at quite young children and their parents would very much prefer their innocence be preserved. I often ask them if they read *Charlotte's Web* as a child and commonly discover that it was one of their favourite books. Generally the penny drops and there is an 'ah-ha' moment as they remember that Charlotte's inevitable death was made bearable by the way her friends honoured her life and carried on with strength. I've had plenty of book stand-offs with parents, for many reasons, and I'm always (sometimes) happy to agree to disagree, because at the end of the day it is the parent's right to decide what is appropriate for their child. However, I talk with them about how it's our job as parents to protect our children from hurts and heartache, but also to develop in them the resilience which will carry them through tough times. I don't know of a better and more gentle way to introduce young people to 'the dark' of life than through age-appropriate, carefully chosen literature while they sit on the lap of a loved adult.

Author Shona Innes is a psychologist working with children and her Big Hug Books series for an early childhood to primary school audience deals with issues such as grief, bullying, family breakdown, body image and online safety. The language in each of the books is spot on and the stories are engaging and appealing to young children. I highly recommend them for every home, school and library collection. Shona shares with us her thoughts on how literature can support young people through the dark times in their life.

Shona Innes

To help a young person through dark times, indeed to help anyone of any age, we need to understand how the problem is for them. What are their experiences? What did they notice? What did they think about?

For the very young, concepts such as thoughts and feelings can be too big for them to understand. As we develop, our brain learns first to deal with the physical, touchable things around us. Only later in development are we able to notice we have thoughts ... and then, later still, we can have thoughts about our thoughts. The very young can express their feelings, but not stand back from their feelings to regulate them. Young children are usually much more in the moment. They can remember things from their past, but they may not be able to articulate those things in words or understand their relevance to how they are feeling and behaving.

To make sense of the world, young children need more tangible and touchable objects to manoeuvre and manipulate. Stories with pictures (sometimes with additional puppets, toys or that thing we just made with boxes and glue) can provide the link between something that happens in the story and a child's own experiences. We can use a picture book to talk about things that are difficult to talk about, and illustrations can help us emphasise emotions and encourage perspective taking. We can also see through a picture book the impact that a character's actions have on other characters. Indeed, the very process of reading together is an intimate activity that usually requires some closeness and undivided attention – safety and attention are two other necessary components of any healing process.

Sharing a book with a child can simply be the start of an important conversation. However, sometimes parents and teachers – because of their own experiences and emotions – can be reluctant to talk about dark topics with children. It is natural that adults want to protect children and I know that some worry that, if they talk to a child who is having a difficult time or needs to know some 'dark' news, they could make things worse instead of making it better.

There's another important concept that psychologists consider when they work with children and that is a process called 'generalisation'. When you give a child some new ideas or ways to manage their troubles they may think about them as things they do just when they are with the psychologist or in the psychologist's room or only with the particular problem you talked about that day. Children can need some help to generalise – to move the ideas from the room or place or time where they've talked about them and take them to use in other places like the playground, bedtime or school. We can help them generalise by practising in different locations and different situations, but we can also help by sharing the concepts used in sessions with other important adults in a child's life. The other adults can then prompt children to use new skills in other places.

It's a very exciting time to be a psychologist helping young people. We now know more than ever before about how children's brains change as they grow. This new information helps us to make sense of so many things we notice as a child moves from infancy through early childhood, the teen years, young adulthood and then into adulthood.

We now know that it is quite 'normal' for teens to experience more strongly felt emotions. Teens can become very interested in dark things and the troubles and dramas of others. They begin to have the capacity to relate and process darker themes. Changes to their developing brains can sometimes lead to differences in how emotions feel and they can go looking for bigger doses of things in order to experience pleasure – louder music, faster cars and juicier gossip. We think this might have something to do with the primal desire to push boundaries and explore new lands so that our gene pool has a healthier, more diverse mix. So, it is unsurprising that teens desire more emotion and excitement in their books. A teen brain wants more from a 'good read' and they can use books to escape and explore emotions and ideas without leaving the comfort of home.

Books can be useful in psychological interventions with children as a way of sharing experiences about dark times, discussing feelings and reflecting on options. They can open pathways to further conversations and provide connection. In the same way you might keep a first-aid kit for minor medical emergencies, having some books about darker issues can serve as your emotional first-aid kit – not a substitute for a professional consultation, but a good way to get conversation rolling to see if more help is necessary.

My own experience reading emotionally complex books to all the children in my professional and family life has led me to believe, quite passionately, that children are more able to deal with the light and the dark of life than we give them credit for. The very best creators of children's books weave sorrow and heartbreak with love and comfort. These books develop empathy and resilience in our children. But books are also an escape – so don't fall into the trap of handing 'books about grief' to a grieving child without also including some humour or fantastical ones. The 'dark' books should be available to, but not forced upon, a child. The truth is that the world is full of love and of devastation. Good writers help their readers to see that the darker shades of this world can be made bearable by offering hope and showing that there is always light, even just a pinprick of it, in the dark. And, of course, my hope is that every child has someone in their life who loves them and will read to them.

The books in the following lists may help to facilitate conversations and deepen understandings around death, dying and bereavement.

PICTURE BOOKS ABOUT GRIEVING

A Story for Hippo: A book about loss by Simon Puttock, illustrated by Alison Bartlett (Scholastic, 2001)

Beginnings and Endings with Lifetimes in Between by Bryan Mellonie, illustrated by Robert Ingpen (Puffin, 2005)

Ben's Flying Flowers by Inger Maier, illustrated by Maria Bogade (Magination Press, 2012)

City Dog, Country Frog by Mo Willems, illustrated by Jon J. Muth (Hyperion Books, 2010)

Courage by Bernard Waber (Houghton Mifflin, 2002)

Cry Heart, But Never Break by Glenn Ringtved, illustrated by Charlotte Pardi (Enchanted Lion Books, 2016)

Death Is Stupid by Anastasia Higginbotham (Dottir Press, 2020)

Duck, Death and the Tulip by Wolf Erlbruch (Gecko Press, 2008)

Finding François by Gus Gordon (Puffin, 2020)

Finn's Feather by Rachel Noble, illustrated by Zoey Abbott (Enchanted Lion Books, 2018)

Fly by Jess McGeachin (Puffin, 2019)

Ida, Always by Caron Levis, illustrated by Charles Santoso (Atheneum, 2016)

Life and I: A story about death by Elisabeth Helland Larsen, illustrated by Marine Schneider (Little Gestalten, 2016)

Life is Like the Wind by Shona Innes, illustrated by Írisz Agócs (Hardie Grant, 2019)

Love Is Forever by Casey Rislov, illustrated by Rachael Balsaitis (Casey Rislov Books, 2013)

Michael Rosen's Sad Book by Michael Rosen, illustrated by Quentin Blake (Walker Books, 2015)

My Big, Dumb, Invisible Dragon by Angie Lucas, illustrated by Birgitta Sif (Sounds True, 2019)

My Brother by Dee Huxley and Tiffany Huxley, illustrated by Oliver Huxley (Working Title Press, 2018)

My Father's Arms Are a Boat by Stein Erik Lunde, illustrated by Øyvind Torseter (Enchanted Lion Books, 2012)

Old Pig by Margaret Wild, illustrated by Ron Brooks (Allen & Unwin, 1995)

Paperboy by Danny Parker, illustrated by Bethany Macdonald (Dirt Lane Press, 2019)

Rabbityness by Jo Empson (Child's Play, 2012)

Shine: A story about saying goodbye by Trace Balla (Allen & Unwin, 2015)

The Gift by Michael Speechley (Puffin, 2019)

The Goodbye Book by Todd Parr (Hachette, 2016)

The Heart and the Bottle by Oliver Jeffers (HarperCollins, 2010)

The Important Things by Peter Carnavas (New Frontier Publishing, 2010)

The Invisible String by Patrice Karst, illustrated by Geoff Stevenson (DeVorss Publications, 2000)

The Memory Tree by Britta Teckentrup (Hachette, 2014)

The Paper Dolls by Julia Donaldson, illustrated by Rebecca Cobb (Pan Macmillan, 2013)

The Present Box by Michelle Jewels-Parsons, illustrated by Ellie Rose Hanham (Michelle Jewels-Parsons, 2019)

The Story of the Sand Man by Glenn Colquhoun (Fiona Hewerdine, 2022)

The Tiny Star by Mem Fox, illustrated by Freya Blackwood (Puffin, 2019)

The Very Best of Friends by Margaret Wild, illustrated by Julia Vivas (Margaret Hamilton, 1989)

The Wattle Tree by John Bell, illustrated by Ben Wood (Hachette, 2012)

Visiting You by Rebecka Sharpe Shelberg and Andrea Edmonds (Exisle Publishing, 2018)

Waiting for Wolf by Sandra Dieckmann (Hachette, 2019)

Yesterday You Were Here by Melissa Little (Wakefield Press, 2018)

You, Me & the Rainbow by Petrea King (Jane Curry Publishing, 2005)

MIDDLE-GRADE AND YOUNG ADULT BOOKS ABOUT GRIEVING

It is important for young people to see their own lives reflected in the books they read, as it helps them to feel less alone in the world. The books in this list provide opportunities to reflect on their grief journey or to develop empathy and understanding for the grief journey of a peer. Books also give young people a space to escape to when the actual world is just too 'noisy'. Books are the quietest of companions ... there when you need comfort, but silent when you need space and solitude. Some of these books are for a mature audience; please consider the maturity level of the intended reader and the themes depicted in each book.

A Monster Calls by Patrick Ness, illustrated by Jim Kay (Walker Books, 2012)

Bailey Finch Takes a Stand by Ingrid Laguna (Text Publishing, 2021)

Blueback by Tim Winton (Penguin, 2009)

Bridge to Terabithia by Katherine Paterson (Puffin, 2005)

Catch a Falling Star by Meg McKinlay (Walker Books, 2019)

Cici's Journal: Lost and Found by Joris Chamblain and Aurélie Neyret (First Second, 2021)

H is for Hawk by Helen Macdonald (Penguin, 2015)

How It Feels to Float by Helena Fox (Pan Macmillan, 2019)

I Heard the Owl Call My Name by Margaret Craven (Picador Classic, 1980)

Leave Taking by Lorraine Marwood (UQP, 2018)

Missing by Sue Whiting (Walker Books, 2018)

One Would Think the Deep by Claire Zorn (UQP, 2016)

The Bird Within Me by Sara Lundberg (Book Island, 2020)

The Elephant by Peter Carnavas (UQP, 2017)

The Fault in Our Stars by John Green (Penguin, 2012)

The Little Wave by Pip Harry (UQP, 2019)

The Messenger Bird by Rosanne Hawke (UQP, 2012)

The Naming of Tishkin Silk by Glenda Millard, illustrated by Caroline Magerl (HarperCollins, 2011)

The Protected by Claire Zorn (UQP, 2014)

The Simple Gift by Steven Herrick (UQP, 2000)

This Is Not a Sad Book (But It's OK to Feel Sad) by Elizabeth Vercoe with Kerry Abromowski, illustrated by Grace Fraraccio (Affirm Press, 2024)

Pie in the Sky by Remy Lai (Walker Books, 2019)

Swashbuckler by James Moloney (UQP, 1995)

CHAPTER FIFTEEN

HOW-TO GUIDES

HOW TO BE AN EXCELLENT BOOK GIFTER

We always give books as gifts for christenings, housewarmings, weddings, kids' parties, new babies, or for any occasion, really. It's become a bit of a joke as we hand over the gift-wrapped book-shaped package. I know that a book is the last thing a three-year-old is going to be excited about at their party, but the parents are usually happy, and the child will be happy later, just not at the party when all they want is shiny new toys.

It's important to choose book gifts with care as the right book will be treasured for many years, even through generations. I have several from my childhood gifted to me by family friends and inscribed that I still hold very dear and will never give away.

We've had many friends comment over the years that they love reading the books we've given to their children. Just the other day a friend sent a message saying they were unpacking a shelf at their new house and noticed that all the books their three children had chosen to keep were from us – I gave myself a mental high five. I often choose books that will appeal to our adult friends as much as to their child: for builder friends I've chosen books with hammers and cubbyhouses; for friends who we spent our youth with at music festivals I gift books written by favourite songwriters; foodie friends get kids' cookbooks or food-focused picture books; and our dentist (and the girls' aunt) often receives books about the tooth fairy or teeth. You wouldn't believe how many books about teeth there are, though I've not yet been game to gift her *Demon Dentist* by David Walliams (illustrated by Tony Ross) just in case she takes offence. No one wants an upset dentist wielding a drill!

The following are some tips for when you are ready for some serious book gifting:

- It is tempting to grab books from the bargain bin, but I urge you to walk past those, unless you see something you know is fabulous and shouldn't be in there to start with. Quality books often cost more, but I can assure you they will be treasured. Work out what you'd spend on a toy for a child and buy one or two beautiful books with that money instead.

- When you find the perfect book gift for an occasion such as a christening or birthday ... buy it in bulk. The year Georgia turned eight I found the perfect set of three books for all parties she attended that year so I purchased ten sets on sale. One of the few times I was organised with presents and, by golly, it felt good! Similarly, I have a particular title that I like to gift for the birth of a first child, *Puffling* by Margaret Wild and illustrated by Julie Vivas. It's a good one for reducing emotional parents to tears and is a total keepsake.

- If you or your child would like to gift something with the book, try and find something in theme. My teen now insists on this because 'I'm so embarrassed that you always give books and so embarrassed that you're a librarian and so embarrassed by ...' She is embarrassed by me in general. We've done lots of packs for five-year-old parties of kids' gardening gloves, glass containers and watering cans with my favourite book on growing terrariums, *Tiny World Terrariums* by Michelle Inciarrano and Katy Maslow.

- Inscribe the books you gift, either with a message that relates to the book and why you gave it to them and/or a personal message. The books I've kept from my own childhood are the ones that are inscribed to me. It's so lovely to see the dates and remember who gave them to us. I also have all my old Miffy books (Dick Bruna) and each has my name written by Mum, with the year it was purchased – such a librarian! Mum still writes in all the books she gives to her grandchildren and they really enjoy 'finding' a book that she has inscribed on their shelves. The first gift that was given to me when I had Ava was the beautiful book previously mentioned, *Puffling*, and I cried. The inscription reads: *One day you'll be big enough, tall enough, strong enough and brave enough to leave your nest and take on the world. But until then your lovely mum and your proud dad will be there for you and will cherish you. We'll be watching. Welcome to the World. The Buckleys.* Okay, I had just had a baby, hadn't slept for about three days and the baby wouldn't stop crying, but I still tear up every time I read this inscription.
- Keep a list. I keep lists in a little notebook of all the books I've given to family members and the children of family friends and some of these lists have been going for ten or so years now. It's super handy to look back so I don't double up on titles.
- Don't go for the obvious. I would rarely gift a classic book or super popular book to a child as they will very likely have it already. Things like *The Very Hungry Caterpillar* (Eric Carle) and *Guess How Much I Love You* (Sam McBratney, illustrated by Anita Jeram) are obvious choices for newborns so I steer well clear of them and go for something just as heartfelt but lesser known.

- Own the 'book aunty/uncle/friend' title with pride. My sister gives money to all the nieces and nephews and the children look forward to this tradition. I'm the book aunt!

HOW TO HOST A BOOK PARTY

I'm a fan of book-themed parties. Aside from the obvious joy of seeing a book come to life, the theming is all done for you thanks to the text and illustrations. Let me take you through the process of creating your very own book-themed party at home, keeping in mind that I am a librarian, not a party planner, and I have no thoughts of a career change anytime soon!

- Select your child's favourite picture book or book series or decide what sort of book party you want and subtly convince your child that it's the best book ever.
- Read the book a number of times and pick out some quotes you could use and some theme ideas based on the illustrations and/or the text. Write a list of any food mentioned in the book and brainstorm what sort of food would go well with the book.
- Decide on a colour theme or over-arching theme and stick with it; don't try to cram every element of the book into a party. Keep it simple, streamlined and cohesive.
- Search online for any teaching notes or worksheets that accompany the book. You'll be surprised how many of your favourite children's books have ready-made ideas for activities and party games. You may even find publisher-produced, copyright-free for personal use images you can use for cupcake toppers, invites and party bags.
- Create invitations for the party using either the cover of the book or any images found on the publisher's website. Issues with

copyright will come about if you commercialise your party or share images of it online, but for a home party the use of the cover to promote the party to friends and family will not cause issues. Similarly, using images found on publisher websites is generally fine if they are for personal use.

- Start the party with a reading of the book and explanation of the themed food and party games.
- Party favours may be a copy of the book, if you can find them at a reasonable price, or copies of any other books which you can source at a low cost. My own children have become quite used to the fact that our party bags are always books. Sometimes I add a lollipop to placate them!

We've hosted many book parties at home and in local parks, and two of my favourites are outlined in a little more detail below, as well as a few others which friends have hosted and are featured on my blog. All of these relate to specific titles but could be adapted to suit other books with similar themes.

Where the Wild Things Are party

This theme was perfect for Georgia's second birthday party because we used to talk about Georgia being a 'wild thing'. Poor thing had terrible reflux as a baby and it wasn't her fault but she did rather yell and roar.

The food and décor for this one was super easy as there is a huge amount of *Where the Wild Things Are* (Maurice Sendak) paraphernalia out there. I found printable cupcake toppers to purchase online, posters and bunting and then went with mustard-yellow as the theme colour. Food was all monster- or jungle-related: chocolate cupcakes with chocolate rocks, chocolate grass and cupcake toppers; chocolate spoons with green and mustard-coloured sprinkles;

homemade sherbet cones filled with green sherbet and green and mustard sprinkles; and a selection of savoury food such as monkey-shaped sandwiches and quiches with jungle palm toppers. The cake was a huge wild chocolate creature with lots of chocolate rocks and jungle leaves.

Activity-wise we did some monster stomping, dancing and statues, pin the tail on the monster, dress-ups for all (lots of monster masks and wigs) and a treasure hunt. *Where the Wild Things Are* badges, stickers and tattoos plus a gift edition copy of the actual book made up the party favours for this great family celebration.

Stomping dinosaur party

At three, Georgia was still cranky, wild and now stomping, and had developed a dinosaur obsession. Her favourite book at the time was one my mother gave her about a little boy who accidentally grows dinosaurs in his garden. It is a very long picture book and Georgia wanted it every night for over a year!

We went with a purple, green and yellow theme for this party as these were the predominant colours in the book, and who doesn't love clashing colours? Partygoers dug for dinosaur fossils in sand, made little dinosaur gardens to take home (in small terracotta pots with succulents and a plastic dinosaur), collaged dinosaurs, painted mud dinosaurs (from another favourite dinosaur book) and danced to dinosaur stomp songs.

The food included sandwiches cut with a dinosaur cookie cutter, dinosaur fossil biscuits, cupcake liners filled with fruit and topped with dinosaur toppers, dino egg scones, cake pops covered in chocolate sand, dinosaur-topped cupcakes and a volcano and dinosaur cake. Party favours were bags with flower seeds to 'grow your own dinosaurs' as in the book.

Other parties we have held were themed on the following books:

- Alice in Wonderland series by Lewis Carroll (Puffin)
- *Little Blue* by Gaye Chapman (Little Hare, 2008)
- Miffy series by Dick Bruna (Hardie Grant)
- Pearlie in the Park series by Wendy Harmer, illustrated by Mike Zarb and Gypsy Taylor (Random House)
- Samurai vs Ninja series by Nick Falk, illustrated by Tony Flowers (Random House)
- *The Complete Book of the Flower Fairies* by Cicely Mary Barker (Warne, 2002)
- *The Fairy Dancers* by Natalie Jane Prior, illustrated by Cheryl Orsini (HarperCollins, 2015)
- Thelma the Unicorn series by Aaron Blabey (Scholastic)
- *Truly Tan* by Jen Storer, illustrated by Claire Robertson (HarperCollins, 2012)

HOW TO CREATE A CHILDREN'S BOOK WEEK COSTUME

I am a Children's Book Week tragic from way back. I have vivid childhood memories of planning my Book Week costumes with my mum. I know some people dread the planning of the Book Week costumes so hopefully this how-to will take away some of the pain and swap it with some fun.

There are a wealth of ideas online for book character dress-ups so there is no need for me to re-create such a list here. Instead I'm adding some ideas into the mix for creating meaningful costumes that can help bring the book to life and allow your child to really step into the shoes of their favourite character.

I always let my children choose their own Book Week characters, within reason – I'm not doing a dragon costume anytime soon! On the whole I find that most children choose characters who look a little like them because they connect with books which reflect their own life. Their costume may then be as simple as them wearing casual clothes in the style of their favourite character and deciding on a motif or element from the book to add to their outfit. One year Ava went as Pippa from Belinda Murrell's *Pippa's Island: The Beach Shack Cafe* and wore shorts and a T-shirt. The book is set on a tropical island and has lots of talk of cupcakes so we added skewers with images of pineapples and cupcakes and a thumbnail of the book cover to her hair bun along with a stack of fake tropical flowers. When these skewers were poked into her hair (those bun doughnut things are like florist foam, I've discovered!), she was instantly transformed into Pippa. Adding those little extra elements that reflect the book is what takes a costume from 'pulled this out of my drawer this morning' to innovative and an expression of the child's love for a book or character.

If the costume doesn't make it obvious who the book character is, I always encourage my children and students to either carry the book with them or make a book cover lanyard to wear around their neck to identify which book they are from. Such a simple addition to a costume but it really does allow everyone to get into the spirit and, as an added bonus, seeing all those book covers around the schoolyard is perfect advertising for what you should read next.

If possible, allow plenty of time to prepare a Book Week costume – perhaps do as I say, not as I do. Lately my costumes are a bit 'on the fly', but in previous years I have taken note through the year of favourite books in our house and start talking about 'who we'll be' months before Children's Book Week. In über-organised years I've set up the chosen book on a shelf and we'll talk about the character and what clothing items best represent them and add elements from home. Anything we need to buy to add to the costume we can then source in plenty of time.

Use what you have at home. From a young age my children have adored dress-ups and I've added to their box over the years so that we now have quite the collection. This comes in handy for Book Week each year, but costumes aren't the only thing you can use. I love seeing netball and soccer uniforms on show and one year I had about eight girls all come in netball uniforms as characters from the Netball Gems series (Lisa Gibbs and Bernadette Hellard). This actually led to a borrowing spree of these books, which is entirely the outcome we librarians want from the Children's Book Week dress-up day! We don't organise the Book Week parade to torture parents, caregivers and teachers – we actually use it as promotion and celebration of books!

Simple is good. Some of the cutest costumes I see are so simple and every year I think, *I must remember that idea for next year.* One year a girl came as the cutest little cat from *The Tales of Mrs Mancini* by Natalie Jane Prior (illustrated by Cheryl Orsini) – she wore all black and had a cat ear headband with a nose and whiskers drawn on her face. She was carrying her *Mrs Mancini* book proudly throughout the parade and was completely in character. Another lovely one was a child dressed up as *Audrey of the Outback* from the book by Christine Harris (illustrated by Ann James), wearing plain clothes but carrying a billycan with a photocopy of the cover stuck to the outside.

Educator costumes

I talk all the time about reading role models, and Children's Book Week is one of those times in the school year where I hope that all teachers, support staff, grounds staff and classroom volunteers try to up the reading ante: to bring books to life and celebrate them and demonstrate that you believe in the power of words and reading. Dressing up for Book Week shows students that you care about books and you have favourite characters too. It can be as easy or as complex as you like, but I urge all school staff to make the effort.

When I was a young classroom teacher, I would spend months planning my Children's Book Week costumes and they became more elaborate each year. As the full weight of just what it meant to be a teacher became clear, the days of going to 90s raves and music festivals in all my tulle/coloured-hair glory disappeared and instead I channelled my love of OTT outfits into my Children's Book Week costumes. Early in my career I went as the White Witch from Narnia and my costume consisted of a very large white ballgown, a very tall crown, which had to be pinned to my head, and a lot of silver glitter on my face, neck and arms. I had a rather long drive to school and my car decided this was the day it would break down, on the side of a busy highway at peak hour. I have never really recovered from this.

Now of an age where too much glitter isn't going to work for me, I've toned down my costumes accordingly. But I still love a good Children's Book Week outfit and there are plenty of simple options for teachers. Morrigan Crow, Jupiter North and Dulcinea Dearborn from the Nevermoor series are popular choices each year. A Mary Poppins costume can be as easy as a fitted white shirt, red bow tie, black skirt and an umbrella; although one year a science staff member made herself the most gorgeous Mary Poppins outfit and I'm certain it inspired some children to hunt down a copy of this book from the library. If you're looking for a group costume, the crayons from *The Day the Crayons Quit* by Drew Daywalt (illustrated by Oliver Jeffers) is a great choice, especially for early childhood educators. I also love seeing schools of teachers dressed as Rainbow Fish (Marcus Pfister). Another fun idea is to be playful with your role at the school – for example, one year all the music department staff came as the musicians from *The Flying Orchestra* by Clare McFadden. Another highlight was when our principal came as Enid Blyton's beloved character Elizabeth Allen from *The Naughtiest Girl in the School* – the students thought it was hilarious!

HOW TO RUN A READERS COMPETITION

For anyone who would like to set up a readers competition or become more involved in an existing one, I highly recommend a Readers Cup or Story Sport–style competition.

The books

Organise multiple copies of the books to be used in the competition considering a range of genres, subject matter and reading abilities. Ensure a mix of male and female characters and authors. Often books you have used for set novels in the past and have multiple copies of are useful for a Readers Cup competition, as are sets of novels purchased as classroom readers. You will need to ensure you can either borrow copies from local schools or public libraries in your area or that the book is in print and easily accessible for families.

Introducing the competition to students

- Arrange class visits or promote the competition during library borrowing times or lunchtimes, or whatever has been agreed.
- Prepare posters (online or paper versions) listing the books to be read, the rules and the dates and times of all heats.
- Select sections to read from some of the books and promote the titles.
- Collect entry forms for teams of four.

Preparing the competition

- Write enough questions for each book (usually four to six per book). Prepare extra questions to cater for the possibility of a tie in the final. Share the reading load with other teachers/teacher librarians. Questions are knowledge-based rather than asking students to philosophise over a particular title.
- We prep approximately thirty general literature questions for audience/parent participation between each student round.
- For several years we have also prepared a 'creative challenge' to include some making in the competition and ensure that all types of learners are catered for. These have included designing a new cover for a book and presenting teams with a 'mystery bag' of materials to design and make something significant from one of the books.
- Prepare a timetable for the heats and the final and publicise this to staff and students.
- We have been using an online quiz tool, Kahoot!, for the past few years in order to blend some technology into our competition. All questions are entered into Kahoot! before the event so that students work in team mode to answer questions about the books. This allows us to use visuals or videos uploaded into the program and adds a different element.
- Organise prizes (decide early on how they will be paid for):
    - First prize – cup/medal for each team member (plus, if funds permit, book voucher/book)
    - Second prize – book voucher/book
    - Third prize – book voucher/book
    - Prizes for participation in the heats – lollies/bookmarks

The format of the competition

- Participants read the selected books in advance.
- Teams of four are usually seated at tables, and may have decorated their table with their team name and/or mascot. They may or may not have a team uniform or costume.
- There is one round of questions for each book, to be asked by an MC (teacher, teacher librarian or guest author).
- After each question is asked by the MC, students are given thirty seconds to one minute to confer as a group and complete their written answer.
- Answers are usually collected at the end of each round and a group of scorers mark them with points given for correct answers, usually two points for a correct answer and part points for an incomplete answer. The MC may give progressive scores, which helps to increase the hysteria, fun, competition and noise factor.
- The team with the highest score wins trophies and books and advances to the next level of the competition, after much cheering and happy crying and screaming!

HOW TO START A BOOK CLUB

Book clubs for children can help with confidence and public speaking, as well as encourage them to read for both pleasure and study. It also affords children the opportunity to discuss and recommend their favourite books, genres and authors with like-minded peers.

A child/tween/teen book club may be purely for recreational reading or it may have a specific goal, such as to engage reluctant readers, extend gifted and talented students, encourage reading amongst EALD students or help young people in their reading transition from primary to high school.

My own Year Six Girl Zone Book Club (for girls and a significant woman in their lives) was for this purpose. Book clubs build literary knowledge and skills and they also create memories and positive reading experiences.

The essentials

A designated meeting space. In the past I have rotated meetings through homes, but the emphasis can become the home itself, rather than the reading! Peers will want to explore each other's rooms and adults want to exchange tips for keeping that houseplant alive, which loses the focus. Some families can find it stressful to entertain and cater when it is their turn to host.

With my own book club I have well and truly gone back to 'we meet in the school library twice per term at 6.30 pm'. This established routine and known location seems to take away one of the barriers to maintaining the book club.

Members. Clearly you can't have a book club of one, no matter how specific your reading tastes are. A book club is all about encouraging a social and shared experience around reading. We co-create meaning from books as we read together and listen to the opinions and thoughts of others. I do highly recommend book clubs with members of a similar age, reading level or interest such as a Nevermoor book club (reading books by Jessica Townsend and then books in a similar style) or a food-themed book club, where young members share favourite recipes, recipe books and food-themed novels. The best way to gather book club members is to clearly advertise your book club, either at school if you're a teacher wanting to start a book club, or via a customer database if you work at a bookstore, or among peers and family friends if you are a parent hoping to start one for your children.

Books to read and ponder. A book club is not a book club without books. You have a few options here:

- Read the same book and discuss it as a group.
- Read different books based around a theme or by the same author and compare and contrast. Share titles at your meeting.
- Bring along whichever books you are reading to recommend and share with your peers.
- Put together a collection of books to be read over the year and share these among members, to be read at their leisure.
- Consider a 'first reader' book club if you are in a school library. All newly ordered books go first to book club members who read and review them.

In my Year Six Girl Zone Book Club we read two books and met twice per term. I chose two to five books to 'book talk' about each meeting and we voted on which books we would read as a group. Except when I decided that book club is not a democracy and I INSISTED that all members read a particular book because it was SO GOOD and I wanted them to read it and agree with me on how great it is. Occasionally this strategy backfired, so I try to stick with the democratic process.

Some literary guidance. For each Girl Zone Book Club I prepare a list of questions based on the book we have just read. These are a guide only and not all have to be answered. I create these questions on sticky notes as I read the book myself and I often also consult any teachers' notes (found online) for further ideas. For me these questions should be open-ended and invite discussion, debate and deep thinking. This is not a comprehension test for an English class; this is mature discussion about literature and should help members to develop their own language around books. I like my questions to guide members to think about how the book connects with their own experience – maybe they see their life reflected in the pages or maybe they feel the book helped them to develop empathy or understanding of a particular topic.

If teachers' notes, author interviews or reviews can be found, I will often send these to book club members before a meeting or print copies for the meeting. I usually find that this 'support material' greatly extends the discussion of a book.

A format for meetings. It's really important to think this through properly. What are your aims? Who is the book club for? You may decide that you want formal and in-depth discussion at your meetings or you may prefer casual chats and an informal vibe.

My format is always the same – each person brings a small plate of food to share and I provide tea and coffee. We start with some food and drinks before we move into our discussion time. My book club has between twenty to forty attendees each meeting so we split into groups of about six. For about half an hour each group discusses the books using the prepared literary questions as a guide, and then reports back to the main group and we chat as a whole. I then talk about title choices for our next read, we vote, chat, eat some more and go home for a bit of bedtime reading.

Some years I have included a hands-on activity as part of the meeting, especially when a book has lent itself naturally to this.

I like to allow ten to fifteen minutes towards the end of the meeting for students to share other books they have enjoyed. I ask them to bring the book along to the meeting as well as a summary of the story and two reasons why they are recommending it.

A code of conduct. This helps to keep members on track and if you are a teacher running a book club it helps to put responsibility into the hands of the students, allowing you to be more a facilitator than teacher. Book club meetings are different to teaching an English lesson and you don't want to be standing up the front running things. At the first meeting of the year I always explain the way an adult book club works to the students. We discuss listening to each other, respecting the opinions of others and ensuring there is a balance of students and adults talking and sharing with the group. I also talk about expectations between book club meetings – that everyone will make a concerted effort to read the book in the set time-frame but that you are still very welcome to come along even if you have not finished it. Setting up a code of conduct adds to the feeling of ownership for all members.

The extras. I have been running book clubs for many years now and mostly I keep the format simple, but each year I always organise an end-of-year outing for the members. We visit a local independent bookstore where the owner gives a talk, over wine (and juice!) and cheese, about her favourite books for the age group, plus some for the adults in the audience. We then shop for Christmas presents or holiday reading material, then wander to a local restaurant for a shared meal.

Some years I have been fortunate to be able to invite an author to book club. A few years ago Kate DiCamillo happened to be in Brisbane and her publisher offered to bring her along to our meeting as we were reading her wonderful novel *Raymie Nightingale*. After I picked my jaw up off the ground at being offered a visit from one of the celebrities of children's literature, I tried to write a sensible 'thank you and YES' email reply with not too many over-excited exclamation marks.

Kate DiCamillo was everything I imagined: delightful, funny, humble, warm (so warm!), kind and so very interesting. Her book club visit remains a career highlight for me. Visits of this ilk are not a regular occurrence but every so often an author comes to talk to the book club and it always adds a level of excitement and wonder to the event.

HOW TO HOST AN AUTHOR OR ILLUSTRATOR VISIT

If you follow these tips you'll ensure that when an author or illustrator leaves your school you will have inspired students and staff who are ready to continue some deep and meaningful work. Plus a speaker who walks away telling others about the amazing kids they met and the dedicated educators who go above and beyond to ignite a passion for story in their students.

- Seek funding from your school P&C or other source by writing or speaking about the many benefits of author or illustrator visits as outlined in pages 115–117.
- Consult with your local speakers agency about the best author or illustrator for your school and whether the format will be a talk or workshop.
- Gather and read many or all of the author's or illustrator's books before their visit and ensure students and staff have read them too. There is very little point in an author or illustrator visit if the students and staff have no idea at all who the speaker is as the entire session is merely spent getting to know them rather than deeply engaging with their work.
- Complete some work ahead of the visit. For example, classes may explore the style and medium that an illustrator uses and create their own pictures using these techniques or they may write compositions based on the text. Most publisher websites will have teaching ideas for particular titles and some will even have extensive curriculum-related teaching notes which have been specifically created for schools.

- Discuss with students what the author may talk about. Brainstorm some rich questions and talk about manners – is it polite or helpful to ask someone how much they earn, how old they are or why they have a bald head? Discuss also the difference between a question and a comment – does the speaker really need to know that you had a banana smoothie for breakfast and the quinoa flakes your mum added made your mouth feel gluggy? (Yes, that was an actual comment I heard once at a literature festival.)
- Create posters or banners to showcase student work and welcome authors or illustrators to the school community.
- Distribute the timetable of the day's proceedings to the school community and to the speaker so they are aware of which age groups they are talking to and how many students will be in each group.
- Organise a local bookseller to sell books on the day and preferably send home an order form in the week before the visit.
- Organise students to introduce the speaker and welcome them, and students to thank them at the conclusion of the talk. We often ask student leaders to take notes throughout the workshop and at the end share their thoughts on what the class might take away from the visit.
- Check dietary requirements and plan meal breaks and a time to sign books if needed.
- Have your camera or phone on hand to take photographs of the speaker. I use these for writing about the event in the school newsletter or on social media, with permission.

ENDNOTES

Chapter 1

1 Justice, L. (2006), 'Evidence-based practice, response to intervention, and the prevention of reading difficulties', *Language, Speech, and Hearing Services in Schools*, 37(4), pp. 284–297.

2 Smith, L. & Gasser, M. (2005), 'The development of embodied cognition: six lessons from babies', *Artificial Life*, 11, pp. 13–29.

3 Noble, C., Cameron-Faulkner, T. & Lieven, E. (2018), 'Keeping it simple: the grammatical properties of shared book reading', *Journal of Child Language*, 45(3), pp. 753–766. Retrieved from: https://doi.org/10.1017/S0305000917000447.

Hoff-Ginsberg, E. (1991), 'Mother-child conversation in different social classes and communicative settings', *Child Development*, 62(4), pp. 782–796. Retrieved from: https://doi.org/10.2307/1131177.

4 Fletcher, K. L. & Reese, E. (2005), 'Picture book reading with young children: a conceptual framework', *Developmental Review*, 25(1), pp. 64–103. Retrieved from: http://doi.org/10.1016/j.dr.2004.08.009.

5 Flewitt, R., Kucirkova, N. & Messer, D. (2014), 'Touching the virtual, touching the real: iPads and enabling literacy for students experiencing disability', *Australian Journal of Language and Literacy*, 37(2), pp. 107–116.

6 Smith, L. & Gasser, M.,'The development of embodied cognition'.

7 Lee, B. (2017), 'Facilitating reading habits and creating peer culture in shared book reading: an exploratory case study in a toddler classroom', *Early Childhood Education Journal*, 45(4), pp. 521–527. Retrieved from: https://doi.org/10.1007/s10643-016-0782-1.

8 *ibid.*

9 Cuskelly, J. (2011), 'A case study using Kodály principles in a language immersion setting', *Australian Kodály Journal*, pp. 22–26.

10 Flint, T. K. & Adams, M. S. (2018), '"It's like playing, but learning": supporting early literacy through responsive play with wordless picture books', *Language*

Arts, 96(1), pp. 21–35. Retrieved from: https://www.jstor.org/stable/26779030.

Flint, T. K. (2018), 'Responsive play: creating transformative classroom spaces through play as a reader response', *Journal of Early Childhood Literacy*, 20(2), 385–410. Retrieved from: https://doi.org/10.1177/1468798418763991.

Evans, J. (2012), '"This is me": developing literacy and a sense of self through play, talk and stories', *Education 3–13: International Journal of Primary, Elementary and Early Years Education*, 40(3), pp. 315–331.

Mantei, J. & Kervin, L. (2015), 'Examining the interpretations children share from their reading of an almost wordless picture book during independent reading time', *Australian Journal of Language and Literacy*, 38(3), pp. 183–192.

Chapter 2

1 Castles, A., Rastle, K. & Nation, K. (2018), 'Ending the reading wars: reading acquisition from novice to expert', *Psychological Science in the Public Interest*, 19(1), pp. 5–51. Retrieved from: https://doi.org/10.1177/1529100618772271.

Department of Education (2023), 'Effective teaching of reading: an overview of the literature', Department of Education, Queensland Government. Retrieved from: https://education.qld.gov.au/curriculums/Documents/literature-review.pdf.

2 UNESCO (2000), 'Education for all: meeting our collective commitments; expanded commentary on the Dakar Framework for Action', UNESCO. Retrieved from: https://unesdoc.unesco.org/ark:/48223/pf0000120240.

3 Snow, P. C. (2020), 'SOLAR: The science of language and reading', *Child Language Teaching and Therapy*, 37(3), pp. 222–233. Retrieved from: https://doi.org/10.1177/0265659020947817.

Hempenstall, K. (2013), 'What is the place for national assessment in the prevention and resolution of reading difficulties?', *Australian Journal of Learning Difficulties*, 18(2), pp. 105–121.

4 Department of Education, 'Effective teaching of reading'.

5 Australian Education Research Organisation (2023), 'Introduction to the science of reading', Australian Education Research Organisation, Melbourne. Retrieved from: https://www.edresearch.edu.au/summaries-explainers/explainers/introduction-science-reading.

6 Scarborough, H. S. (2001), 'Connecting early language and literacy to later reading (dis)abilities: Evidence, theory, and practice' in Neuman, S. & Dickinson, D. (Eds), *Handbook of Early Literacy Research*, Guildford Press, New York, pp. 97–110.

Kinnane, D. (2022), 'Children with rich and educated parents have an unfair advantage when it comes to early language development', Banter Speech & Language. Retrieved from: https://www.banterspeech.com.au/children-with-rich-and-educated-parents-have-an-unfair-advantage-when-it-comes-to-early-language-development/.

Di Sante, M. & Potvin, L. (2022), 'We need to talk about social inequalities in language development', *American Journal of Speech-Language Pathology*, 31(4), pp. 1894–1897. Retrieved from: https://doi.org/10.1044/2022_ajslp-21-00326.

7 Cox, R., Feez, S. & Beveridge, L. (Eds) (2019), *The Alphabetic Principle and Beyond: Surveying the landscape*, Primary English Teaching Association Australia (PETAA).

Buckingham, J. (2020), 'Systematic phonics instruction belongs in evidence-based reading programs: a response to Bowers', *Educational and Developmental Psychologist*, 37(2), pp. 105–113. Retrieved from: https://doi.org/10.1017/edp.2020.12.

Swain, N. (2024), *Harnessing the Science of Learning: Success stories to help kickstart your school improvement*, Routledge.

Primary English Teaching Association Australia (PETAA) Position (2024). Retrieved from: https://petaa.edu.au/w/About/PETAA_Position.aspx.

Snow, P. C. (2021), 'SOLAR: The science of language and reading'.

8 Farrar, J. & Simpson, A. (2024), 'Pre-service teacher knowledge of children's literature and attitudes to Reading for Pleasure: an international comparative study', *Literacy*, 58(2), pp. 216–227. Retrieved from: https://doi.org/10.1111/lit.12360.

9 Smith, R., Snow, P., Serry, T. & Hammond, L. (2021), 'The role of background knowledge in reading comprehension: a critical review', *Reading Psychology*, 42(3), pp. 214–240. Retrieved from: https://doi.org/10.1080/02702711.2021.1888348.

10 *ibid.*

11 Severs, J. (2020), 'Why learning should not be led by a child: child-led learning simply does not work, argues Professor David C Geary', *Tes Magazine*. Retrieved from: https://www.tes.com/magazine/archive/why-learning-should-not-be-led-child.

12 Dehaene, S. (2019), *Reading in the Brain: The new science of how we read*, Penguin.

13 Severs, J., 'Why learning should not be led by a child'.

14 Shanahan, T. (2006), 'Relations among oral language, reading, and writing development', in MacArthur, C., Graham S. & Fitzgerald J. (Eds), *Handbook of Writing Research*, Guildford Press, pp. 171–183.

15 Ehri, L. C. (2022), 'What teachers need to know and do to teach letter–sounds, phonemic awareness, word reading, and phonics', *The Reading Teacher*, 76(1), pp. 53–61. Retrieved from: https://doi.org/10.1002/trtr.2095.

16 Dehaene, S., *Reading in the Brain*.

Chapter 3

1 Merga, M. K. (2021), 'Libraries as wellbeing supportive spaces in contemporary schools', *Journal of Library Administration*, 61(6), pp. 659–675. Retrieved from: https://doi.org/10.1080/01930826.2021.1947056.

Ivey, G. (2014), 'The social side of engaged reading for young adolescents', *The Reading Teacher*, 68(3), pp. 165–171. Retrieved from: https://doi.org/10.1002/trtr.1268.

2 American Library Association (2013), 'A history of making'. Retrieved from: http://americanlibrariesmagazine.org/features/02062013/manufacturing-makerspaces.

3 Slatter, D. & Zaana, H. (2013), 'A place to make, hack, and learn: makerspaces in Australian public libraries', *The Australian Library Journal*, 62(4), pp. 272–284. Retrieved from: https://doi.org/10.1080/00049670.2013.853335.

4 Colegrove, T. (2013), 'Editorial board thoughts: libraries as makerspace?' *Information Technology and Libraries*, 32(1), pp. 2–5.

Chapter 4

1 Lopatovska, I., Carcamo, T., Dease, N., Jonas, E., Kot, S., Pamperien, G., Volpe, A. & Yalcin, K. (2018), 'Not just a pretty picture part two: testing a visual literacy program for young children', *Journal of Documentation*, 74(3), pp. 588–607.

Hattwig, D., Burgess, J., Bussert, K. & Medaille, A. (2011), 'ACRL visual literacy competency standards for higher education', Association of College & Research Libraries. Retrieved from: www.ala.org/acrl/standards/visualliteracy.

2 Lukehart, W. (2011), 'Wordless books: picture perfect', *School Library Journal*, 57(4), pp. 50–54.

Serafini, F. (2014), 'Exploring wordless picture books', *The Reading Teacher*, 68(1), pp. 24–26.

3 Greenhoot, A., Beyer, A. & Curtis, J. (2014), 'More than pretty pictures?

How illustrations affect parent-child story reading and children's story recall', *Frontiers in Psychology*, 5. Retrieved from: https://doi.org/10.3389/fpsyg.2014.00738.

4 Fichner-Rathus, L. (2008), *Foundations of Art and Design*, Wadsworth.

Chapter 5

1 Freeman, G. (2007), 'Reinventing the library' in Kresh, D. (Ed.), *The Whole Digital Library Handbook*, American Library Association, Chicago, pp. 370–374.

2 Lackney, J. (2007), '33 Educational design principles for schools and community learning centers', School Design Studio. Retrieved from: http://schoolstudio.typepad.com/school_design_studio/33-educational-design-pri.html.

3 Groundwater-Smith, S. (2004), 'Transforming learning: transforming places and space for learning', CEFPI Conference: Faculty design and learning: has the paradigm changed?, Conservatorium of Music, Sydney.

Chapter 6

1 Horbec, D. (2012), 'The link between reading and academic success', *English in Australia*, 47(2), pp. 58–67.

Hiebert, E. H., Wilson, K. M. & Trainin, G. (2010), 'Are students really reading in independent reading contexts? An examination of comprehension-based silent reading rate', in Hiebert, E. H. & Reutzel, D. R. (Eds), *Revisiting Silent Reading: New directions for teachers and researchers*, International Reading Association, Newark, DE, pp. 151–167.

Larson, L. C. (2015), 'E-Books and audiobooks: extending the digital reading experience', *The Reading Teacher*, 69(2), pp. 169–177.

National Endowment for the Arts (2007), *To Read or Not to Read: A question of national consequence* report, National Endowment for the Arts, Washington, DC. Retrieved from: https://www.arts.gov/sites/default/files/ToRead.pdf.

2 Horbec, D., 'The link between reading and academic success'.

3 Shanahan, T. (2006), 'Relations among oral language, reading, and writing development', in MacArthur, C., Graham, S. & Fitzgerald, J. (Eds), *Handbook of Writing Research*, Guildford Press, New York, pp. 171–183.

Sedita, J. (2022), *The Writing Rope: A framework for explicit writing instruction in all subjects*, Brookes Publishing.

Chapter 7

1 Rutherford, L., Singleton, A., Reddan, B., Johanson, K. & Dezuanni, M. (2024), *Discovering a Good Read: Exploring book discovery and reading for pleasure among Australian teens*, Deakin University, Geelong.

2 Centre for Youth Literature (2009), *Keeping Young Australians Reading* report, State Library of Victoria.

3 Newman, N. (2017), 'What is middle-grade fiction and should you write it?', *Australian Writers' Centre* (blog). Retrieved from: https://www.writerscentre.com.au/blog/what-is-middle-grade-fiction/.

Chapter 8

1 Moynihan, K. E. (2009), 'Local authors in the classroom: bringing readers and writers together', *The English Journal*, 98(3), pp. 34–38.

2 DeFauw, D. L. (2018), 'One school's yearlong collaboration with a children's book author', *The Reading Teacher*, 72(3), pp. 355–367. Retrieved from: https://doi.org/10.1002/trtr.1726.

Chapter 10

1 Kalantzis, M., Cope, B., Chan, E. & Dalley-Trim, L. (2016), *Literacies*, Cambridge University Press, Port Melbourne, Australia.

Pahl, K. & Rowsell, J. (2005), *Literacy and Education: understanding the new literacy studies in the classroom*, Paul Chapman Publishing, London.

Bock, M., Pachler, N. & Kress, G. (2013), *Multimodality and Social Semiosis Communication, Meaning-making and Learning in the work of Gunther Kress*, Routledge, New York.

2 Larson, L. C. (2015), 'E-Books and audiobooks: extending the digital reading experience', *The Reading Teacher*, 69(2), pp. 169–177.

Moyer, J. (2011), '"Teens today don't read books anymore": a study of differences in interest and comprehension in multiple modalities', in *Proceedings of the 2011 iConference*, pp. 815–816. Retrieved from: https://doi.org/10.1145/1940761.1940918.

Lysenko, L. & Abrami, P. (2014), 'Promoting reading comprehension with the use of technology', *Computers & Education*, 75, pp. 162–172. Retrieved from: https://doi.org/10.1016/j.compedu.2014.01.010.

3 Grover, S. & Hannegan, L. D. (2012), *Listening to Learn: Audiobooks supporting literacy*, American Library Association, Chicago, IL.

4 Gander, L. (2013), 'Audiobooks: the greatest asset in the library', *Library Media Connection*, 31(4), p. 48.

Chapter 12

1 Jha, A. P., Krompinger, J. & Baime, M. J. (2007), 'Mindfulness training modifies subsystems of attention', *Cognitive, Affective, & Behavioral Neuroscience*, 7(2), pp. 109–119. Retrieved from: https://doi.org/10.3758/CABN.7.2.109.

Zylowska, L., Ackerman, D. L., Yang, M. H., Futrell, J. L., Horton, N. L., Hale, T. S., et al. (2007), 'Mindfulness meditation training in adults and adolescents with ADHD: a feasibility study', *Journal of Attention Disorders*, 11(6), pp. 737–746. Retrieved from: https://doi.org/10.1177/1087054707308502.

Hodgins, H. S. & Adair, K. C. (2010), 'Attentional processes and meditation', *Consciousness and Cognition*, 19(4), pp. 872–878. Retrieved from: http://doi.org/10.1016/j.concog.2010.04.002.

Tarrasch, R., Berman, Z. & Friedmann, N. (2016), 'Mindful reading: mindfulness meditation helps keep readers with dyslexia or ADHD on the lexical track', *Frontiers in Psychology*, 7(May), p. 578. Retrieved from: https://doi.org/10.3389/fpsyg.2016.00578.

2 *ibid.*

3 Australian Curriculum, Assessment and Reporting Authority (ACARA) (2022), 'The Australian Curriculum'. Retrieved from: https://www.acara.edu.au/curriculum.

Chapter 13

1 Australia Council for the Arts (2007), *Protocols for Producing Indigenous Australian Writing*. Retrieved from: https://creative.gov.au/first-nations-arts/protocols-for-using-first-nations-cultural-and-intellectual-property-in-the-arts.

Harrison, J. interviewed by Adeney, A. (2017), 'Question your motives', Writers Victoria. Retrieved from: https://writersvictoria.org.au/writing-life/.

2 Heiss, A. (2014), 'Writing Indigenous characters: an interview', *Anita Heiss* (blog). Retrieved from: https://anitaheiss.wordpress.com/2014/11/14/writing-indigenous-characters-an-interview/.

3 BlackWords. https://www.austlit.edu.au/BlackWords.

Atkinson, M. (2017), 'Read, listen, understand: why non-Indigenous Australians should read First Nations writing', *The Conversation*. Retrieved from: http://theconversation.com/read-listen-understand-why-non-indigenous-australians-should-read-first-nations-writing-78925.

Tan, M. (2016), 'Indigenous writer Bruce Pascoe: "We need novels that are true to the land"', *The Guardian*. Retrieved from: https://www.theguardian.com/books/2016/feb/18/indigenous-writer-bruce-pascoe-on-why-australias-literary-giants-have-failed.

Sheldon-Collins, D. (2014), '"Getting it right": Anita Heiss on Indigenous characters', The Wheeler Centre. Retrieved from: https://www.wheelercentre.com/news-stories/2014/getting-it-right-anita-heiss-on-indigenous-characters.

4 Birch, T. interviewed by McLaren, M. (2015), 'Approaching Indigenous characters and culture', Writers Victoria. Retrieved from: https://writersvictoria.org.au/writing-life/.

Roger, M. (2016), 'Taking control of our stories', Writers Victoria. Retrieved from: https://writersvictoria.org.au/category/writing-life/featured-writers/.

5 Heiss, A. (2016), '20 reasons you should read Blak', *Anita Heiss* (blog). Retrieved from: https://anitaheiss.wordpress.com/2016/02/21/20-reasons-you-should-read-blak/.

Heiss, A. (2011), 'Anita's Black Book Challenge (BBC)', *Anita Heiss* (blog). Retrieved from: https://anitaheiss.wordpress.com/2011/04/23/anitas-black-book-challenge-bbc/.

6 World Health Organization, *Disability*. Retrieved from: www.who.int/health-topics/disability.

7 Australian Bureau of Statistics (2024) 'Disability, ageing and carers, Australia: summary of findings'. Retrieved from: https://www.abs.gov.au/statistics/health/disability/disability-ageing-and-carers-australia-summary-findings/latest-release.

8 Australian Institute of Health and Welfare (2019), 'People with disability in Australia 2019: in brief'. Retrieved from: https://www.aihw.gov.au/reports/disability/people-with-disability-in-australia-in-brief/contents/how-many-people-have-disability.

9 Cooperative Children's Book Center (2020), 'The numbers are in: 2019 CCBC diversity statistics', University of Wisconsin-Madison. Retrieved from: https://ccbc.education.wisc.edu/the-numbers-are-in-2019-ccbc-diversity-statistics/.

10 Maclean, M. J., et al, (2017), 'Maltreatment risk among children with disabilities', *American Academy of Pediatrics*, 139(4). Retrieved from: https://doi.org/10.1542/peds.2016-1817.

11 Purkiss, A. (2019), 'The ethical responsibility of representing disability in children's literature', *The Sociological Review*. Retrieved from: https://thesociologicalreview.org/collections/politics-of-representation/the-ethical-responsibility-of-representing-disability-in-childrens-literature/.

12 BookTrust (2022), 'Representation of people of colour among children's book creators in the UK'. Retrieved from: https://www.booktrust.org.uk/resources/find-resources/representation-of-people-of-colour-among-childrens-book-creators-in-the-uk/.

13 Adam, H. (2021), *Transforming Practice: Transforming lives through diverse children's literature*, Primary English Teaching Association Australia (PETAA), Sydney.

14 Bishop, R. S. (1990), 'Mirrors, windows, and sliding glass doors' in Moir, H., Cain, M. & Prosak-Beres, L. (Eds), *Collected Perspectives: Choosing and using books for the classroom*, Christoper-Gordon Publishers.

15 Harper, L. (2016), 'Preschool through primary grades: using picture books to promote social-emotional literacy', *YC Young Children*, 71(3), pp. 80–86.

Wee, S. J., Kim, S. J., Chung, K. & Kim, M. (2021), 'Development of children's perspective-taking and empathy through bullying-themed books and role-playing', *Journal of Research in Childhood Education*, 36(1), pp. 96–111. Retrieved from: https://doi.org/10.1080/02568543.2020.1864523.

Koopman, E. & Hakemulder, F. (2015), 'Effects of literature on empathy and self-reflection: a theoretical-empirical framework', *Journal of Literary Theory*, 9(1), pp. 79–111. Retrieved from: https://doi.org/10.1515/jlt-2015-0005.

Pearson, R. M. & Pillow, B. H. (2016), 'Mother–child conversation and children's social understanding during middle childhood', *The Journal of Genetic Psychology*, 177(4), pp. 103–121.

Tamir, D., Bricker, A., Dodell-Feder, D. & Mitchell, J. (2016), 'Reading fiction and reading minds: the role of simulation in the default network', *Social Cognitive and Affective Neuroscience*, 11(2), pp. 215–224. Retrieved from: https://doi.org/10.1093/scan/nsv114.

Wild, N. R. (2023), 'Picturebooks for social justice: creating a classroom community grounded in identity, diversity, justice, and action', *Early Childhood Education Journal*, 51(4), pp. 733–741.

16 Adam, H., *Transforming Practice.*

Esteves, K. J. (2018), 'Fostering global perspectives with children's literature', *Kappa Delta Pi Record*, 54(2), pp. 72–77. Retrieved from: https://doi.org/10.1080/00228958.2018.1443673.

Walton, J., Priest, N., Kowal, E., White, F., Fox, B. & Paradies, Y. (2016), 'Whiteness and national identity: teacher discourses in Australian primary schools', *Race Ethnicity and Education*, 21(1), pp. 132–147. Retrieved from: https://doi.org/10.1080/13613324.2016.1195357.

Yared, H., Grové, C. & Chapman, D. (2020), 'How does race play out in schools?: A scoping review and thematic analysis of racial issues in Australian schools', *Social Psychology of Education*, 23(6), pp. 1505–1538.

17 Priest, N., Walton, J., White, F., Kowal, E., Fox, B. & Paradies, Y. (2014), '"You are not born being racist, are you?" Discussing racism with primary-aged children', *Race Ethnicity and Education*, 19(4), pp. 808–834. Retrieved from: https://doi.org/10.1080/13613324.2014.946496.

18 Ben, J., Kelly, D. & Paradies, Y. (2020), 'Contemporary anti-racism: A review of effective practice' in Solomos, J. (Ed.), *Routledge International Handbook of Contemporary Racisms*, Routledge, London, pp. 205–215. Retrieved from: https://www.taylorfrancis.com/chapters/edit/10.4324/9781351047326-16/contemporary-anti-racism-jehonathan-ben-david-kelly-yin-paradies.

Compton-Lilly, C., Ellison, T. L., Perry, K. & Smagorinsky, P. (Eds), (2022), *Whitewashed Critical Perspectives: Restoring the edge to edgy ideas*, Routledge, London.

19 Strouse, G. A., Nyhout, A. & Ganea, P. A. (2018), 'The role of book features in young children's transfer of information from picture books to real-world contexts', *Frontiers in Psychology*, 9.

Kotaman, H. & Balci, A. (2017), 'Impact of storybook type on kindergarteners' storybook comprehension', *Early Child Development and Care*, 187(11), pp. 1771–1781.

Larsen, N. E., Lee, K. & Ganea, P. A. (2018), 'Do storybooks with anthropomorphized animal characters promote prosocial behaviors in young children?', *Developmental Science*, 21(3). Retrieved from: https://doi.org/10.1111/desc.12590.

20 Gamble, N. (2019), *Exploring Children's Literature: Reading for knowledge, understanding and pleasure*, Sage Publications, London.

Tschida, C. M. & Buchanan, L. B. (2018), 'Unpacking the paradox', in Shear, S. B., Tschida, C. M., Bellows, E., Buchanan, L. B. & Saylor, E. E. (Eds), *(Re)Imagining Elementary Social Studies: A controversial issues reader*, Information Age Publishing, pp. 111–128.

21 Arizpe, E. & Styles, M. (2015), *Children Reading Picturebooks: Interpreting visual texts*, Routledge, London.

CONTRIBUTOR BIOGRAPHIES

Kathryn Apel is a born-and-bred farm girl who's scared of cows. Kathryn has released a number of kids' books and verse novels, including *Mad Cows*, *Miss Understood*, *What Snail Knows*, *Too Many Friends*, *On Track* and *Bully on the Bus* to much acclaim. A trained teacher and literacy coach, Kathryn now shares her passion for words at schools and festivals. katswhiskers.wordpress.com

Stephen Axelsen has been a children's book illustrator and author for time immemorial, specialising in humour and fantasy. He has a long history of making 'sequential art', in the shape of cartoon series for *The School Magazine* and graphic novels. He is best known to a close circle of family and friends.

Katie Bryant is a passionate educator committed to early years literacy. As Curriculum Leader for Early Years Literacy at St Peters Lutheran College in Brisbane, and a Year One teacher, she champions the Science of Reading and Learning, driving impactful, evidence-based literacy instruction. Katie's leadership in establishing a bespoke literacy program earned her the 2022 Head of College Award at St Peters Lutheran College, followed by the 2023 ACEL Pivotal People Leadership Award for her influence on teacher practice and student outcomes. Dedicated to evidence-based instruction and professional learning, Katie continues to shape the future of early years education by sharing her ideas at conferences and through papers in educational journals.

Des Crump's Gamilaroi family is from the Goondiwindi district. He has a teaching background working in primary teaching, secondary guidance and curriculum policy prior to establishing his own consultancy where he continues to work in Aboriginal education but also with Aboriginal and Torres Strait Islander languages. Des is the Industry Fellow (Indigenous Languages at The University of Queensland. Qualifications include: Masters of Indigenous Languages Education; Masters of Education (Guidance and Counselling); Bachelor of Education; Graduate Diploma in Aboriginal Education; Graduate Diploma in Education Studies (Careers); Diploma of Teaching (Primary).

Tony Flowers is an acclaimed illustrator, known for his intricate and humorous drawings, with over fifty titles to his name. His recent picture books include *Grandma's First Tattoo*, *You, Me and Community* and *Advance Australia Fair*. His latest project as author and illustrator is *Divi and Frey*, a graphic novel that blends traditional illustration techniques with 3D optical illusions. He holds a master's degree in visual communication and teaches design at the University of Tasmania. Tony is also known for his academic work in the area of visual literacy.

Kate Foster is a bestselling and award-winning children's author living on the Gold Coast with her family and second-hand dogs. Her novels are published internationally and include *Paws*, *The Bravest Word*, *Harriet Hound*, *The Unlikely Heroes Club* and *Small Acts* (co-written with Kate Gordon). Kate founded the ASLA Diversity in Australia and Aotearoa New Zealand Children's Book Award which celebrates and spotlights books that push boundaries and challenge stereotypes. She is passionate about encouraging and teaching a wider understanding of autism and mental illness via a positive approach and representation in both her books as well as her presentations and talks.

Tracey Hand is the co-founder of Optimise Learning and an experienced educator who is passionate about assisting students to engage in learning and achieve to their full potential. Tracey has extensive classroom experience and has held a variety of roles within school settings in Australia and Singapore. Tracey is a qualified Reading Recovery teacher, a QSA-trained Preparatory Facilitator and a QSA-trained Curriculum Assessment and Reporting Framework Facilitator. A skilled presenter, Tracey has held workshops for a number of organisations.

Jacqueline Harvey is one of Australia's most popular authors for children, having sold over a million copies of her Alice-Miranda and Clementine Rose series in Australia alone. She is the author of the spy series, Kensy and Max, and the adventure series, Willa and Woof. Her picture book *The Sound of the Sea* was a CBCA Honour Book. A highly experienced teacher and presenter, Jacqueline has delivered thousands of talks and workshops at schools and festivals around the world.

Shona Innes is a clinical and forensic psychologist with many years of experience helping others. As well as individualising psychological interventions for a wide range of people and behaviours, Shona has advised organisations, big and small, about promoting better mental health, safe behaviours and the right kind of ways to manage and support others with problem behaviour or in troubling situations. Her children's book series, The Big Hug Books, grew out of individual therapy sessions with children and their families.

Will Kostakis is a writer of all things, from celebrity news stories that score cease and desist letters, to tweets for professional wrestlers. He's best known for his award-winning YA novels, including *The Sidekicks*, *The First Third* and *The Greatest Hit*. *We Could Be Something* won the Young Adult Literature Prize at the 2024 Prime Minister's Literary Awards. He has written two fantasy novels, *Monuments* and it's sequel, *Rebel Gods*.

Georgina Manning is the director of Wellbeing for Kids and a counsellor and psychotherapist. Georgina runs regular parent seminars in schools, training for school staff and is a national speaker for wellbeing events. Georgina has created the 'Peaceful Kids' and 'Peaceful Parents' Mindfulness and Positive Psychology programs and holds training for school staff and mental health professionals across many states in Australia.

Sophie Masson is the award-winning, internationally published author of more than sixty books for children, young adults and adults. She is a founding partner and co-director of Christmas Press, an acclaimed boutique children's publishing house specialising in beautiful illustrated books for children, from picture books featuring retellings of traditional tales by well-known authors, as well as anthologies, novels, plays and poetry, and books featuring both established and emerging writers and illustrators.

Kelly McDonough is a registered nurse turned full-time mother of five. She shares her passion for beautiful and realistic home interiors through her blog *The Styling Mama*, with a focus on children's spaces. She writes for a number of online and print publications, sharing parenting advice, tricks and DIY hacks.

Belinda Murrell is a bestselling, internationally published children's author with a history of writing in her family that spans over 200 years. Her titles include four picture books, her fantasy adventure series The Sun Sword trilogy and her seven time-slip adventures, *The Locket of Dreams*, *The Ruby Talisman*, *The Ivory Rose*, *The Forgotten Pearl*, *The River Charm*, *The Sequin Star* and *The Lost Sapphire*. For younger readers (aged six to nine) Belinda has the popular Lulu Bell series about friends, family and animal adventures in a vet hospital, and a middle-grade series called Pippa's Island. Her most recent series for junior readers is The Daredevil Princess.

Dr Lyndal O'Gorman is a senior lecturer in the School of Early Childhood and Inclusive Education at Queensland University of Technology. Lyndal has taught in primary schools in Brisbane and Far North Queensland. Her current teaching and research at QUT explores early childhood and primary arts education, education for sustainability, play pedagogies, interdisciplinary learning and teaching, and early childhood leadership. She is particularly interested in the intersection of the arts and education for sustainability.

Natalie Jane Prior is the author of numerous books for children and young adults. Her work includes the classic picture book *The Paw* and its sequels (illustrated by Terry Denton), and the internationally successful fantasy series Lily Quench, which has well over half a million copies in print, and which was broadcast on BBC Radio in 2006. Natalie's books have won the Aurealis Awards (for fantasy and science fiction), the Davitt Awards (for crime writing), and have been Honour, Shortlist and Notable Books in the CBCA Awards. Her most recent series is Naughty Dragons (illustrated by Simon Howe).

Allison Rushby is the internationally published author of many middle-grade novels, including *The Mulberry Tree*, the Davitt Award–winning *The Turnkey* and its sequel *The Seven Keys*, as well as *When This Bell Rings*, *The Ghost Locket* and the Miss Penny Dreadful series. She has also written a junior fiction series, The Wish Sisters, and two YA novels – *The Stand In* and *The Fifth Room*. www.allisonrushby.com

Award-winning author **Pamela Rushby** has worked in advertising, as a preschool teacher, and a freelance writer. She was a writer and producer of educational television, audio and multimedia for the Queensland Department of Education for sixteen years, and now freelances in children's and young adult fiction and non-fiction; scriptwriting; and multimedia writing/designing. Pamela Rushby has over 200 books to her credit and is passionately interested in children's books and television, ancient history and Middle Eastern food.

Emma Sainty is an early childhood educator who has taught across Australia. She has taught in a variety of before-school settings using a number of curriculums, including the International Baccalaureate, the Early Years Learning Framework and the Queensland Kindergarten Learning Guidelines. Emma has also completed her Master of Education in Leadership and Management.

R. A. Spratt is a bestselling author and television writer. She is known for a number of popular series, including Nanny Piggins; Friday Barnes; The Peski Kids and Shockingly Good Stories. Spratt has written for dozens of different television shows and specialised mainly in children's animation, but she has also had extensive experience writing jokes, sketch comedy and political satire. Her most recent YA novel is *Hamlet is Not OK*.

Allison Tait (A. L. Tait) is the internationally published bestselling author of middle-grade adventure series The Mapmaker Chronicles and The Ateban Cipher. A multi-genre writer and accomplished speaker, Allison also co-hosts the top-rating *Your Kid's Next Read* podcast and teaches creative writing for adults and kids at the Australian Writers' Centre.

Jennifer Teh is the founding director of Hush Little Baby Early Childhood Music Classes. Jen has taught everything from primary, high school and university music, directed choirs, taught private singing lessons, presented workshops, written papers for national and international conferences and symposia in music education and carved out a career as a professional live and studio singer. Jen's passion lies in early childhood music education, and this is supported by a huge body of research around the positive benefits of sharing music with infants and children.

Lotte ten Hacken is an experienced educator who is lucky enough to have her dream job of being a primary school teacher librarian. She is in the final stages of her PhD candidature and also works as a Casual Academic at The University of Queensland teaching English curriculum. Her professional goals include harnessing the power of picture books to make the world a better place, especially through dialogue and critical literacy. During her doctoral research she developed a teaching model, known as 'Picture book talks', to bring other teachers along on this quest. She is currently a CBCA Book of the Year judge for the Picture Book and New Illustrator categories (2024 and 2025).

Joe Visser has been reviewing books at bookboy.com.au since he was twelve and, in 2018, aged fourteen, was the first teen member of the #LoveOzYA committee. Joe blogs less regularly these days, focusing instead on his burgeoning career as a singer/songwriter (you can hear his music on his website: joevisser.com). But he continues to read voraciously.

Michelle Witheyman-Crump is an author and teacher librarian. Her first book, *Original Girl*, was the story of her Indigenous daughter. As the eldest child of three, with parents who were foster carers, Michelle grew up with many children from various cultural backgrounds sharing her home, and many of these experiences have shaped her as a person and as an author. She is a teacher librarian in Ipswich, editor for the Ipswich District Teacher Librarian Book Week Publication and on the committee of the StoryArts Festival Ipswich.

ACKNOWLEDGEMENTS

The very first thanks in this second edition must go to my family, Ava, Georgia, Sam, James and Murray as well as my parents Robyn and Geoff Dean, without whom I would not be a reader and writer. Special mention to Murray Arkadieff AKA The Beekeeper – thank you for loving me without question, for parenting alongside me, for shepherding me into my office (and making me stay there), for being so terribly wise and your pure love of our family (chaos!). Daniel John Daley was no doubt involved in our meeting and is definitely chuckling at us from above.

Many thanks also to the fabulous Mrs Malta AKA Ana CoutinhoMalta who makes my working days in the school library a delight. I wish a Mrs Malta on every school library! Thank you also to my teaching partner and wing woman Lotte ten Hacken.

Allison Tait – co-host and creator of the *Your Kid's Next Read* podcast. There is not enough words and correct pronunciations to thank you for all you give to me in this kidlit space and for our weekly quality waffle. To the third member of Team YKNR, Allison Rushby – while your books often spook me out, I am ever grateful for your wisdom and writing prowess.

My ever-patient, ever-encouraging crew of Jessica Rudd, Joanne Curry, Kym Potts and Mel Kroeger – thanks for reading my daily essays. One day our WhatsApp will the form the basis of the memoirs of each of us.

Helen Giaquinta, your kid wrangling has provided many of the hours of editing needed for this book and our kids' lives are so much richer for having you.

Thank you to the entire team at UQP, especially Cathy Vallance and Jacqueline Blanchard who have wrangled this second edition expertly. And to Kristina Schulz without whom this book would not exist.

www.ingramcontent.com/pod-product-compliance
Ingram Content Group UK Ltd.
Pitfield, Milton Keynes, MK11 3LW, UK
UKHW041857190726
13854UKWH00002B/952

9 780702 268984